The Boys of '76

THE ALARM.

THE BOYS OF '76.

A HISTORY OF

THE BATTLES OF THE REVOLUTION.

By CHARLES CARLETON COFFIN,

AUTHOR OF

"THE STORY OF LIBERTY," "OLD TIMES IN THE COLONIES," "MY DAYS AND NIGHTS ON THE
BATTLE-FIELD," "FOLLOWING THE FLAG," "FOUR YEARS OF FIGHTING ,"
"WINNING HIS WAY," "OUR NEW WAY ROUND THE WORLD," &c.

Illustrated.

The Boys of '76

Published by Maranatha Publications, Inc.
Copyright © 1998 by Maranatha Publications

Introduction prepared by Rose Weiner.

Printed in the United States of America

International Standard Book Number: 0-938558-82-X

Library of Congress Catalog Card Number 97-076379

2nd Printing
August 2000

Contact for more information:

MARANATHA PUBLICATIONS
P.O. Box 1799
Gainseville, FL 32602
(904) 645-3965 phone
(904) 645-3966 fax

website: http://www.mpi2000.net

TO MY NEPHEWS,

HENRY L. LITTLE, LUTHER B. LITTLE,
AND HERMAN L. SAWYER,

WHOSE ANCESTORS TOOK PART IN THE BATTLES OF THE REVOLUTION,

THIS VOLUME

Is Affectionately Dedicated.

Charles Carleton Coffin, Author

Journalist, (Civil War Correspondent), Popular Lecturer, (1823-1896)

I accept the Bible because it contains, immeasurably beyond all other books, moral precepts which are the rules of all right conduct; because it is the foundation of all just government; because it tells the truth about men; because its spiritual teachings satisfy the longings of my heart, giving me joy, peace, comfort, rest, and hope of a better and larger life beyond the present.

I regard Jesus Christ as God in human form; as revealing the character of God to the human race. All my conceptions of justice, righteousness, goodness, truth, love, compassion, tenderness, forgiveness, all moral qualities and holy affections are found in Him. Through Him my fellow men become my brothers, and we all may come into sweet and holy relations with the Father, and enjoy ineffable spiritual blessedness.

I believe in Jesus Christ as my Saviour, Redeemer, Brother, and best Friend. All history centers around Him. He is the life and light of the world-the One absolutely perfect human being of all time-stainless and immaculate in everything. His teachings, if followed, will settle all disputes between man and man-between individuals and nations alike; will banish misery and woe, and make the world a paradise of happiness. I accept Him for what He claimed to be—the Son of God and the Son of Man.

A NOTE FROM THE PUBLISHER

> At the birth of each new Era,
> with a recognizing start,
> Nation wildly looks at nation,
> standing with mute lips apart,
> And glad Truth's yet mightier man-child
> leaps beneath the Future's heart.
> from "The Present Crisis"
> by James Russell Lowell

As the British laid down their arms at the end of the Revolutionary War, the British soldiers played an old tune "The World Turned Upside Down." The British surrender at Yorktown, Virginia, in 1781, after eight years of conflict with her American colonies was important not only for America, but because it marked a turning point in the progress of civilization. Since the time that the young nation of Israel had demanded the rule of a king, men and women have had to exist in a world full of empires, kingdoms, lords, and hierarchies of rulers of all kinds. Until the founding of America, 99% of the human race has had to live under the tyranny of ruler's law. Because God understood the darkness that lurked in the unredeemed human heart, He had given Israel a representative government in the wilderness that would be guided by His law and commandments. However, Israel was not satisfied with this, rejected God's government, and demanded a king so she could be like every other nation. Of course, God warned the Israelites of the cruelty, enslavement, and oppression that awaited them under the rule of kings. God cautioned that a king would force their sons into military duty, would take the best of their fields, their vineyards, their flocks, and would take away their liberties and possessions. Israel, however, refused to listen. Consequently, with the momentary exception of ancient Anglo Saxon law, which for a brief moment in history was based on something uniquely similar to Moses government in the wilderness, the majority of mankind has suffered under the kings, the despots, and the tyrants.

The Bible and history furnish many examples of the blood and terror of ruler's law. The chief baker of Pharaoh was thrown into prison and later hanged for not baking the bread the way Pharaoh liked it. Joseph was thrown into prison without a trial and spent many years there under false charges. Israel suffered the cruel yoke of slavery and oppression under the Pharaohs for hundreds of years. Elijah feared for his life because Queen Jezeabel wanted him killed. During the reign of King Ahasuerus, gallows were prepared for Mordecai and the Jewish people were scheduled for execution because of Haman's deep resentment for Mordecai. The Babylonian magicians were subject to death if they could not tell the king his dreams.

Shadrach, Mesach, and Abed-nego were thrown into the fiery furnace for refusing to bow down and worship the golden image the king had set up. Daniel was thrown in the lion's den for continuing to pray to his God.

After the coming of Christ, the tyrants continued to rage. King Herod, seeking to kill the Christ child, ordered the slaughter of all the male infants in Bethlehem.

When Jesus began his ministry he read from the prophet Isaiah;

> The Spirit of the Lord is upon Me because the Lord has anointed Me to preach deliverance to the poor, He has sent Me to heal the broken hearted, to proclaim liberty to the captives, and the opening of the prison to those who are bound. (Luke 2:1-4)

Jesus' mission was not limited to personal reformation alone. He was also promising civil freedom along with all the social and economic blessings the gospel can bring to society. He knew that as men and women became free from sin they would eventually establish governments, institutions and economies that would be based on moral virtue and biblical law.

Jesus died and rose from the dead to make all men free. He instructed His disciples to take the gospel not only to the individual, but to all nations, teaching the nations to observe everything that He commanded. Jesus brought to man the possibility of a new birth, of a new life, of internal freedom from slavery to sin and self. It was the power of that gospel that eventually overthrew the Roman Empire. It was the departing from those primitive tenets of Christianity and the embracing of idolatry in the Roman Church that plunged Europe into Medieval darkness.

When Jesus was born in Bethlehem, a multitude of heavenly hosts had announced his birth to shepherds who were keeping watch in the fields of Ephratha. The angels ended their glad tidings praising God and saying, "Glory to God in the highest, and on earth peace, goodwill toward all men." The angelic proclamation was the fulfillment of Isaiah's prophecy;

> For a Child will be born to us; a Son will be given to us; and the government will rest on his shoulder's; and His name will be called Wonderful Counselor, Eternal Father, Prince of Peace. There will be no end to the increase of His government or of peace, on the throne of David and over His kingdom, to establish it and to uphold it with justice and righteousness from then on and forevermore. The zeal of the Lord of Hosts will accomplish this. (Isa, 9:6-7)

From these passages it will be noticed that peace with God and peace among men were among the blessings the Messiah came to bring. This peace on earth was to begin from Messiah's first advent and would increase and grow in the earth until the nations hammered "their swords into plowshares and their spears into pruning hooks and ...never again" learned war. (Isa. 2:4) Although only a small stone as foreseen by Daniel's prophecy, the kingdom of God, being set up in the hearts of men, would eventually lead to the destruction of all tyrannical kingdoms, and would become a great mountain that filled the entire earth. (Dan. 2:35,44)

After Christ's resurrection, as Christianity began to grow and spread, the Ceasars realized that the very foundations of their despotic rule were threatened by this new religion. They threw Christians to the lions, boiled them in oil, and burned them as human torches. The power of Rome eventually fell, but the gospel continued.

Later, during the time of the Protestant Reformation, the papal hierarchy carried on the same tyrannical acts in their efforts to root out heretics, and coerce people to renounce salvation by faith alone, a doctrine which opposed the Catholic teaching of forgiveness of sins through buying pardons, etc.. Although Messiah's peace was gaining ground in the hearts of men through reconciliation with God, Messiah's peace had not yet gained a foothold in civil government.

Down through the ages, practically every government has had its roots in covetousness and greed and has been structured to exploit its people, to reduce them to poverty and to marshal their intimidated youth into predatory wars against nearby nations. The long history of this type of government has been one of blood and terror, both in ancient and modern times. Those in power have reveled in luxury while the lot of the common people was one of excessive taxation, stringent regulations, and a continuous existence in misery.

Individuals lived not only under the tyrant's threat within their own homeland, they also lived under the threat of attack from enemies without. People were for the most part very warlike. Among the warlike nations of Europe, no person could appear in public without his arms, consisting of a sword, lance, and buckler. Wherever they sat down to eat, each man had a servant who stood behind him to hold his lance and buckler. When they finished eating, each man resumed his arms and wore them at all times, whether they were playing, dancing, or engaging in other exercise.

In the history of Western Europe, we find that England was held under conquest by the Romans for 500 years. After the Romans left, the Britons were threatened by their enemies the Scots and Picts. They invited the Saxons to come to their assistance, were received with joy by the Britons, and united with them to help them defeat their enemy. Later, however, the Saxons decided that they liked England and wanted to take the land for themselves. They invited reinforcements to come to England, made peace with the Picts and began to quarrel with the Britons. The Britons realized that their new-found friends had become their enemies.

In the early ages, the men were devoted to war and the chase. Slavery was an institution as old as the human race. In war, conquered kingdoms were enslaved by their captors. The great bulk of human history reveals that the greater portion of the energy of the human race has been spent in war, conquest, and self defense. One of the major purposes of the king was to lead his kingdom in their wars. Warriors disliked the drudgery of work which they left to the old men, the women, and the children. The love of war was a trait in the character of the Gothic and Teutonic nations. When they were not engaged in a war with nations, the chiefs would sometimes invade their neighboring chiefs to seek booty or to revenge an injury. Deadly feuds existed at all times between different tribes producing quarrels and bloodshed. They also had a hatred for slavery and would rather see their whole family killed than taken captive. When advancing to battle, the women would sometimes mingle with the troops and, with cries and tears, urge them to fight bravely. If any of the men retreated the women would rush among them and compel them to renew the battle and either win or perish in the attempt.[1]

In the 13th century, during the reign of King John of England, the king ordered the country people to drive their cattle into camp to supply his soldiers with food, but they refused. To teach them a lesson, John seized twenty-eight sons of the chief families, threw them into prison, and had them put to death. The noblemen were so incensed that they organized themselves into the "Army of God" and marched to his castle to seize him. Compelled by fear, John rode out to meet the men. They presented him with a document to sign called the Magna Carta which prohibited the king from levying taxes and taking the possessions of the people at will. The Magna Carta also established a parliament made up of barons who would decide what taxes should be levied and prohibited any free man from being punished without a trial by a jury of his peers. This was one of the first documents that ensured some sort of peace and liberty to the individual. It was one of the first signs of the blessings of Christianity to appear in civil government.

Before the establishing of America which gave birth to the "dream" of liberty, there was little hope of liberty for the average man of courage and good will. The ambitions of a ruling class conspired against liberty of speech, liberty of conscience, liberty of the person, and liberty of economic opportunity. Most of human energy and strength, as well as physical resources, were spent in fighting wars caused by greed, hereditary hatreds, jealousies and ancestral thirsts for vengeance. There was little spiritual freedom, certainly no economic or political liberty, and little hope for the chance of it.

It was at the dawn of the Reformation, a little before Martin Luther dusted off a copy of the Bible from the monastery shelves and began to discover the basic truths of God's word, that one of the greatest ironies in history occurred. God used the greed and wrath of man to "praise Him." Perhaps the most ruthless and wicked of all European rulers were the infamous leaders of the Spanish Inquisition, King Ferdinand and Queen Isabella of Spain. These Spanish rulers had confiscated the lands of their most prosperous citizens and either exiled or killed the owners. They had martyred multitudes of Protestants, Jews, and Moslems alike who had refused to embrace Catholicism, leaving their children to wander homeless in the streets and forbidding anyone to assist these children. Seeking for a quicker way to obtain the gold and silk of India and Cathay so they could enrich their treasuries, the Spanish monarchs sent Christopher Columbus and his crew to seek for a quicker route to the Indies. What they found over the Western horizon was instead what would become common man's second chance to escape those rulers. In short, they found a land in which the common man would have a chance to "live." As God lifted the curtain on the New World to reveal a land destined to be the new home of those who wished to worship God freely and who would eventually live free from those oppressive governments, He used the finances of the greatest persecutors of true Christianity and religious freedom to fund the voyage. America was destined to become a land in which mankind could find those things which they desired the most—freedom of opportunity, freedom of thought, freedom to worship God.

When the Reformation swept Europe, the Bible became available to the masses. As the traditions of the Roman Church and Medieval government began to be weighed in its light, men and women began to question those teachings which appeared to violate God's word. True Christians desired to see the faith that Christ taught re-established, to see the church purified. The doctrine of the "Divine Right of Kings" began to be questioned and examined in the Bible's light. (This doctrine upholds the idea that the king's right to rule came directly from God, rather than from the consent of his subjects, that he can do no wrong, and that his word is law.) The fundamental principles of right and wrong as recorded in the Bible were the fundamental principles that made up the Reformation world view.

This New World became the desired destination of the Pilgrims who left the familiarity of a civilized Europe in search of a land where they could worship God freely without fear of reprisal. The Pilgrims were destined to carve out of the American wilderness a nation which would insure religious liberty. The primitive Christianity practiced by the Pilgrims gave a new direction for external freedom and eventually gave rise to a new form of civil government, a government free from the savagery of demagogues and kings.

English jurist William Blackstone, whose commentaries were accepted as the primary analysis of law in the colonies and used extensively in early America, expounded that it was self-evident that God was the source of all laws, whether found in the Bible or observed in nature. Samuel Rutherford in *Lex Rex, The Law and The Prince,* challenged the "Divine Right of Kings," asserting that the basic premise of government and law must be the Bible— the Word of God, rather than the word of any man. All men, including the king, Rutherford argued, were under the law and not above it. As concepts of government began to be revolutionized in the minds of men, the stage was set for the American Republic.

Although still under the oppressive rule of a king at the time of the

Declaration of Independence, England was more advanced in the rule of law than any European nation. However, the king and Parliament as well began to oppress and overly tax the British colonists in America. Because the Colonists considered themselves to be free Englishmen, they invoked the Magna Carta, the basis of English law and the document that guaranteed certain liberties and rights to Englishmen. They believed that the king was bound to honor this covenant and respect their rights. The Colonists also believed that the right to own private property without fear of seizure, a principle upheld by the Magna Carta, was as sacred as the law of God because God had stated in the Ten Commandments that a man should not covet or steal anything that belonged to his neighbor. Concerning the importance of private property rights, John Adams states, "The moment the idea is admitted into society that property is not as sacred as the laws of God . . . anarchy and tyranny commence. Property must be secured or liberty cannot exist."[2]

In the Declaration of Independence, Thomas Jefferson carefully listed 27 violations of those rights by King George III. Among these infringements were: dissolving representative houses for opposing the king's invasion on the rights of the people, imposing taxes without the consent of the American colonists, cutting off their trade with all parts of the world, depriving them in many cases of trial by jury, suspending the colonial legislatures and declaring that they could legislate for the colonists in all cases, plundering American vessels at sea, burning their towns, destroying peoples lives, capturing American citizens while they were at sea and forcing them to bear arms against the colonies, stirring up Indians to attack the inhabitants of the frontiers whose known rule of warfare was complete destruction of all people regardless of age, sex, or conditions.

Jefferson concluded these numerous violations by stating:

> In every stage of these oppressions we have petitioned for redress
> in the most humble terms. Our repeated petitions have been
> answered only by repeated injury. A prince, whose character
> is thus marked by every act which may define a tyrant, is unfit to
> be the ruler of a free people.

Jefferson concluded the Declaration by stating that the United Colonies had a right to be "free and independent states" and dissolved all ties to Great Britain.

As a consequence, the American Colonies were thrown into revolutionary war to defend and protect the rights to govern themselves that they claimed were God given. Because the Bible taught that rulers were to be a terror to those who do evil, "an avenger to execute wrath on him who does evil," the founding fathers believed that it was the chief end of government to protect the life and liberty, and property of it's citizens (Rom.13:4). The Bible clearly states, "Because the sentence against an evil deed is not executed quickly, therefore the hearts of the sons of men among them are given fully to do evil." (Ecc.8:11). Just as there are evil men who murder and steal and need to be brought to justice by an unbiased application of law to all under it, so there are nations who do evil, attack the innocent, steal, and murder. They too must be brought to justice. This usually can be done only through a state of war as the armed forces of the nation which has been attacked tries to defend its citizens and bring the renegade nation to justice. To avoid this state of war is one great reason why men establish nations. As long as there is a judge on earth that can settle the dispute by appeal, the state of war is avoided and the controversy is decided by that power. But, when there is no earthly judge, the appeal lies with God, the judge in heaven. The children of Israel demonstrated this appeal when threatened by the Ammonites. With no earthly judge to settle the dispute, the leader of Israel called on God to act as judge, and then led his army out courageously to battle. The Founding Fathers based their separation from England on this same appeal. To support their Declaration the Founders made an appeal to "Divine Providence and mutually pledged" their "lives," "fortunes," and their "sacred honor."

As Patrick Henry expressed it:

> If we wish to be free, we must fight! . . . An appeal to arms and to the God of Hosts is all that is left us! . . . Three millions of people, armed in the holy cause of liberty, and in such a country, are invincible by any force which our enemy can send against us. We shall not fight alone. A just God presides over the destinies of nations. . . There is no retreat, but in submission and slavery . . . Is life so dear, or peace so sweet, as to be purchased at the price of chains and slavery? Forbid it, Almighty God. I know not what course others may take; but as for me, give me liberty or give me death!

George Washington, recognizing the right of an appeal to Heaven, prayed accordingly during the Revolutionary War:

> And now Almighty Father; if it is Thy holy will that we shall obtain a place and a name among the nations of the earth, grant that we may be enabled to show our gratitude for Thy goodness by our endeavors to fear and obey Thee. Bless us with wisdom in our councils, success in battle, and let all our victories be tempered with humility. Endow also our enemies with enlightened minds that they may become sensible of their injustice, and willing to restore our liberty and peace. Grant the petition of Thy servant for the sake of Him whom Thou hast called Thy Beloved son; nevertheless, not my will but Thine be done.[3]

On the shores of America, the doctrine of the "Divine Right of Kings" was finally overthrown and the concept of self-government, the foundation stone of the United States of America, was established in its place. Thus America was the first nation to exist without a king since Israel rejected the theocracy of God and demanded a king during the days of Samuel.

Noah Webster, author of the Webster's Dictionary, was a man the framers of the Constitution relied upon to help explain the Constitution to the American people through his New York newspaper. A friend observed:

"They are saying, Mr. Webster, that it is you and your daily newspaper that is leading us to a new awareness of our civil liberties."

Mr. Webster exclaimed, "My dear friend, it is One long before I who gave birth to civil liberties. The religion which has introduced civil liberties is the religion of Christ and His apostles! To this we owe our free constitutions of government."[4]

The Constitution provided the political climate that gave "eagle's wings to the human spirit." When the first settlers arrived in New England, they differed little from the ancient pioneers who had begun earlier civilizations in the world five thousand years before. They had come through a long and hazardous journey in a boat no larger and no more commodious than those of the ancient sea kings. Their tools still consisted of a shovel, an ax, a hoe, and a stick plow. These tools had been only slightly improved over those which were used in the ancient civilizations of Egypt, Persia, China, and Greece. These pioneers harvested their grain and hay-grass with the scythes of the same primitive design. They wore clothes which were made of thread, spun on a wheel, and then woven by hand. Their medications were superstitious concoctions that did little to heal anything. Their transportation was by cart and oxen. Most of them died young.

Soon two hundred years had passed into history. As the world entered into the later half of the twentieth century, the noble experiment of religious liberty, free enterprise economics, and a representative government of, by and for the people had produced some phenomenal results. The floodgates of progress were opened up as people regained their God-given right to own property and to keep the rewards of individual labor. By the end of the nineteenth century, the entire human race had benefited from America's prosperity economics. Although at the time America contained less than six percent of the earth's population, they were producing approximately half of the world's goods.

A deluge of inventions, advances in science, medicine, and technology came pouring out of America to bless the nations. During the 20th century, the number of ideas exported to the nations from the United States alone enabled "from less than one percent of the world's people living in any reasonable level of comfort to go to more than half of them living at a standard virtually unimagined at the turn of the twentieth century."[5]

The promise that America held caused multitudes to come seeking to share in the destiny of a nation built on Christian principles. In less than 100 years after her Independence 34 million men, women, and children came through Ellis Island. The Statue of Liberty which was erected in New York harbor to greet all those who came to this land seeking freedom bares this inscription carved on her base:

Give me your tired, your poor,
Your huddled massed yearning to breathe free,
The wretched refuse of our teeming shore,
Send these the homeless tempest tossed to me,
I lift my lamp beside the golden door!

The Statue of Liberty came to visualize, over a hundred years later, the hope that America would offer to the rest of the world. Her design with the broken shackles under Liberty's feet represent triumph over tyranny. The seven rays of her crown symbolize liberty radiating to the seven continents and the seven seas. Marvin Trachtenberg, in his enlightening book, *The Statue of Liberty*, explains the statue's symbolism:

Although shields and open books were common sculptural devises
for displaying inscriptions, stone tablets were comparatively
rare. When not in the hands of Moses himself they generally
embody a Mosaic reference, as in figures of the Synagogue and
Faith who usually display the Old Law on a tablet. Liberty's
tablet, particularly the way it is borne forward, is an unmistakable
allusion not only to political events (July 4, 1997), but to
the Mosaic tablet of the patriarch, but her radiant crown also
may allude to the "rays of light" about his face after the revelation.
Thus she is, along with everything else, a seer and prophetess
Considered in this way, her tablet bears not so much a
remembrance as an implicit commandment—"Seek Liberty!"
and a prophecy: "Liberty, as achieved in America in 1776 shall
spread throughout the world.[6]

In the entire history of human mobility, nothing stands out in the scope, speed, and magnitude as the American migration. Most who came were of humble origins. Seeking religious freedom, driven by famine and economic hardships, fleeing from fierce persecutions and political oppression, they came seeking above all else, the freedom to worship God, individual liberty and a better way of life.

Two and a half million new immigrants crossed the Atlantic Ocean the decade before the Civil War. Sixteen million pilgrims were added to their number before 1924. One newspaper avowed that there had been nothing to compare with the American migration in diversity "since the encampments of the Roman Empire."[7]

The spirit of liberty which swept across America and spread to other nations gave the world the gigantic new power resources of harnessed electricity, the internal combustion engine, jet propulsion, computer technology, exotic space vehicles and all the wonders of nuclear energy. Communications were revolutionized by telegraph, telephone, radio, television, and satellite.

The world was explored from pole to pole. The depths of the sea were plummeted. Men left the earth in rocket ships and actually walked on the moon. Space planes were developed which could be maneuvered and landed back on the earth by the flight crew.

The average life span increased. Homes, food, textiles, communications, transportation, central heating, central cooling, world travel, millions of books, surgical miracles, medical cures for age-old diseases, entertainment at that the touch of a switch, instant news. . . in two hundred years, the human race had made a "five thousand year leap."[8]

In just two hundred years, the United States of America rose from a nation in its infancy to become the leader of the free world. God poured out His blessings upon this land and permitted us to try every good thing we have been able to think of. We have been granted great success. While we have had the privilege of partaking of all these blessings of liberty, it was not without a cost.

The Boys of '76 records the suffering, the hardship, the victories and the providence of God during our war for independence that made our free form of government possible. That it cost many Americans everything will be clearly seen in the record of this war. Many of those who fought for our liberties are among those of "whom the world was not worthy."

Henry Armit Brown, delivering the Centennial Oration at Valley Forge to commemorate the courage and the mission of these Revolutionary soldiers declared:

> The blood that stained this ground did not rush forth in
> the joyous frenzy of the fight; it fell drop by drop from the
> heart of a suffering people. They who once encamped here
> in the snow fought not for conquest, not for power, not for
> glory, not for their country only, not for themselves alone.
> They served here for posterity; they suffered here for the human
> race; they bore here the cross of all the peoples; they died here
> that Freedom might be the heritage of all. It was Humanity
> which they defended; it was Liberty herself that they had in
> keeping.
>   She that was sought in the wilderness and mourned for by
> the rivers of Babylon...Driven by the persecution of centuries
> from the older world, she had come with Pilgrim and Puritan,
> and Caviler and Quaker, to seek a shelter in the new. Attacked
> once more by her old enemies, she had taken refuge here. Nor
> she alone. The dream of the Greek, the Hebrew's prophecy, the
> desire of the Roman, the Italian's prayer, the longing of the
> German mind, the hope of the French heart, the glory and honor
> of old England herself, the yearning of all the centuries, the

aspiration of every age, the promise of the Past, the fulfillment of the Future, the seed of the old time, the harvest of the new—all these were with her and here, in the heart of America, they were safe.

The last of many struggles was almost won; the best of many centuries was about to break; the time was already come when from these shores the light of a new civilization should flash across the sea, and from this place a voice of triumph make the Old World tremble, when from her chosen refuge in the West, the spirit of Liberty should go forth to meet the rising sun and set the people free!

Americans: A hundred years have passed away and that Civilization and that Liberty is still your heritage. But think not that such an inheritance can be kept safe without exertion... The memory of this spot shall be an everlasting honor for our fathers, but we can make it an everlasting shame for ourselves if we choose to do so. . . It is well to commemorate the past, but it is not enough.

If they could return...if in the presence of this holy hour the dead could rise and lips dumb for a century find again a tongue, might they not say to us: 'You do well, countrymen, to commemorate this time. You do well to honor those who yielded up their lives here'. Theirs was a perfect sacrifice, and the debt you owe them you can never pay. Your lives have fallen in a happier time. The boundaries of your Union stretch from sea to sea. You enjoy all the blessings which Providence can bestow; a peace we never knew; a wealth we never hoped for; a power of which we never dreamed. Yet, think not that these things only can make a nation great.

We laid the foundations of your happiness in a time of trouble, in days of sorrow and perplexity, of doubt, distress, and danger, of cold and hunger, of suffering and want. We built it up by virtue, by courage, by self-sacrifice, by unfailing patriotism, by unceasing vigilance. By those things alone did we win your liberties; by them only can you hope to keep them. Do you revere our names? Then follow our example. Are you proud of our achievements? Then try to imitate them. Do your honor our memories? Then do as we have done. You yourselves owe something to America, better than all those things which you spread before her with such lavish hand— something which she needs as much in her prosperity today, as ever in the sharpest crisis of our age! For you have duties to perform as well as we. It was ours to create; it is yours to preserve. It was ours to found; it is yours to perpetuate. It was ours to organize;

it is yours to purify! And what nobler spectacle can you present to mankind today, than that of a people honest, steadfast, and secure—mindful of the lessons of experience—true to the teachings of history—let by the loftiest examples and bound together to protect their institutions at the close of the Century, as their fathers were to win them at the beginning, by the ties of "virtue, honor, and love of country."

The endless generations are advancing to take our places as we fall. For them as for us shall the Earth roll on and the seasons come and go...For them as for us shall the years march by in the sublime procession of the ages. And here, in this place of sacrifice, in this vale of humiliation, in this valley of the shadow of death, out of which the life of America rose, regenerate and free, let us believe with an abiding faith, that to them Union will seem as dear and Liberty as sweet and Progress as glorious as they were to our fathers and are to you and me, and that the institutions which have made us happy, preserved by the virtue of our children, shall bless the remotest generations of the time to come. And unto Him, who holds in the hollow of His hand the fate of nations, and yet marks the sparrow's fall, let us lift up our hearts this day, and into His eternal care commit ourselves, our children, and our country.[9]

Centennial Oration at Valley Forge
Henry Armit Brown
June 10,1878

During the course of our short history, there have been times we have had to fight and die for what we have as a nation. Abraham Lincoln resolved when he dedicated Gettysburg during the Civil War:

...that these dead men have not died in vain; that this nation should have a new birth of freedom; that this nation of the people by the people and for the people shall not perish from the earth.

America went on into the twentieth century defending the cause of freedom not only for themselves, but for many nations throughout the world. President Ronald Reagan related a story about a old Dutch grandmother who came to visit him at the Whitehouse. They sat and talked for a while, then Reagan asked her what the most memorable event of her life was. Was it when she got married? Was it when she had her first child?

"No," she said, " it was none of these things. It was one day during World War II when Holland was occupied by Hitler. I was standing at my kitchen sink. I looked out the window for a moment, and there to my amazement, I saw a group of US Marines coming up the cobblestone road, and I knew at that moment I was free! I cannot express to you the incredible feeling of that moment." As she spoke, tears were flowing down both of their faces. The price of freedom has not been cheap. 120,000 American soldiers lost their lives defending freedom in World War I, 400,000 more died in World War II, 54,000 young Americans perished in Korea, 66,000 in Vietnam. Have these fallen American patriots died in vain? Have we preserved the one nation under God they fought to preserve? That liberty and freedom, brought to birth on the shores of America and nursed from infancy through sacrifice, blood, and tears, is now the desire of the world.

In his Farewell Address, President Ronald Reagan said:

> I have been reflecting on what the past eight years have meant and mean—and the image that comes like a refrain is a nautical one — a small story about a big ship and a refugee and a sailor. It was back in the early '80s... A sailor was hard at work on the carrier Midway which was patrolling the south China Sea. The crew spied on the horizon a leaky, little boat and crammed inside were refugees hoping to get to America.
>
> The Midway sent a small launch to bring them to the ship and safety. As the refugees made their way through the chopping seas, one refugee saw the sailor standing on deck and called out to him, 'Hello, American sailor! Hello, Freedom man!' A small moment, but a big meeting...When I heard the story I couldn't get it out of my mind, for that's what it was to be an American... After 200 years, two centuries, she still stands strong and true on the granite ridge, and her glow has held steady no matter what storm. And she's still a beacon, still a magnet for all who must have freedom, for all the pilgrims from all the lost places who are hurtling through the darkness toward home.

Reflecting on the American success in their experiment with civil government and the failure of Russia's experiment with Communism, President Bush proclaimed in his Inaugural address:

> We live in a world refreshed by freedom. A new breeze is blowing... the day of the dictator is over. The totalitarian era is passing and its old ideas are blown away like leaves from an ancient lifeless tree. A new breeze is blowing and a nation refreshed by freedom stands ready to push on. There is new ground to be broken and new action to be taken...Great nations of the world are moving toward democracy through the doors of freedom... From free market, free speech, and free elections, and to exercise a will unhampered by the state...
>
> For the first time in perhaps all history, man does not have to invent a system by which to live. We don't have to talk late into the night about which form of government is better. The people of this world agitate for free expression and free thought through the door to the moral and intellectual satisfaction that only liberty allows. We know what works. Freedom works! We know what is right. Freedom

is right! We know how to secure a more just and prosperous life for man on earth. We don't have to arrest justice from the kings. We only have to summon it from within ourselves. We must act on what we know is right.

But, have we acted on what we know is right? Have we been a faithful steward of the liberty and freedom God has given us? There is evidence that we haven't. As Americans, we have disregarded God, forgotten His laws, and have fallen into a fatal lapse of memory, congratulating ourselves for our achievements and forgetting the power and grace of God that has preserved us as a nation. Enslaved to materialism, filled with selfish ambition, sensuality, violence, and pride, we have allowed and tolerated indecency, immorality and perversion which was forbidden by every state in the union by laws which were established on God's standards of right and wrong. When God's holy standards fade from national conscience, almost anything can be justified.

The Reformation doctrine of Rex Lex, that proclaims that the prince is not above the law of God— a foundation stone of our free government, a safeguard against the tyranny of man's unrestrained passions—has eroded away. Man has become maker of his own laws which are in accordance with his fickle whims.

We have this caution against disobedience from the word of God: "And it shall be, when the Lord your God brings you into the land of which He swore to your fathers. . . then beware, lest you forget the Lord . . . and you say in your heart, My power and the might of my hand has gotten me this wealth." (Deut 6:10-12; 8:17)

Inscribed on the walls of the Jefferson Memorial is a similar admonition from the author of the Declaration of Independence:

> God who gave us life, gave us liberty. Can the liberties of a nation
> be secure when we have removed a conviction that these liberties
> are the gift of God? Indeed I tremble for my country when I
> reflect that God is just, that His justice cannot sleep forever.

The time is late, for God's judgments are already taking their toll throughout our nation. We have eaten our inheritance and a skeleton remains. All of our wealth, ability, and effort cannot hold back the destruction of our nation if we continue to flaunt our wickedness and turn our back on God. We are in a great spiritual battle between the very forces of Heaven and Hell. Our good intentions are like trying to put a Band-Aid on a mortal wound. Immorality has reached epidemic proportions.

Yet, even in all this there is hope. The spiritual conflict that America faces today does not have to bring about her death. It can instead become the labor pains of a new birth of vision and purpose. God has given us this wonderful promise from His word;

> If my people which are called by My name will humble themselves
> and pray and seek My face and turn from their wicked ways, then

will I hear from Heaven and will forgive their sin and heal their land. (II Chron 7:14)

During a time of great decadence and idolatry in Israel a very young boy named Josiah came to the throne and began to reign as king. The books of the law which had been lost for many years were found and Josiah had them read. Grieved at the depraved condition of Israel, he rose up in the spirit of the Lord and cleansed the nation of Israel from idolatry and turned the nation back to God.

It is our hope that the young people of this generation will through the study of history from a Christian perspective come to gain an understanding of the hand of God in American history, the price that liberty has cost, and our responsibility as American Christians to preserve that liberty and to lead this nation and the world in truth and righteousness. It is our hope that like Josiah, this generation of young Americans will rise up and turn our nation back to God, and her God given call to bring truth, liberty, and the light of the gospel to all the nations of this world. The call of God on America has not yet been revoked.

Rose Weiner
Maranatha Publication, Inc.

---

[1] Noah Webster, History of the United States (New Haven: Durie O Peck, 1832) 18-21.

[2] Charles Francis Adams, ed., The Works of John Adams, (Little, Brown and Co.) 280.

[3] William Johnson, George Washington the Christian, (Milfor, MI:, Mott, 1981) 127.

[4] Nancy DeMoss, ed., The Rebirth of America, (St. David's Center, St. David PA: Authur DeMoss Foundation, 1986) 32,

[5] Skousen, The Making of America, (Washington, DC: The Center for Constitutional Studies, 1985) 219.

[6] Richard H. Schneider, Freedom's Holy Light, (Nashville, TN: Thomas Nelson Publishers, 1985) 46.

[7] Leslie Allen, "Liberty" (Summit Books, 1985) 43. and, "Miss Liberty's Children," Newsweek Special Edition, (July, 1986), p. 30.

[8] Cleon Skousen, The Five Thousand Year Leap, (Washington, DC: The Center for Constitutional Studies, 1981) 1-4.

[9] Verna Hall, The Christian History of the American Revolution, (San Francisco: Foundation for American Christian Education, 1976) 66-68.

CONTENTS

CONTENTS

ILLUSTRATIONS

ILLUSTRATIONS xi

PREFACE

THE story of the American Revolution—what our fathers accomplished, their hardships, heroism, and self-denial, in securing the independence of the country and in advancing liberty and happiness throughout the world—will have an interest and charm of its own so long as the desire for freedom exists in the hearts of men.

In this volume an attempt has been made to give a concise, plain, and authentic narrative of the principal battles of the Revolution as witnessed by those who took part in them.

Although the name of Elijah Favor may not be found on the Ryefield muster-roll, yet we have more than his counterpart in the person of Alexander Scammell, who fought at Bunker Hill, became Washington's trusted adjutant-general, and who gave his life to his country at Yorktown; while Dodifer Hanscom, Esek Earl, and Nicholas Dolof are representative boys of the time.

More than a century has passed since "the Boys of '76" shouldered their muskets and fought for their liberties. The sufferings, hardships, hatreds, and barbarities of that struggle all have passed away, and Americans and Britons are brothers; but the story of the struggle—the patriotism, self-denial, and devotion—will never be forgotten. That a perusal of these pages may deepen the love of the boys of the present generation for their country, and quicken their love for liberty and the rights of man, is the earnest hope of

C. C. C.

The Boys of '76

Chapter 1
THE ALARM

ELIJAH FAVOR lived in Ryefield, up among the New Hampshire hills. On the morning of April 20th, 1775, as he was milking the cows, he heard a clattering of hoofs, and, looking up, saw Deacon Clyde coming as fast as his old mare could bring him, and that was not fast enough to suit the deacon, for he was striking the creature with a switch and digging his heels into her sides. He was leaning forward; his coat-tails were streaming in the wind. The mare was striking fire on the gravel and leaving a cloud of dust behind.

"Turn out! turn out!" shouted the deacon. As there was no one in the way, Elijah wondered if the good man had gone crazy.

"Alar-um! alar-um!" he cried. Elijah thought that surely the man had lost his reason.

"Alar-um! alar-um! The red-coats are out, cutting and slashing all before 'em! they have killed a lot of folks at Concord! Go—the minute-men are parading!" the deacon shouted to Elijah's father, who was standing in front of the house. The deacon did not stop—did not slacken his speed even, but rode on, and in a moment disappeared behind a cloud of dust.

1

Mr. Favor stepped into the house, seized his gun and fired it, reloaded and fired again, and a third time. Almost before the reports had ceased to echo, there were answering guns from the neighbors up the road, a half mile away.

They were alarm guns—the signal agreed upon for alarming the country, if the services of the minute-men were needed. Mr. Favor was an old soldier and a minute-man. He fought at Louisburg in 1745, at Ticonderoga in 1756, and at Quebec, with General Wolfe, in 1759, and now he was enrolled to be ready to go at a minute's notice to defend the country against the British troops.

Elijah ran into the house. He was sixteen years old, stout and hearty. He found his father taking down his powder-horn and bullet-pouch.

"Let me go in your place, father," said Elijah. His blood was up. The news brought by the deacon had set him on fire. "Let me go; I am young and strong, and can stand it better than you can."

Mr. Favor knew that Elijah had spoken truly, for he was well along in life; the gray hairs were hanging about his ears, and the rheumatism was racking his bones. Yet he was ready to go, to defend his own rights and the rights of his countrymen.

"If either of you must go, let it be Elijah," said Mrs. Favor.

That settled it. Mr. Favor handed the powder-horn to Elijah; Mrs. Favor bustled around, and in a few minutes had his knapsack filled with bread and cold meat, besides a pair of stockings and a shirt.

"Don't show the white feather to the red-coats, my boy!" said Mr. Favor.

"Take good care of yourself. Don't get sick, and God bless you, 'Lijah!" said Mrs. Favor.

"You'll come back again, 'Lije, won't you?" said his sister Dolly, who threw her arms about his neck and kissed him. He saw a tear on her cheek; it was that which made something come up in his throat, but he gulped it down, shouldered his gun, said "Good-bye," and started for the meeting-house.

"YOU'LL COME BACK AGAIN, 'LIJE, WON'T YOU?"

3

He could hear a drum beating the long roll. Men were running, with guns in their hands. He could see that the minute-men were parading on the green. When he arrived at the meeting-house, he found Captain Abbot and the other officers, and nearly all the members of the company. Among them were three of his playmates—Dodifer Hanscom, Nicholas Dolof, and Esek Earl—who were going in the place of their fathers.

The boys took their places in the ranks. Just before the company was ready to start, the old gray-haired minister, Rev. Mr. Truegrace, stood upon the horse-block, and all took off their hats while he offered prayer. When he had finished, Captain Abbot stepped to the head of the company, drew his sword, and gave command.

"'Tention, comp'ny! Trail arms! By the right flank—file right—march!"

The drummer and fifer struck up "Yankee Doodle," and, with Deacon Clyde on the right of the line, and Captain Abbot at the head, in advance of the drummer and fifer, the Ryefield minute-men filed across the green and turned into the road leading to Boston, leaving their friends and neighbors—old men, leaning on their canes, and women and children—standing on the steps of the meeting-house and around the horse-block, gazing after them with throbbing hearts and tearful eyes.

Captain Abbot and his men knew what they were on the march for—to defend their rights. They understood the whole question at issue between England and the colonies. Elijah, Dodifer, Nicholas, and Esek had read the speeches of James Otis and Samuel Adams, the eloquent patriots of Boston. Elijah could repeat by heart what they had said in Boston town-meetings about the rights of the colonies to be represented in Parliament. He knew what John Hancock had said, the rich merchant of Boston, who had been in England, and was present at the king's coronation, and who was now President of the Congress in session at Philadelphia. He had read the letters of the Pennsylvania farmer, John Dickenson, and the speeches of Edmund Burke and Colonel Barre, who had maintained the right of the colonies to be represented in Parliament, and who had contended that without such representation Parliament had no right to tax them. He knew all the arguments that had been put forth by Lord North and Lord Grenville on the other side, maintaining that, as the debt of England was largely contracted in driving the French out of Canada, the colonies ought to help pay it. He had heard all about the Stamp Act, and had rejoiced to hear that the people in Boston had thrown a lot of tea into the harbor rather than have it landed. But the king's ministers had undertaken, in revenge, to destroy the liberties of the people. They had a bill passed by Parliament, called the Regulation Act, which took away the rights and liberties of the people of Massachusetts. Under the charter the people elected their councilors and representatives, but under the new law the number of councilors was changed. There might be twelve, or thirty-six, and they were to be appointed by the king through the governor, who could remove them at any time and appoint others. The sheriffs, judges, justices, and all officers who, under the charter, had been appointed by the governor and council together, were to be appointed by the governor alone. The governor was to say what salaries all officers were to receive, and the people were to have nothing to say about it.

As the governor was appointed by the king, such a law made the king the government, but, as the king was three thousand miles away, it virtually made the governor the government. The people were not permitted even to elect jurors; that was to be done by the sheriffs. Twice a year the people might meet in town-meeting, and elect town officers and representatives; but nothing else was to be done, nor could any other meeting be held without the permission of the governor.

Troops had been sent over from England to enforce these laws, and Governor Hutchinson had been instructed to arrest Samuel Adams and John Hancock, and send them to England to be tried for treason.

This was in 1774. Parliament had also passed a bill, called the Boston Port Bill, shutting up the port of Boston, so that no ships could arrive or depart except war-ships. General Gage had been ordered to Boston, to take command of the troops and enforce these laws.

On the first day of June, 1774, Governor Hutchinson sailed for England, and when the clock on the old brick meeting-house in Cornhill struck twelve on that day, the Boston Port Bill went into effect.

What that bill was, and what effect it had upon Boston, Elijah Favor learned from a letter written by his cousin, Peter Tremont, who lived in Boston:

"Boston, January 1st, 1775.

"COUSIN ELIJAH,—You can't think how dull it is here in Boston. Six months ago this was the liveliest town in America. Every body was busy, the streets were filled with people, the shop-keepers were selling their goods, the carpenters were putting up houses, the shipwrights were building vessels, the calkers and rope-makers were all at work, ships were coming and going: but now it is just like Sunday. Not a ship can come into the harbor, nor can one go out. The war-ships are anchored in the channel, and the guns at the castle are kept loaded, ready to fire upon any vessel attempting to pass. A fishing smack can't go down to Cohasset to catch cod, nor a dory even to Spectacle Island to catch mackerel or cunners.

"The people of Watertown or Newton can't load a gundalow with cordwood and bring it down Charles River, and unload it at Boston; nor can the farmers who cut hay on the Medford marshes load a scow and bring it down the Mystic, and deliver it at the Blue Anchor or any other stable.

"The brick-makers at Leechmere's Point can't load a boat with bricks and take them across the water to this town. The people of Charlestown have some nice cabbage-gardens out on the road leading to Charlestown Neck, but they can't bring a cabbage or turnip across the ferry and sell it in market.

"A man who owns an apple orchard on Bunker Hill, and some pear-trees on Breed's Hill, just beyond Charlestown, when he wanted to market his fruit last fall, couldn't bring it across the ferry, but had to take his apples in a cart, out over Charlestown Neck, round through Cambridge and Roxbury, to get to market. Nothing can come or go by water.

"Perhaps the king and his ministers think that they can bring us to terms by corking us up, as if we were so many flies in a bottle; but they will find themselves mistaken. The people are more determined than ever not to give in.

"It is hard on the poor. There are hundreds of sailors lounging around the taverns and boarding-houses, drinking grog, with nothing to do. Hundreds of ship-carpenters, house-joiners, and mechanics are idle. The wharves are rotting; grass will grow in the streets in the spring. The town looks as if half the people were dead, and the other half were attending their funeral.

"The town is full of soldiers. The Common is covered with tents, cannon, and baggage-wagons. Sentinels are posted everywhere. Every morning and evening, and at midday, we hear the drums beating.

"People all over the country are sympathizing with us, in a practical way, by sending provisions. The people in Hartford, Connecticut, were the first to inform us that they would help us, but the Windham County folks got ahead of them. They sent two hundred and fifty-eight sheep in July. A few days later, Colonel Israel Putnam, who is an old soldier, and who fought against the French and Indians with Governor Gage, and who was with Lord Howe at Ticonderoga when he was killed, came with one hundred and thirty sheep. From almost every town in New England the people have sent something — rye, wheat, flour, pease, beans, cattle, sheep, or fish. The people of Wilmington, North Carolina, have raised £2000 for us. A ship-load of rice has been sent by the people of Charleston, South Carolina, to be landed at Newport, for, of course, it could not be landed

"There Are Hundreds of Sailors Lounging Around."

here. Mr. Gadsden, who wrote a letter to the people here, is full of pluck. 'Don't pay a cent for the tea,' he writes, using an oath to make it emphatic. The French and English at Quebec have sent one thousand bushels of wheat.

"Lord North planned a mean game. He thought that he would play off Marblehead against Boston, making that place the port of entry. He reckoned that the Marblehead merchants would be so eager to get the trade, that he could get up a rivalry which would divide the people of the colony. Some of the traders of Marblehead jumped at the bait, and were mean enough to solicit General Gage for his patronage, but one hundred and twenty-five others signed an address to General Gage, in which they say: 'Nature, in the formation of our harbor, forbids our being rivals in commerce to Boston. And were it otherwise, we must be lost to all the feelings of humanity, could we indulge one thought to seize on wealth and raise our fortunes on the ruin of our suffering neighbors.'

"Do you think that Boston is going to give in, so long as the whole country, except here and there a Tory, is with her?

"When Colonel Putnam was here, he stopped with Dr. Warren. He is well acquainted with most of the officers in the regiments here, and went out to the camps on the Common to see them. He had a good talk with Major Small. 'If Boston don't give in, she may expect twenty ships of the line and twenty regiments over here pretty soon,' said Small. 'If they come, I shall treat them as enemies,' Putnam replied.

"General Gage finds it difficult to get the machinery of the new government into working order. He has appointed a set of councilors, but some won't accept, and others who have accepted have been obliged to resign. Timothy Paine, of Worcester, accepted, but the people of that town turned out one night, formed a hollow square, and made Paine stand in the centre, take off his hat, and resign the office. Then they started—about fifteen hundred of them—for Rutland, where Mr. Murray, another councilor, lives; but Murray took to his heels, and they couldn't find him.

"Mr. Willard, another councilor, who lives in Lancaster, happened to be down in Connecticut, and the people there, hearing of it, made him march six miles, and so frightened him that he promised never to take his seat. Out of thirty-six appointed by Gage, more than twenty have backed out, while the others are sneaking round like dogs that have been stealing sheep.

"Gage don't have any better success with the judges whom he has appointed. When the time came for holding the court at Springfield, where Gage's new judge was to sit, about two thousand people formed in procession, and, with drums beating, marched to the court-house, set up a black flag, and told the judge that if he entered the court-house it was at his peril. One of the officers of the court—Williams, of Hatfield—had to go round a large circle and ask the people's forgiveness. Two others got down on their knees and resigned their offices. The crowd put old Captain Mirrick, of Monson, upon a cart, drew him round a while, and threatened to give him a coat of tar and feathers for accepting office; but, as he is an old man, concluded not to do it.

"Any man can lead a horse to water, but a whole army can't make him drink, and that is what Gage is just finding out. When the Superior Court was opened the other day here in the State-house, every man who had been selected as juror refused to take the oath.

" 'Why do you refuse?' the chief-justice (Oliver) asked of Thomas Chase.

" 'Because the chief-justice of this court, Judge Oliver, has been impeached by the late representatives of this province,' was the fearless reply. Three cheers for him!

"General Gage called a meeting of his new council at Salem, but not enough for a quorum obeyed the summons, and so, though it is contrary to the Regulation Act for the council to meet in Boston, he had to adjourn it to meet here, on the pretense that it can't do business unless protected by the troops. He is the first to break the new law!

"The people are in earnest, as General Gage and all his officers will soon find. Judge Myrie, who lives up in Monson, is one of Gage's councilors. He has made himself obnoxious to the people, and not long ago they treated him to a free ride in a dung-cart.

"An outrage was committed on the morning of September 1st. The province powder-house is at Quarry Hill, almost on the line between Medford and Cambridge. The powder there belonged to the different towns, and Gage concluded to seize it. About daylight two hundred and sixty soldiers got into boats at Long Wharf, rowed up the Mystic, and landed at Mr. Temple's farm; marched to the magazine; took away two hundred and fifty half-barrels (all there was); then went on to Cambridge and seized two field-pieces, and returned as if they had been making an excursion into the enemy's country.

"The next day there was a lively time in Cambridge. All Middlesex was aflame, to say nothing of the towns in Worcester. The people came flocking into town—several thousand of them. Dr. Warren and some of the other patriots rode out and persuaded the citizens not to do any thing rash. They found old Judge Danforth standing on the Court-house steps, promising never to have any thing more to do with Gage's government. He is a councilor. Then the sheriff was called upon to resign.

"The boys are as wide awake as the men. They hoot at the Tories and pin papers to their backs. The Tories do not like such notoriety; but so long as they uphold the unjust measures of the king, they must expect to be hooted at.

"The people in the country towns are organizing companies of minutemen, who are to be ready, in case of an alarm, to start at a minute's notice. A ship just in from England brings word that a lot more of troops are to be sent over to force us to submit, and the prospect is that, sooner or later, we shall have to fight for our liberties; for as to submitting to such tyranny, we will not.   PETER."

Elijah, Esek, Nicholas, and Dodifer were equally determined with Peter that they never would submit to such tyranny, and so they were hastening toward Boston. So rapidly did they march that they found themselves at Medford, only five miles from Boston, at the end of the second day, having marched nearly sixty miles. The New Hampshire troops were assembling in that town. The Essex County (Massachusetts) troops were in Chelsea. Other Massachusetts troops were at Cambridge. Some Connecticut troops were there. The Rhode Island soldiers were in Roxbury. In all, there were twenty thousand.

The New Hampshire troops were commanded by Colonel John Stark, an old Indian fighter. When he was a young man, he was captured by the Indians while out hunting on a stream called Baker's River, one of the branches of the Merrimac. He was taken to Canada. When he arrived there, the Indians told him that he must run the gantlet, and they formed themselves into two lines, with clubs in their hands, to give him a blow as he passed. His fellow-prisoner, named William Stinson, ran first, and was terribly beaten. Stark had no intention of suffering that way, and when it came his turn to run, he wrenched the club from the hands of the first Indian, then, swinging it with all his might, knocked the Indians right and left, tumbling them one upon another, and getting through without receiving a blow, but leaving many aching heads behind him. Instead of punishing him for what he had done, the Indians patted him on the back, and called him a "brave," and wanted him to be their chief.

One day they set Stark to hoeing corn. That was degradation, for the squaws hoe corn—the braves never. Stark pretended that he did not know corn from weeds, and so cut it up. They threatened to punish him, whereupon he threw the hoe into the river. The Indians found that they could do nothing with him as a prisoner, and were glad to sell him his freedom. He came back to New Hampshire, and, when war broke out between England and France in 1755, he went to Lake Champlain as a captain of the New Hampshire Rangers, and fought the French and Indians, made many a weary march through the wilderness, and did the enemy all the damage he could. Now he was ready to do what he could in defense of his rights.

The soldiers felt their blood flow more quickly through their veins as they listened to the story of what had occurred at Lexington and Concord. This is the way it was: the Sons of Liberty saw that in all probability they would have to fight for their liberties. Samuel Adams, John Hancock, and men from all parts of Massachusetts, had met in convention to deliberate upon the dangers that threatened them. They collected some cannon, powder, balls, flour, fish, and rice at Concord. Governor Gage heard of it, and on the 20th of March sent two of his officers, Captain Brown and Ensign De Bernicre, dressed as citizens, to see what the Sons of Liberty were doing. General Gage had ten regiments of troops in Boston, and he resolved to send out a party secretly, and destroy the cannon, seize the supplies, and also to capture Hancock and Adams, who were stopping with Rev. Jonas Clarke, in Lexington. It was eighteen miles to Concord, and about twelve to Lexington.

The Sons of Liberty in Boston kept a sharp lookout on all of Gage's movements. One of the most active of them was Paul Revere, who cleaned watches and clocks, and who had tried his hand at engraving. Another was Ebenezer Dorr, who dressed calf-skins. Another was Henry Knox, a young man who kept a book-store in Cornhill, where the British officers of a literary turn used to lounge when they had nothing else to do. Another was Mr. Hall, who kept a grog-shop. Another was Mr. Devens, an adjutant in the militia. All of these, and scores more, had their eyes open.

Mr. Hall was in his grog-shop on the evening of the 18th of April, when a woman stepped in. She was a poor creature who lived in the barracks of the Forty-third regiment. She had been drinking, and was a little tipsy, but wanted another drink.

"The troops are going out to Concord to-night," said the woman.

Mr. Hall pricked up his ears. Out to Concord! The cannon were there—and the powder. Mr. Hall had an apprentice, William Baker. He took William one side, whispered in his ear, and in a short time William was going upon the run to see Adjutant Devens. And a few minutes later, the people who

MR. HALL TOOK WILLIAM ONE SIDE AND WHISPERED IN HIS EAR.

13

lived at the north end of the town were surprised to see two lighted lanterns hanging in the belfry of the North Meeting-house. Little did they think that those two tallow-candles would throw their feeble rays far down the centuries. But people over in Charlestown and Cambridge, who were on the watch, understood the signal, that the British troops were going to cross from Boston to the main-land in boats, instead of march-ing out over the "Neck" to Roxbury. William Baker was meanwhile upon the run toward the north end of the town. The sentinels knew him, and did not stop him, for he served them with grog. He found a boat, and pulled across the river to Charlestown, and ran to see good Deacon Larkin, who had a fast horse. The deacon heard what William had to say, and ran to his stable, and saddled and bridled the horse. A moment later the ingenious watch-maker and engraver, Paul Revere, leaped into the saddle and disappeared in the darkness, riding north-west along the road to Charlestown Neck and Medford.

"A hurry of hoofs in a village street,
A shape in the moonlight, a bulk in the dark,
And beneath from the pebbles, in passing, a spark
Struck out by a steed flying fearless and fleet;
That was all! and yet, through the gloom and the light,
The fate of a nation was riding that night;
And the spark struck out by that steed in his flight
Kindled the land into flame with its heat.
He has left the village and mounted the steep,
And beneath him, tranquil and broad and deep,
Is the Mystic meeting the ocean tides;
And under the alders that skirt its edge,
Now soft on the sand, now loud on the ledge,
Is heard the tramp of his steed as he rides.
It was twelve by the village clock
When he crossed the bridge into Medford town;
He heard the crowing of the cock
And the barking of the farmer's dog,
And felt the damp of the river fog,
That rises after the sun goes down."

People who had just gone to bed heard the clattering of hoofs, and wondered who was riding at such a break-neck speed.

He halted at houses here and there, thundering at the doors. "The Regulars are out," he says, and the next moment is away.

While Paul Revere is riding out through Medford, Ebenezer Dorr, mounted on an old plod-jogging horse, with his saddle-bags flopping at every step of the animal, is going out over Boston Neck. The British sentinels say to themselves, "He is a countryman," never once mistrusting that as soon as the rider is past the last sentinel the old mare will be going like the wind toward Cambridge.

Ebenezer reaches Cambridge, stops a moment with the Committee of Safety, and then, with the old mare all afoam, is riding toward Lexington with a letter from Dr. Warren to John Hancock.

About eight hundred British are on the march, under Lieutenant-colonel Smith, of the Tenth regiment, and Major John Pitcairn, of the Marines.

Paul Revere has the start of Mr. Dorr, and comes thundering up to Rev. Mr. Clark's at midnight. Sergeant Monroe and eight men are guarding the house.

"You can't come in, and you mustn't make a noise," the sergeant says.

"You'll have noise enough before morning," the rider replies.

"I can't admit strangers at this time of night," the good minister says.

John Hancock knows the watch-maker's voice.

"Come in, Revere; we know you," he shouts from the chamber window.

They hear the exciting news.

"Ring the bell!" says Hancock; and a few minutes later the people of Lexington hear the bell ringing as it never has rung before. They hear it saying, "The Regulars are coming! the Regulars are coming!"

John Hancock, young and full of fire, is cleaning his gun. His lady-love, Dorothy Quincy, is there at Mr. Clark's. Will not her presence make him brave?

"John, it isn't our business to fight to-night; we belong to the Committee," Samuel Adams says, with his hand on John's shoulder, and John goes with him to the next town, Burlington, to write his name, a year later, so large, upon the Declaration of Independence, that King George can read it without putting on his spectacles.

' Up in Lexington village, young Jonathan Harrington, fifer to the minute-men, is sleeping; but his mother hears the bell, and hastens to Jonathan's chamber.

"Get up, Jonathan! The Regulars are coming, and something must be done."

The minute-men with the guns are running to Mr. Buckman's tavern.

Half-past four in the morning, Thaddeus Brown comes running up the road to Buckman's.

"The red-coats are almost here!"

The drummer beats the long roll out on the green, in front of the meeting-house. The minute-men come out from the tavern and form in line. Captain Parker is their commander. He sees in the dawning light the long column of British troops coming up the Boston road. He has only fifty men; they will be powerless against eight hundred.

"Disperse—don't fire!" is the order of the cool-headed captain. Just as they begin to disperse, Lieutenant-colonel Smith and Major Pitcairn ride forward. The major is sixty years old. People say he is a kind and genial man, but he has lost his head this morning. He is a terrible swearer.

"Lay down your arms, you rebels, and disperse!" he shouts, with an oath, and fires his pistol.

"Fire!" It is Lieutenant-colonel Smith who issues the order, and the British open fire, killing eight and wounding ten of the minute-men. The others flee, and the British give a hurrah over the victory, which is nothing but a massacre.

At two o'clock, Paul Revere rode into Concord. A few minutes later, the meeting-house bell was ringing, and the whole town was astir. The cannon, powder, balls, flour, and supplies must be saved. Some of the farmers came with their ox-carts, others with their horses, to convey the articles to places of safety. The cannon carriages, poor things, roughly made by the country wheelwrights, were taken across Concord River to Colonel Barrett's house. It was thought best to bury the cannon, and some of the pieces were dragged into a field, a trench dug, the cannon laid in it, the earth thrown over them; then a farmer began to plow the field. Some of the flour was carted away to barns and covered with hay. No sleep in Concord after two o'clock; but men and women are astir, doing what they can to secure every thing before the British make their appearance.

Although it is the 19th of April, the season is far advanced. The fields are green, the peach-trees in bloom, and the birches and maples are putting forth their leaves. The robins are building their nests, and the sparrows are chirping in the thickets, on this bright, sunny morning.

Seven o'clock. The people of Concord hear a drum beat, and the shrill notes of the fife, playing the "White Cockade." The fifer down by Lexington played "Yankee Doodle," and a boy laughed to hear him.

"What are you laughing at, boy?" asked Major Pitcairn.

"The Yankees will make you dance it before night," said the boy.

Perhaps the fifer was tired of "Yankee Doodle," and so struck up the "White Cockade" for a change.

And now the people, looking down the Boston road, behold the even ranks of the British. Major Pitcairn and Lieutenant-colonel Smith are on horseback. Above the advancing column waves the cross of St. George, which has waved in triumph over many a battle-field. The sunlight glints from the bright gun-barrels and bayonets. Proudly, defiantly, the column moves on.

The people of Concord know nothing of the slaughter at Lexington. Fifty or more minute-men have gathered under Major Buttrick, ready to defend their homes and fight for their rights, if need be. Oh, if they only knew what had been done at Lexington! But no word has reached them. What can fifty farmers do against eight hundred disciplined troops? Not much. They have succeeded in secreting most of the cannon and nearly all of the powder, and some other things. They have done what they could. The flag that waves above them is not so gorgeous as the banner of the king; it is only a piece of cloth with a pine-tree painted upon it, but brave men are marshaled around it. The minister of Concord, Rev. Mr. Emerson, is there, with his gun on his shoulder.

"Let us stand our ground," he says.

"We are too few; we had better retreat to the other side of the river," says Major Buttrick. He is no coward, but is cool-headed, and gives wise counsel. The minute-men march up the street, cross the bridge, but come to a halt by Mr. Hunt's house.

The British troops halt in the road by the meeting-house. Colonel Smith and Major Pitcairn dismount, leave their horses, go into the burial-ground, and with a spy-glass look across the river to see what the minute-men are doing. Some of the troops—about two hundred—cross the river to Colonel Barrett's, and set the gun-carriages on fire. Other squads are sent to search the houses and barns of the people. They find a barrel of musket-balls and throw them into a well, break off the trunnions of the cannon which the people had not time to bury, and stave in the heads of fifty barrels of flour.

The troops have marched all night, are weary, hungry, and thirsty. They call for breakfast, which the people give them— bread and milk or bacon and eggs. The officers pay liberally, in some instances handing out a guinea and refusing to take any change. Major Pitcairn and some of the officers go into Mr. Wright's tavern and call for brandy. Major Pitcairn stirs the grog with his fingers.

"I mean to stir the Yankee blood as I stir this before night," he says, with an oath.

The minute-men are all west of the river. From the west come men from Acton, the next town, under Captain Isaac Davis. He has kissed his wife, Hannah, good-bye, saying to her, "Take good care of the children, Hannah," and here he is wiping the sweat from his brow, for he and his men have come up on the run. The Sudbury men are coming from the south, and the Bedford men from the west. They meet near the north bridge, in front of Major Buttrick's house. They can see smoke ascending from the town and from Colonel Barrett's, where the gun-carriages are burning, but think that the British have applied the torch to their houses. The party of British which have been to Colonel Barrett's house have returned to the bridge, and are taking up the planks.

"They are burning the town. Shall we stand here and permit it?" says Adjutant Hosmer.

"Let us march and defend our houses. I haven't a man that is afraid to go," says Major Buttrick.

"Neither have I. Let us go," says Captain Davis.

They are five hundred now. Colonel Barrett is commander.

"File right; march to the bridge. Don't fire unless you are fired upon," is his order.

John Buttrick and Luther Blanchard, fifers, strike up the "White Cockade," the drums beat, and the men move on in double files, Captain Davis and the Acton men leading, the Sudbury, Concord, Lincoln, and Bedford men following.

The British, one hundred and fifty, are on the east side, and the Americans on the west side, of the river. They are not ten rods apart. A British soldier raises his gun. There is a flash, and the fifer, Luther Blanchard, feels a prick in his side. A dozen British fire. Captain Davis leaps into the air and falls with a ball through his heart. Nevermore will Hannah, the beloved wife minding the children at home, feel the lips of the brave man upon her cheek. Abner Hosmer also falls dead.

"Fire! for God's sake, fire!" Major Buttrick shouts it. He raises his gun, takes quick aim, and fires the shot which Rev. Mr. Emerson's grandson says, "is heard around the world."

Captain Brown is a Christian. He never swore an oath in his life, but his blood is up, and he utters a terrible curse, and shouts, "They are firing balls! Fire, fire!" he shouts, takes aim, and a British soldier falls, the first in the affray. "Fire! fire! fire!"

The shout runs along the line. Two or more of the British

fall killed or wounded, and the others flee toward the village.

"The war has begun; and no one knows when it will end," says Noah Parkhurst, one of the Lincoln men.

It is eleven o'clock. Lieutenant-colonel Smith and Major Pitcairn are alarmed. They send out messengers to bring in the scattered troops. The Yankee blood is getting hotter than Major Pitcairn thought possible. He has stirred it effectually, and his own life will yet go out in the fire he has kindled.

Colonel Smith marshals the troops in front of Elisha Jones's house.

It is high time he was on his return to Boston. Yet he does not like to go, for fear the Yankees will think he is afraid. He will not be in a hurry. But the Yankees are gathering in larger force. He can see them down by the river. They are marching round through the meadows to cut off his retreat. Twelve o'clock. The

At Every Corner the Minute-men Attack the Retreating Troops.

British move out of the town, but instantly from behind the fences rise up unseen faces. There is a rattle of muskets, and British soldiers drop by the roadside. The minute-men are no longer in line. Every man fights for himself. He is his own general and captain. Colonel Smith is wounded in the leg, and Major Pitcairn in the arm. He tumbles from his horse, and the horse escapes. The Americans see it running wild in the fields and capture it. The British are upon the run now. Down the road toward Lexington they flee, stopping now and then to load and fire, then running again, with men dropping from the ranks at every step.

The Billerica and the Reading minute-men have arrived to harass them, and there is a sharp fight at Merriam's Corner.

At every corner, every turn, in every orchard, in every wood, the minute-men attack the retreating troops.

Back to Lexington they hasten. Oh, what a welcome sight is that which they behold! Lord Percy, with eleven hundred men and two pieces of cannon, are at Lexington. The fugitives are worn out. Their tongues hang from their mouths, like the tongues of deer when hunted by hounds, as they throw themselves upon the ground under the protection of the sheltering cannon.

And now it is a battle all the way to Charlestown. The shades of evening fall as the British troops rush across the narrow neck of land to Charlestown. Seventy-three of their number have been killed, and one hundred and seventy-two wounded, and twenty-six missing. Of the minute-men, forty-nine have been killed and thirty-six wounded. Men from thirty-one towns have followed them. Such the story.

It was no great hardship for Elijah and Dodifer, Esek and Nicholas, to spread their blankets in a barn and sleep on a haymow, for many a time, while out hunting raccoons, they had slept on the ground.

From Medford they could look across the salt-marshes and see the steeples of the meeting-houses in Boston, and at night, when all was quiet, could hear the clock on one of the steeples striking the hours.

Colonel Stark drilled the regiment every day. The boys had enough to eat, the nights were warm, the days beautiful, and so the time passed swiftly by.

Chapter 2
BUNKER HILL

BOOM!"

It was day-break on the morning of the 17th of June, when the roar of a cannon went over the marshes toward Medford and Cambridge. Elijah, and Dodifer, and Nicholas, and all the other soldiers, sprung to their feet and rushed out-of-doors.

"Boom!" it came again. And now, looking toward Charlestown, they saw a white cloud enveloping the war-ship *Lively*, which was at anchor in the stream between Boston and Charlestown. There was a bright flash, and again the deep, heavy thunder of the cannon came rolling over the green marshes.

They wondered what was going on, but as the day brightened they could see that not only the *Lively*, but the other ships, were firing at an embankment of earth which had been thrown up during the night on a hill overlooking Charlestown. When the sun rose, they could see men at work with picks and shovels. The firing soon ceased, but the work went on. Soon it was rumored through the camp that Colonel William Prescott, with about one thousand men, part of his own regiment, about one-third of Colonel Bridge's, and a third of Colonel Frye's, and one company of Connecticut men, under Lieutenant-colonel Knowlton, had started from Cambridge the evening before, to construct a fort on one of the hills near Charlestown. Before they started they paraded on Cambridge Common, in front of the meeting-house; and the President of Harvard College, Rev. Mr. Langdon, offered prayer. Two sergeants with dark lanterns led the way, and the soldiers marched in silence, followed by two carts loaded with picks and shovels They crossed Charlestown Neck about eleven o'clock, but it was after midnight before a shovelful of earth was thrown up; and there they were, working like beavers, with the cannon-shot flying around them.

About nine o'clock an officer came to Medford, where Colonel Stark had his head-quarters, with a message from General Artemus Ward, who was commander-in-chief of all the troops around Boston. His head-quarters were at Cambridge. A few minutes later the adjutant of the regiment came out of Colonel Stark's quarters with an order for Lieutenant-colonel Wyman to march with two hundred men to Charlestown to re-enforce Colonel Prescott. Dodifer had been transferred to another company, and his was one of those ordered to march.

"I wish that our company had been selected," said Elijah.

"Don't be in a hurry, boy," said the old soldier, who had fought at Quebec. "Likely as not you'll have a chance to show your pluck before night, for what our boys are doing on the hill there is like giving General Gage's nose a tweak. Ye see, our boys can fire right plum-down upon the ships; and if he don't try to drive 'em out, then I'm mistaken."

Elijah looked across the marshes once more and saw that the tide was coming in, and that the *Lively* and another warship, the *Symmetry*, were floating up-stream. The *Symmetry* came well up toward Charlestown Neck and dropped anchor. The firing from the ships had stopped, but now it began again louder than ever. The church bells were ringing in Cambridge, and there was a general commotion in all the camps.

About eleven o'clock another officer came in haste from Cambridge to see General Stark. A minute or two later, the drummers came out with their drums and began to beat the long roll.

"Fall in! fall in!" shouted the officers.

The boys seized their powder-horns and bullet-pouches and guns, and took their places in the ranks. The regiment marched to Colonel Stark's quarters, and each man received a gill of powder and several bullets and an extra flint. Colonel Stark came out, drew his sword, and turned to the regiment.

"By sections, quick step, shoulder arms, march!" was his order. The drums beat, the regiment moved down the street, crossed a bridge spanning the Mystic River, and took the road leading to Charlestown.

The bell on Medford meeting-house was ringing for twelve o'clock when they started. An hour's march brought them to an elevation called Plowed Hill, from whence they could look down upon the harbor and upon Charlestown. The *Symmetry*, with twenty guns, threw shot across Charlestown Neck, over which they must march. Farther down the harbor, near the ferry between Charlestown and Boston, was the *Lively*, with twenty guns; beyond it the *Glasgow*, with twenty-four guns; the *Cerberus*, with thirty-six guns; and the *Somerset*, with sixty-eight guns. Admiral Graves's flag was floating in the breeze above the quarter-deck of the *Somerset*. The *Symmetry* was sweeping the Neck with its guns, while the other ships were firing at the bank of yellow earth on the hill.

The regiment marched on, and came to some troops that had halted in the road, as if afraid to cross the narrow isthmus leading to Charlestown. Elijah saw Major Maclary, of Colonel Stark's regiment—a tall man, for whom he had great respect—step forward to see what the trouble was.

"Why don't you go ahead?" Major Maclary asked.

The halting troops made no reply.

"If you ain't going, step one side, will you, and give us a chance."

The troops stepped to the side of the road, and the regiment marched on.

"Bang! bang! bang!" went the cannon of the *Symmetry*. Suddenly the air was full of horrifying noises. Something unseen went by with a terrible screech. Something plowed a furrow in the ground and threw the gravel stone into the boys' faces. Something came with a terrible whirr, and passed over their heads. Their hair stood on end. They wished that they were not there, and wanted to turn and run. They never were so frightened before. Colonel Stark was marching, at the head of the regiment, a slow and measured step. They wished he would go faster.

"Don't you think it would be well to go across upon the double-quick?" Captain Dearborn asked.

"No; one fresh man is worth two tired ones," the colonel replied, keeping the same steady step. They crossed in safety. As they passed up the hill on the other side, they met some soldiers who had been at work through the night upon the intrenchments.

"What's the news?" Elijah asked.

"The red-coats are landing at Moulton's Point," said one.

"A cannon-shot killed one of our men—Asa Pollard, of Billerica," said another.

"But ain't you going the wrong way?" Esek Earl asked.

"We have worked all night and through the forenoon without a wink of sleep, nor have we had any thing to eat or drink," said one of the retiring soldiers.

The regiment came to some houses, where Colonel Reed's New Hampshire regiment was quartered. It was under arms, and followed Colonel Stark's up a hill, and over it to a rail-fence, which ran from the water straight up the hill, toward the intrenchment.

The farmers had been mowing their grass the day before, and had raked some of it into cocks and windrows. As they came to the fence, Elijah saw the Connecticut troops under Colonel Knowlton at work, tearing down another rail-fence and setting it up against the one behind which they had halted, and stuffing the space between with hay. Colonel Stark told his men to do the same. The boys laid down their guns, and in a few minutes had a hay breastwork, which, if it would not stop a bullet, would at least screen them from the red-coats.

Colonel Stark got over the fence, went out about eight rods, and drove a stake into the ground.

"There, boys," he said, "if the red-coats attack us, wait till they get to this stake before you fire."

"THE RED-COATS ARE LANDING AT MOULTON'S POINT."

The boys had shot partridges farther away than that, and they thought that a red-coat would stand a poor chance at that distance.

All the while, Dodifer was in the intrenchment on the top of the hill. He could look over the breastwork and see all that was going on. At first he did not dare to look, the cannon-balls flew so thick; but he soon got accustomed to hearing them fly past, and took a look now and then.

Colonel Stark Went Out About Eight Rods, and Drove a Stake into the Ground.

There was a great commotion in Boston. Officers were riding furiously through the streets, and soldiers were marching from their barracks to Long Wharf. The roofs of the houses were covered with people. Cannon on Copp's Hill were flaming and thundering, sending their shot across the water. The harbor was alive with boats bringing soldiers from Long Wharf to Moulton's Point.

One of the hills was owned by Mr. Breed, and the other by Mr. Bunker. The fortifications were on Breed's Hill, but the engagement is known as the battle of Bunker Hill.

Behind him, Dodifer saw an embankment of earth, extending from the north-east corner of the intrenchment down the hill. There were few soldiers in the intrenchment at this moment—not more than three hundred. The rest—worn and tired, hungry and sleepy—had straggled away, except a few, whom Colonel Prescott had sent down into the village of Charlestown.

Dodifer was glad when he saw the rest of the regiment, followed by Colonel Reed's, march down to the fence, and when some soldiers from Colonel Nixon's, Colonel Little's, and other regiments, arrived, to help defend the intrenchments. An officer on a white horse was riding furiously about. One moment he would be at the intrenchment, talking with Colonel Prescott; then he would gallop to the rail-fence and talk with Colonel Reed and Colonel Stark, and with the men; then he would be away to the rear, hurrying up re-enforcements, and planning another intrenchment on Bunker Hill.

Colonel Prescott Stepped upon the Embankment.

"That is 'Old Put.' He is a tiger at fighting; I was with him at Ti," said a soldier who had fought the French and Indians at Ticonderoga. It was Israel Putnam, from Connecticut.

A noble-looking man, well dressed, and in the prime of life, entered the intrenchment. Dodifer saw some of the soldiers take off their hats to him. "That is Dr. Warren, of Boston, one of the truest patriots that ever lived. He has just been made a general," said a soldier.

Dr. Warren went up to Colonel Prescott and shook hands with him.

"I yield the command to you," said Colonel Prescott.

"Oh, no; I come as a volunteer," the doctor replied, and looked around for a gun.

The cannon-balls were flying thicker than ever, and some of the soldiers were frightened. To inspire them with courage, Colonel Prescott stepped upon the embankment and walked backward and forward, telling the soldiers not to fire till the British were so near that they could see the whites of their eyes, and then to aim at their belts. The soldiers admired him, he was so cool. They fixed their flints, looked at the priming, and waited for the coming-on of the British.

Chapter 3
BATTLE of BUNKER HILL

THE sun was shining from a cloudless sky, and Dodifer could see all that was going on down in the harbor. The British troops were landing and forming on the beach. While the boats went back to Boston for more soldiers, those already landed sat down upon the grass and eat their dinners. When all had arrived, the regiments formed in a field. There were five of them—the fifth, the thirty-eighth, forty-third, forty-seventh, and fifty-second, and a battalion of marines; nearly three thousand men in all. The officers were noble-looking men. General Howe was commander-in-chief; General Burgoyne and General Pigot commanded under him.

It was a grand sight—the long lines, the red coats faced with buff, the white pantaloons of the soldiers, the white cross-belts, the bright buckles, the tall caps, the sunlight gleaming from the guns and bayonets, the moving columns, the drums beating, the fifes playing, the bugles blowing, the ships all aflame, and great white clouds rolling high above the masts, another white cloud ascending from Copp's Hill in Boston, the roofs of the houses covered with people: all together it was the grandest sight Dodifer had ever seen—so grand that he almost forgot that he was standing there to fight those advancing columns of Old England. The thought came: what chance would he and his fellow-soldiers have, men and boys as they were, without discipline, knowing nothing of war, without bayonets, with only their shot-guns, with a few bullets, and only a gill of powder in their horns—what chance would they have of defeating troops that had fought the veteran soldiers of France and Spain? Not much. Yet it was no time to flinch. He resolved to do his best.

Similar thoughts came to Elijah, Esek, and Nicholas, as they lay upon the grass behind the fence. They could hear the cannon roaring, and, as they looked along the water toward Moulton's Point, could see the light-infantry and grenadiers getting ready to advance.

The British troops were in motion, advancing slowly. They were yet at a considerable distance, when there was a flash, a puff of smoke.

"Down! down!" shouted everybody. The boys dropped behind the fence, and the next moment a cannon-ball went screaming over their heads.

"It whistles a lively tune," said Esek.

Behind the intrenchments there was a good deal of excitement just at this moment. Some of the men had rifles, and they had been accustomed to bring down a buck or a wolf at long range. They laid their rifles on the top of the intrenchment and took aim and fired, and men down in the British ranks suddenly threw up their hands and fell headlong.

"Stop firing!" shouted Colonel Prescott; and an officer jumped upon the embankment and kicked up the rifles.

"Save your powder. Wait till they get within eight rods," he said, and the soldiers reloaded their rifles and waited.

The light-infantry and grenadiers were getting nearer to the fence. Elijah peeped through the hay and saw the soldiers of the front rank come to a halt. He heard the colonel commanding them say, "Take aim!" They leveled their pieces. "Fire!" he shouted. There was a flash, a white cloud, and the air was filled with leaden hail which struck into the ground, splintered the rails of the fence, or flew above the heads of the boys and their fellow-soldiers.

"Keep quiet, boys; don't be in a hurry," said Captain Abbot, as he walked up and down the line.

Another volley came, and another. The bullets were whistling close to Elijah's ears. He was getting nervous, for the British troops were only a few rods away—so near that he could hear their tramping. He cocked his gun—he was down on one knee, with the muzzle resting on a rail. There was a clicking of locks all along the line.

"Don't get flustered; keep cool," said Captain Abbot.

"Aim low," said an old soldier at Elijah's right hand.

"Take good aim," said one at the left.

"Pick off the officers," said Esek.

Elijah ran his eye along his gun-barrel and took aim at a white belt. It was a good mark to aim at, a white belt on a red coat, and many a soldier died that day, as there has on many other battle-fields, simply because the showy uniform of Old England is the best of targets.

The white pantaloons and red coats were up to the stake which Colonel Stark had driven. There was a sudden crack, a rattle, a roar. The boys fired, then sprung to their feet and loaded their guns as quick as they could. There was a white cloud along the fence from the water up the hill almost to the embankment. Looking through the smoke, Elijah could see men reeling and falling to the ground. Some were down on their knees trying to get up. Some were trying to save themselves from going down. The front rank was broken up. Some were running; officers were flourishing their swords, and trying to stop them. Elijah fired again as quick as he could, and so did all around him. The second line of the British was tumbling to pieces, and the third; and a moment later all except the officers took to their heels and ran back through the fields to Moulton's Point.

The boys off with their hats, swung them over their heads, and hurraed as loud as they could. And now the intrenchment on the hill was all aflame, and the regiments under General Pigot were fleeing.

ELIJAH WAS DOWN ON ONE KNEE, WITH THE MUZZLE OF HIS GUN
ON A RAIL.

35

"Hurra! hurra! hurra!" came from the hill. The back-woodsmen were a match for the troops of Old England.

There was a great commotion at Moulton's Point. Officers were running here and there rallying the men, telling them how disgraceful it was for them to be whipped by a handful of Yankees. After a while the lines were reformed, and the British troops advanced a second time.

There were some brick-kilns in one of the fields, and the artillery came past them, wheeled into position, and began to fire upon the breastwork. The light-infantry and grenadiers came on again, but not quite so proudly as before. They halted, fired, advanced, and fired again. The bullets came through the hay. A soldier close to Elijah was wounded. At first Elijah, Esek, and Nicholas had trembled, but now they were as cool as if waiting to get a shot at a deer.

The British came on. Click, click, click, went the gun-locks again. They were so near that Elijah could see the whites of their eyes.

Again there was a ripple and a deafening roar. When the smoke cleared away there was a heap of dead and wounded— a windrow of men. Some staggered a few steps before they fell, while others dropped as nine-pins drop when the ball goes down the alley. Again the British troops were fleeing, and vain were all the efforts of the officers to stop them.

While this was going on in front of the fence, Dodifer and the men behind the intrenchment were waiting for the advance of the troops under General Pigot. The British went slowly up the hill. They almost reached the intrenchment when the parapet blazed, and the ranks went down as the grass falls before the mower, and those who could get away fled to Moulton's Point. Again there was a hurra.

"We can lick the lobsters," shouted Dodifer in his enthusiasm.

"We'll drive 'em into the sea," shouted another.

Nearly a third part of the British had been killed or wounded. General Howe saw his fine army melting away. Thus far he had been defeated, but it never would do to give it up so.

What would the king say? What would all England say? He must drive the rebels out of the fort, or his honor and every thing else would be lost.

"It is murder," said the British soldiers. "No troops can stand such a fire."

General Clinton was in Boston, and now he came across the harbor with four hundred men to help in a third attack.

The British soldiers laid aside their knapsacks and prepared for a last desperate attempt. General Howe had learned a lesson from the New Hampshire boys behind the fence. He would not have any more men slaughtered there; he would only make believe that he was going to attack them; he would march a few soldiers in that direction, but would hurl his main body upon the handful of men behind the intrenchment on the hill. He had discovered the weak place in the intrenchment: it was at the north-east corner.

Suddenly a black smoke rolled up from Charlestown, growing blacker every moment. The town was on fire. A shot, called a carcass, had been fired across the water from Boston, with the intention of setting the town on fire, and now the flames were leaping from window and roof and steeple.

In a few minutes four hundred houses were on fire. While the town was burning, the light-infantry, as before, marched toward the fence, but when the troops reached the brick-kilns they turned to the left and marched toward the intrenchment. Elijah and the men at the fence saw them turn, rank after rank, and fired at them, but they were a good distance away, and the balls fell short and the ranks pressed on. Dodifer and the few soldiers in the fort fired as fast as they could, but their powder was gone, for they had only a gill at the outset. The British came nearer. Dodifer heard a hurra behind him, and saw them leaping over the parapet at the north-east corner. He had no bayonet, nor had many of those by his side. Some used the butts of their guns to beat out the brains of the British, but they were quickly shot or bayoneted. He saw Dr. Warren in the thickest of the fight. A British soldier was aiming at him, and the next moment the noble man fell.

"Retreat!" said Colonel Prescott.

The British had already cut off Dodifer's escape toward the north-east. He ran to the west side, leaped over the embankment almost into the faces of the British that were coming up on that side. A red-coat stabbed at him, but did not hit him. Bullets whizzed past him. One soldier fired in his face. The smoke covered him, and the grains of powder from the gun made his cheeks smart, but the bullet did not touch him. He escaped past the advancing line. He was going to throw away his gun, that he might run faster, but concluded he would not. He reached a rail-fence, sprung over it, and fell upon the other side. The bullets came against the rails like hail-stones in a shower. He was out of breath, and concluded to lie still a moment.

"We've stiffened that young Yankee," said a British soldier.

"They think that they have hit me," said Dodifer to himself. He heard the tramp of those who

Dodifer Saw Elijah and Esek Carrying a Wounded Soldier.

were fleeing, and the shouts and hurras of the British. He recovered his breath and started once more. The balls flew around him, but in a minute he was so far away that he dropped into a walk.

Colonel Stark, Colonel Reed, and Colonel Knowlton were coming up from the fence. Dodifer saw Elijah and Esek carrying a wounded soldier. Getting nearer, he saw that it was Nicholas—a ball had gone through his foot. He helped them, and together they went to Bunker Hill. General Putnam was there, riding to and fro, shouting and swearing.

"Stop here, you cowards! We can beat 'em here!" he cried. He was wet with sweat and covered with dust.

The soldiers would not stop, and as the boys went down the hill toward the "Neck," they could hear him still shouting, "Stop here! we can lick 'em here!"

The ships were firing faster than ever across the "Neck." Just in advance of the boys was Major Maclary, the brave man who had opened the way for the regiment in the morning. They saw him fall, struck by a grape-shot. He lived only a few minutes. The shot flew all around them, but they got across the "Neck" safely, and carried Nicholas into a house where a surgeon had set up his hospital.

It was sunset when they reached the high ground on Plowed Hill. They were tired and hungry. They had no tents, but kindled fires in the field and cooked their supper, and through the evening talked over the events of the day.

They were sorry to learn that one hundred and forty of their number had been killed, and two hundred and seventy-one wounded. But the loss of the British was terrible—two hundred and twenty-six killed, and eight hundred and twenty-eight wounded.

The old soldiers lighted their pipes, threw themselves upon the grass, and told stories of the days when they fought the French and Indians. A Connecticut soldier told about General Putnam's exploits.

"He has smelled gunpowder before," he said. "He is as brave as a lion. I never heard him swear, though, before to-day; he is a member of the church, but it made him mad to see the retreat, when we had all but beaten the British. I was with Old Put at Fort Edward in '55. One hot day in August, he and Captain Robert Rogers, of the New Hampshire Rangers, and a dozen of us took a tramp to see what the French and red-skins were doing at Crown Point. We got close up to the fort. Rogers and Put crept up under the walls and made what discoveries they could, but stumbled upon two French soldiers. One of the Frenchmen seized Rogers's gun, and the other was about to stab him, when Put up with his gun and split the fellow's head open. The other Frenchman took to his heels, and gave an alarm; and the whole garrison, French and Indians, several hundred, swarmed out like so many hornets when you give the nest a stirring-up; but we all got back safe and sound.

"The next year, in '57, we were at Fort Edward. One day a party of wood-choppers and a guard of fifty British soldiers were surprised by a legion of Indians. The captain of the guard sent to the fort for help. General Lyman was commander, but was afraid to send out any troops. Old Put boiled over at that, and started upon the run with the Rangers. Lyman called to him to stop; but Put was deaf just then, and we rushed into the woods yelling like so many devils. We poured a volley into the Indians and drove them.

"I was there with Putnam all the next winter," the old soldier went on to say, "and one morning the barracks took fire. We rushed out with our camp-kettles, formed a line down to the river, and passed the kettles from hand to hand to Putnam, who climbed upon the roof and dashed the water on the fire, which was close to the magazine, where all our powder was stored. A single spark lighting on the powder would have sent him and all the rest of us sky-high quicker than you can say Jack Robinson.

"Colonel Haviland was our colonel, and he ordered the captain to get down, but Putnam refused, and kept throwing water till the fire was put out. His hands and face were badly blistered, and it was a month before he got out of the hospital.

"The next summer we had a nice scrimmage with five hundred French and Indians under Molong. Putnam, and sixty of us soldiers, were ordered to go to Lake Champlain to see what the French and red-skins were up to. We built a stone wall on the shore of the lake for a breastwork, planted a lot of pines and hemlocks in front of it, so that from the lake you never would have mistrusted that a wall had been built there. We were as still as mice. The canoes came, got abreast of us, when one of the Rangers hit his gun against a stone. Quick as a flash the Indians stopped paddling.

" 'Let 'em have it!' shouted Old Put, and we sent a lot of red-skins heels over head into the lake. But we were only a handful, as they could see by our firing, and the French captain landed to cut us off. We saw what he was up to, and got ahead of him, and all hands returned without a scratch.

They Tied Him to a Tree and Were Going to Burn Him at the Stake.

"A few days later we were out on a scout, and the French and Indians, under Molong, ambushed us. We sprung behind trees and fought like tigers. Putnam shot four Indians and aimed at another, but his gun missed fire, and, before he could fix the flint, the Indians sprung upon him, and seized his gun. They had surrounded us, and we had to surrender.

"The Indians had a special spite against Putnam because he had killed so many of 'em; so at night, when we halted, they tied him to a tree, got a lot of wood, heaped it around him, and were going to burn him at the stake; but it was raining hard, and put the fire out. They kindled it again; but the French captain, Molong, found out what the red-skins were about, rushed up, kicked away the brands, and took him to his own tent, and so saved his life.

"The next year General Amherst sent Putnam up to Oswegatchie (Ogdensburg), and he captured a lot of French and Indians. He was with Wolfe at Quebec. In '62 he fought the Spaniards in Cuba; and in '64, when that red-skin Pontiac got up his conspiracy, Putnam commanded the Provincials that were sent away up the lakes to Detroit. I guess there ain't a man in America who has seen more fighting than Old Put. He has had lots of hair-breadth escapes. He is as generous as he is brave. He drove a flock of sheep to Boston last summer when the people were almost starving after the port was shut up. He had a square talk with General Gage and Lord Percy. He is well acquainted with them, for all three were together in Canada. Gage laughed at the idea of our fighting.

" 'Why, with five thousand troops I can march from Massachusetts to Georgia,' said he.

" 'So you can,' says Putnam, 'if you behave yourself, and pay for what you eat; but if you attempt to do it in a hostile manner, the women will give you a drubbing with their skimmers.'

"Putnam has a farm in Connecticut, and keeps a tavern. He has a picture of General Wolfe on the sign. When the news came of the battle of Lexington, he was plowing. He unharnessed his team, left the plow in the furrow, mounted his horse, and, without stopping to change his clothes, started. "If there is any fighting to be done, he is always 'round."

The old soldier had finished his pipe, and now threw himself on the ground on the leeward side of the fire.

"The smoke will blow in your face," said Esek.

"That won't hurt me; but let me tell you a thing worth knowing, my boy," said the soldier. "Always sleep on the leeward side of the fire. True, you will get the smoke, but the heat will dry up the dampness and keep you from having the rheumatiz. If you don't want your bones to ache by-and-by, sleep on the side where the smoke blows."

The boys saw the philosophy of it, and lay down by his side, and so spent their first night after a battle.

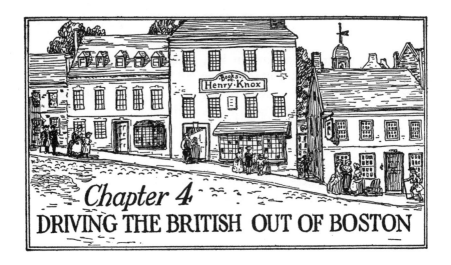

Chapter 4
DRIVING THE BRITISH OUT OF BOSTON

NOW came hard work with the spade and shovel. While some of the soldiers kept guard, others threw up intrenchments, till from Winter Hill, where Colonel Stark's regiment was stationed, around to Dorchester, were fortifications, completely shutting the British army in Boston.

There came an important day—the 3d of July. Congress had appointed General George Washington commander-in-chief, and he had arrived at General Ward's headquarters in Cambridge. The boys had heard of him—that he had been a surveyor, and had accompanied General Braddock in his disastrous campaign against Fort Du Quesne, and had shown himself to be a brave and able commander.

On the morning of the 3d of July, the regiment paraded and marched to the colleges in Cambridge, and were drawn up in brigades on the Common. They saw a noble-looking man, accompanied by General Putnam, General Ward, and nearly all the generals in the army, ride out from General Ward's head-quarters. The cavalcade drew up under a great elm.

The regiments presented arms, the drums beat a salute, General Washington raised his cocked hat, and then, replacing it on his head, drew his sword, and rode along the lines. He was in the prime of life. He wore a blue coat with buff trimmings, buff breeches, and high top-boots, an epaulet on each shoulder, and a black cockade on his hat. He sat splendidly on his horse. There were decision and energy in all his movements. He was reputed to be rich, and owner of a great estate on the banks of the Potomac; but he had left all to take command of the army. The soldiers regarded him with great respect, and his coming gave them renewed confidence.

Elijah Rolled a Handbill Round a Stone and Threw It at the British Sentinel.

A strict guard was kept everywhere, and the British troops in Boston soon found themselves in want of fresh provisions. They could get no vegetables, nor fresh meat. Somebody in the American camp got up a handbill and printed it. Elijah took a copy when he went out on picket at Charlestown Neck. He was so close to the British sentinel, that they could talk with one another. Elijah rolled the handbill round a stone, and threw it at the British soldier, who picked it up, and this is what he read:

AMERICAN ARMY.	ENGLISH ARMY.
1. Seven dollars a month.	1. Three-pence a day.
2. Fresh provisions in plenty.	2. Rotten salt pork.
3. Health.	3. The scurvy.
4. Freedom, ease, affluence, and a good farm.	4. Slavery, beggary, and want.

The red-coat put it into his pocket; but the next night a deserter came over to the Americans—the next night another; and so many came that General Howe was much perplexed, and shot several who tried to escape.

In September, volunteers were called for to go on a secret expedition through the woods of Maine to capture Quebec. Dodifer joined the expedition, and bid good-bye to Elijah and Esek. Where he went, and what he saw, will be narrated in the next chapter.

Elijah, Esek, and Nicholas remained with the army digging trenches, standing as sentinels, or acting as guards at Washington's head-quarters in Cambridge.

There was a scarcity of arms in the American ranks around Boston, but there came a day of great rejoicing, for an American vessel, the *Lee,* commanded by Captain Mosely, captured the English brig *Nancy,* and took it to Marblehead, with two thousand muskets, one hundred thousand flints, thirty thousand cannon-shot, thirty tons of musket-balls, and one thirteen-inch mortar. The Essex County farmers turned out with their oxen, and drew the ammunition into camp. When the long line of teams wound over the Medford marshes and reached Cambridge, the soldiers cheered till they were hoarse.

Elijah and Esek worked with levers and crow-bars, helping place the mortar behind one of the intrenchments. When they got it in position, General Putnam, in his enthusiasm, mounted it, with a bottle of rum, and drank to its new name, "The Congress," and soon sent a shell whizzing through the air into Boston.

On a foggy morning in December, 1775, Elijah and Esek were sent with other soldiers to a little round hill called "Cobble Hill," almost down to the edge of the water, to throw up an intrenchment. There was a British war-ship at anchor only a short distance away, but the fog was so thick that they worked all the forenoon without being discovered. At last the fog lifted, and then the ship's cannon began to thunder, and the balls came so thick that they had to quit. In the night they went back with a cannon and placed it in position—a thirty-four-pounder.

As soon as it was light enough in the morning, Captain Smith sighted the cannon, and sent a ball whizzing over the marsh that went plump into the side of the vessel, and followed it up till the captain raised his anchor, hoisted his sails, and made all haste to get away.   The soldiers shouted so loud that the British on Bunker Hill heard the hurra, and began to let their cannon roar in reply.   They wasted a great deal of powder, doing no harm to any body.

General Washington established strict discipline, and looked carefully after the health of the army.   Provisions were plenty. This is what Elijah and Esek had served to them during a week:

MEATS.

Corned beef or pork, half a pound per day, four days in a week.
Fresh beef two days.
Salt fish one day.

FLOUR.

One pound of flour per day.
Three pints of pease or beans during the week.
Half a pint of rice once a week.

OTHER THINGS.

Potatoes, onions, cabbages, turnips, butter, molasses, and a quart of spruce-beer every day, with now and then a glass of grog.

The determination of the Americans to resist the aggressions of the king and his ministers was not confined to New England, but extended to all the colonies.   It was a common cause, and the people of Virginia and the Carolinas were just as ready to take up arms in defense of their rights as the people of Massachusetts.

One day there came marching into camp a regiment from Virginia, from the beautiful valley of the Shenandoah.   It was commanded by Daniel Morgan.   The men wore frocks trimmed with fur, and fur caps ornamented with buck-tails.   On their breasts were the words uttered by Patrick Henry in the House of Burgesses in Virginia, "Liberty or Death!"   They were armed with rifles, and had marched all the weary way from beyond the Potomac, to have a hand in driving the British out of Boston.

General Washington was riding out to inspect the intrenchments, and met the brave riflemen. General Morgan saluted the commander-in-chief.

"From the right bank of the Potomac, general!"

From the Potomac! Then they were old neighbors. He must shake hands with them; and the commander-in-chief dismounts, goes along the line, and, with tears upon his cheeks, shakes hands with the hardy huntsmen of the Shenandoah, who have shown such devotion to their country.

The 2d of January, 1776, was an eventful day. The regiments were paraded to receive the new flags which had been agreed upon. Up to this time some of the regiments had carried the pine-tree flag; other regiments, those from Connecticut, with flags bearing this motto, *"Qui transtulit sustinet"* ("God, who hath transported, will sustain"); but now the regiments were to fight under a common flag. The drums beat a salute, the soldiers presented arms, and the flags were unfurled—each flag with thirteen stripes, red and white, with the Union Jack in place of the stars. Thirteen guns were fired, and the regiments marched back to their camps with the flags waving above them.

Just about the time the flags were received the sentinels at Charlestown Neck saw a British officer coming down to the picket-line with a flag of truce. An officer went to meet him, to see what he wanted, and found that he had a proclamation which had just been received from England, sent over by the king. The king said that the Americans had turned rebels, and were carrying on a war for the purpose of establishing an independent empire, and that the British nation would never give up the colonies. He had enlisted thousands of soldiers, and was negotiating with the Prince of Hesse, in Germany, for a large number of troops to aid in putting down the rebellion.

If the American soldiers would lay down their arms and go home, he would not punish them; but if not, they must take the consequences.

"YOU ARE TO MARCH IN SILENCE. NO TALKING."

The proclamation was read in camp, and the soldiers laughed at it; they swung their hats, and cheered louder than ever. Lay down their arms! Not they.

Henry Knox, the young book-seller, whose store was on Cornhill, a stout, thick-set man, was placed in command of all the artillery. He went to Ticonderoga, where there were many cannon, engaged ox-teams, and one day in February the army saw forty-two sleds drawn by oxen come into camp, loaded with cannon and powder and balls. "Now we will drive the redcoats out of Boston," said the soldiers. They went to work with a will, and soon had forty-nine cannon and six mortars in position to send shells and solid shot across the water into the town. One ball struck Brattle-street Church, and imbedded itself in the wall. On the night of the 3d of March the cannon and mortars were thundering from sunset till sunrise. One shot went into the British guard-house, and wounded six men. Very little sleep in Boston that night.

Elijah did not know, nor did any one in the army know, that behind all this cannonading General Washington had a grand plan.

The next night, the cannon began to roar again. As soon as it was dark, the soldiers in Roxbury under General Thomas were paraded—two thousand in number.

"You are to march in silence. No talking allowed," said the officers.

The regiments came out from their camps into the road leading to Dorchester Neck, and found a long line of carts, drawn by oxen and horses—three hundred carts in all. In the carts were gabions—great baskets which had been made in Dorchester in an alder swamp. Some were loaded with picks and spades. The teamsters had wound wisps of hay around the felloes, so that the wheels would make no noise.

The troops marched down the road across the marsh, followed by the carts. The teamsters were not allowed to speak to their teams, but in silence all moved on. The moon was shining brightly, but all the while the cannon were flashing and thundering, sending shot and shells into the town.

The soldiers crossed the lowlands and came to the hills on Dorchester Neck, overlooking the harbor. They marched up the steep ascent on the south-west side, reached the top, seized the gabions, placed them on the ground, filled them with earth, and soon had a line of strong intrenchments. Besides gabions, the carts contained a large number of barrels. These the soldiers filled with stones, and laid them in position, so that by pulling away the trigs they would go rolling down the steep hill. If the British attempted to march up the hill, they would be crushed to death by the barrels.

General Howe, in Boston, listening to the cannonade, never mistrusted what was going on over on the hills of Dorchester Neck.

Admiral Shuldham, commanding the fleet down in the harbor, never dreamed that the Yankees were getting ready to send a plunging fire down upon his decks. The sailors on the watch and pacing the deck of the *Glasgow*, frigate, and calling out "All is well," through the night, did not even catch a glimpse of the swarm of men on the hills, close at hand, till daylight streaked the east. They opened their eyes wide, and informed the admiral of what was going on. The admiral came up from his cabin and opened his eyes very wide, and sent a boat off in all haste to Boston with a message to General Howe, that if the Yankees were not driven from the hill, they would soon be able to drive the fleet out of the harbor.

There was a sudden stir that morning in Boston. Officers were riding furiously through the streets, and orders were given for the whole army to be ready. Boats were collected, and General Howe intended to start from Long Wharf and land his troops on Dorchester Neck, and march up the hill; or get in rear of it, and cut off the retreat of the Americans, and so defeat them. General Washington was as wide awake as General Howe. He sent more troops, and had the whole army ready to march at a moment's notice. A high wind arose. The waves rolled in from the sea. General Howe could not embark his troops, and before the waves calmed the Americans were so strongly intrenched that he saw the only thing for him to do was to get out of Boston.

On Sunday morning, the 17th of March, the British troops went on board their ships, with a large number of the citizens who adhered to the cause of the king. It was a sad day to them —to leave their comfortable homes and sail away, never again to set foot in these streets. As the British troops went down the harbor, the Americans marched into the town over the Neck. Elijah noticed that the fortifications which General Howe had erected were very strong. General Howe sailed for Halifax, and General Washington took possession of the town. The people who remained welcomed him as a deliverer. A hard time they had had—cooped up for eleven months with thirteen thousand soldiers, and nothing to eat except salt beef and fish— no milk, no fresh meat or vegetables. The only thing that they could have in abundance was rum, and that they could get at three-pence a quart.

Once, in the month of August, General Gage sent some ships around Cape Cod to Connecticut with soldiers, who landed and stole a few flocks of sheep and some cattle, so that the army and the citizens had a taste of fresh meat. A few months later, a ship came from London bringing a file of newspapers. One paper, *The London Chronicle,* contained some lines ridiculing General Gage's operations:

"In days of yore, the British troops
  Have taken warlike kings in battle.
But now, alas! the valor droops,
  For Gage takes naught but harmless cattle.

"Britons, with grief your bosoms strike;
  Your faded laurels loudly weep!
Behold your heroes, Quixote-like,
  Driving a timid flock of sheep!"

General Howe had torn down several hundred houses, and used the lumber for fuel. The Old South Meeting-house was used for a riding-school. One of the officers had taken Deacon

Wheelock's pew, and used it for a pig-pen. The other meeting-houses had been used for hospitals, and the city was in a sad plight.

To pass the time away, the British officers opened a theatre in Faneuil Hall, and brought out a play during the winter, written by General Burgoyne, entitled "The Blockade of Boston."

The Audience Thought It Was Part of the Play.

On the evening when it was to be enacted, General Howe and all the officers were there to see it. It happened that on the same evening General Putnam sent two companies of soldiers, about two hundred in all, to burn some houses at Charlestown Neck, in which the British outposts were quartered; and when they attacked the pickets, drove them in, and set the houses on fire, the whole British army was alarmed. The play had just begun when a soldier rushed upon the stage.

"The Yankees are attacking Bunker Hill!" he shouted.

The audience thought it was a part of the play, and cheered his vigorous acting.

"I tell you they are attacking Bunker Hill!"

Just then a cannon was heard.

"Officers to your commands!" shouted General Howe, and all hands made haste. It was the end of the play for that night.

Chapter 5
EXPEDITION TO QUEBEC

IN August, after General Washington took command of the army, a committee from Congress, sitting in Philadelphia, reached Cambridge to confer with him about sending an expedition secretly to Canada, through the woods of Maine, to capture Quebec. General Philip Schuyler was on Lake Champlain getting ready to capture St. John's and Montreal. Captain Benedict Arnold, of Connecticut, who started in life as an apothecary, but who had bought horses in Quebec and knew all about the town, believed that if an expedition were sent up the Kennebec River to cooperate with an army sent from Lake Champlain, Canada might be secured to the colonies. He thought that the French would take up arms against the British. The plan was agreed upon, and Captain Arnold was made a colonel and appointed to command the expedition. It was a great undertaking to march so far through a wilderness, where there were no paths, and of which very little was known. Only one white man had been over the route—Captain Montressor, of the British army.

There were thirteen companies. Two of the captains were Captain Dearborn, who had fought bravely at Bunker Hill, and Captain Daniel Morgan, from Virginia. There were two lieutenant-colonels; one was Christopher Green, of Rhode Island, and the other Timothy Bigelow, of Worcester, Massachusetts. There were about eleven hundred men in all.

On the 13th of September, Dodifer bade Elijah and Esek good-bye in Cambridge, slung his knapsack on his shoulders, and marched to Medford, and from there to Malden. The next night the battalions camped at Beverly, and the next day, Friday, reached Newburyport.

It Was Harder Work the Next Day, for the River Was Rapid.

The good people of that town opened the Presbyterian Meetinghouse for them to sleep in. On Sunday, Dodifer heard Rev. Mr. Parsons preach. After meeting, the troops marched down to the wharves, went on board the vessels in waiting, and the fleet, sixteen vessels in all, sailed down the river, out into the ocean, and steered eastward. On the second morning they were in the Kennebec, and sailed up that river to Mr. Gardner's town, where boats were in waiting. Now came hard work. The boats were heavy and leaky, and were loaded with provisions—barrels of pork and bread and flour. They rowed up the river five miles to Fort Western, and from there to Fort Halifax, which stood at the mouth of a small river which the Indians called Sebasticook.   There the boats were unloaded, and every thing carried about eighty rods past some falls.   Then the boats were drawn up by ropes and reloaded.   The river was so rapid that half the time Dodifer had to be in the water, lifting the boats over the rocks.   At night the soldiers built arbors, kindled great fires, and dried their clothes, but the air was chilling, and they shivered before morning.

It was harder and colder work next day, for the river was rapid.   The boats leaked badly, wetting their flour and sugar. The night was so cold that their clothes froze, but every body was in good spirits.   At night the boats had to be unloaded again, and the barrels of pork and flour carried up a steep ledge, and the boats dragged past Skowhegan Falls, where the river boiled and foamed fearfully.

The next day the water was smoother.   Seven miles brought the expedition to Norridgewock Falls.   Colonel Arnold had sent oxen and sleds in advance to this point, and the soldiers loaded the teams and dragged boats and provisions a mile and a quarter through the woods.   The flour was examined, and it was found that a great deal of it was spoiled.

From Norridgewock it was only thirteen miles to Carrytunk, or the Devil's Falls, where the river leaps over a ledge and falls sixteen feet.   The boats were unloaded again.   Seven miles beyond the Devil's Falls there was another unloading, and every thing was packed on sleds and dragged through the woods four miles.   The expedition had passed the last settlement; beyond was a pathless wilderness.   One of the riflemen shot a moose as large as an ox, and the soldiers had a delicious supper.

Colonel Arnold had so few teams that the soldiers unheaded the pork barrels, slung the thick slices of pork on poles, and so helped get the provisions over the carrying places; but it was hard work, staggering over the hillocks and fallen trees.   Again the boats were launched, but could go only a short distance before they were again unloaded.   There were trout in the streams, and Dodifer and the other soldiers caught fine strings of them, which they cooked for supper.

A hard time they had the next day at the seventh carrying place, which was across a bog. At times Dodifer found himself sinking in the mire up to his knees, while staggering along with pork on his shoulders.

On October 13th, the army had been a month on its way, and was now moving up Dead River, a branch of the Kennebec. The mountains were white with snow. Lieutenant-colonel Bigelow thought that perhaps Quebec might be seen from the top of one of the highest mountains, and climbed it. He could see mountains all around, but no shining steeples. Quebec was far, far away. The mountain from that day to this has been called Mount Bigelow.

The next day Colonel Arnold sent a man, with two Indians, ahead to some of his friends in Quebec, to let them know he was on his way, that they might be ready to aid him. It would have been better if he had not sent the letter, as we shall see.

Dodifer's company was in advance of the others, and the next night they had a light supper, for the provisions were behind, and there were only six pounds of flour for sixty men. The next day they had no flour, and only a small piece of pork. The night set in dark and rainy; the rain poured in torrents, and the river rose suddenly. The banks were low, and at midnight they found the water sweeping around them. The drift-wood was floating down stream—old logs started by the freshet—and they could hear the water roaring louder and louder. They stood still, not knowing which way to go. Before daylight the water was up to their knees, but they reached dry ground at last.

On the 23d of October the soldiers came to their eleventh carrying place early in the morning. Getting past that, and going two miles, they came to the twelfth; a half mile beyond that they came to the thirteenth. Getting past that, they went seven miles, but the stream was rapid and swollen, and filled with drift-wood, and six of their boats were destroyed on the rocks, and all their salt washed away.

AT TIMES DODIFER FOUND HIMSELF SINKING INTO THE MIRE UP
TO HIS KNEES.

Snow had fallen, and the river was full of ice. From morning till night Dodifer was wet to the skin. Many times during the day he had to stand in the water and lift the boats over the rocks. His shoes were wearing out. His feet and legs were black and blue, and his ankle-joints began to swell. The last ox had been killed; he could have no more fresh meat. The flour and pork were nearly gone.

Colonel Arnold decided to send back the sick. Forty-eight men, with a sergeant, started. Some of the well men lost heart. Captain Williams and Captain Scott, and their men belonging to Major Enos's battalion, decided to return. The rest of the captains and their men would not turn back. It was a tearful parting.

"I wish you success, but I never shall see you again. You will perish in the wilderness," said Captain Williams to those who were going on.

"I am ready to go on and meet whatever fate awaits me; but my officers and men will not go," Major Enos replied, tears upon his cheeks.

Major Enos and his men turned their faces homeward, and the brave-hearted set their boats up stream. The wilderness, hardship, starvation, ice, snow, disease, possible failure, imprisonment, and death, were before them; but they would not turn back.

On the 26th of October the expedition passed three carrying places. The night was very cold. The soldiers had very little supper and less for breakfast; but they pushed on.

Oh, brave hearts! What a day is this 28th of October! In the morning they pass a carrying place, come to a pond, and then to the long carrying place, four miles and a quarter. They are on the dividing line between the Atlantic and the St. Lawrence. Weak, staggering under their burdens, over bogs, along steep hill-sides, through the dense forest, breaking the ice in the streams with the butts of their guns as they wade through them, sinking knee-deep in the mud of the bogs—yet they push on. Rheumatism seizes them. Some are burning up with fever, others shaking with ague. But there is no turning back. On they toil. They know not how far it is to Sertigan, the place where they can get something to eat. They reach a little stream running north leading to Lake Megantic. They have passed their last carrying place. Twenty-four times they have dragged their boats past the rapids.

No pork to carry now; the last mouthful gone; seven pints of flour to each man left. They measure it out, a gill to each in the morning, stir it up with water, lay it on the coals, bake it a few moments, shoulder their guns, and move on. At noon each man has two gills of flour, at night one gill. They are so weak that a stick trips them, and when they are down in the snow, it takes them a long time to get up.

Dodifer and his company lose their way. There is no path. They have a compass, and steer by that west-north-west, for Canada lies in that direction. Colonel Arnold, with Captain Hanchet and sixty men, have started to make a rapid march to Sertigan—how far it is they do not know, but sixty or seventy miles. They will hasten back with provisions. Oh, the gnawing within! and the gill of flour makes but a mouthful. The last morsel of meat is gone; but there are the hides of the oxen which they had killed, lying in one of the boats, which they have dragged four miles across the dividing ridge. They have made some of the hides up into cartridge-boxes. The skins are musty, but perhaps there is nourishment in them. Dodifer cuts a skin into pieces, boils it in a camp-kettle, and makes hide soup. He broils a piece, and tries to chew the burned leather. One of the soldiers cooks his moccasins. Another has an old pair of moose-leather breeches, which he boils for supper.

Captain Dearborn has a large Newfoundland dog, which is killed and eaten, entrails and all. They chew the leather, then scrape away the snow, cut a few hemlock boughs with their hatchets, and lie down to sleep, to rise before daylight, eat the two mouthfuls of cake and another piece of broiled leather, and then stagger on toward Canada.

There are women in the party. Mrs. Grier, wife of Sergeant Grier, a large, athletic woman, has accompanied her husband, to take care of him, if he should be sick or wounded. She wades through the streams, carries her heavy pack, eats her gill of flour, lies down to sleep in the snow, thus helping to secure liberty to the country. Everybody treats her with respect. Mrs. Warner, wife of a soldier, accompanies her husband. The soldier is weak and faint, and the wife shoulders his knapsack and trudges by his side. He staggers and falls—strength gone, hope gone, courage gone. He leans his head against a tree. He is ready to welcome death in any form. His wife urges him on, but he can not stand upon his feet.

Dodifer would gladly help him, but the expedition can not halt for any one. Others have dropped by the way, never to rise again. The ranks are growing thinner. Dodifer beholds the wife standing with the knapsack on her back, the gun on her shoulder, trying to lift her husband to his feet. It is the last view. The column moves on, leaving them there.

Joyful news! Colonel Arnold has reached Sertigan, and a messenger has arrived with the information that a party of Frenchmen are on their way with cattle and flour.

Hurra! hurra! They make the forest ring. Six pints of flour left for each man. That will keep them alive till the cattle arrive. They launch their boats upon the Chaudière. One is smashed in the swift stream—another, another, six—every thing on board lost. All their flour gone! God help them now! In the wilderness, and nothing to eat. They have dragged their boats across the great divide to no purpose. They must march. There is no road; but on, picking their way over rocks and fallen trees, eating pine bark, so the seven hundred, like a long line of shadows, move on, ever toward Quebec.

God be praised! The cattle have come. The French have arrived. A bullet is sent through the brain of an ox; fifty knives gleam in the air. Before the flesh has ceased to quiver it is broiling on the coals. Saved; strength returns. The desponding pluck up heart. They break out into singing, and move on.

While on the march, Dodifer made the acquaintance of a young officer (Aaron Burr) who was acting as aid to Colonel Arnold, and who was only twenty years old. He was from Pennsylvania; had left home, and joined the army against the wishes of his friends. He was a very agreeable young man, and Dodifer set it down that he would be heard from in the future, if they ever reached Canada.

With buoyant hopes the men go on. They do not mind the snow, the cold nights, the fording of streams, the hardships, now that they have something to eat. But they are weak, some have swollen limbs, some are afflicted with rheumatism, some are burning up with fever; yet they are approaching Sertigan, where the French have an abundance of provisions. The French are delighted to see the Boston men, as they call Colonel Arnold's party; but they are shrewd enough to charge high prices for all they sell. Refreshed, strengthened, glad to know that they are out of the wilderness, the army marches up the Chaudière, and on the 9th of November reaches the St. Lawrence. For thirty-two days the seven hundred and fifty have struggled in the wilderness. Colonel Arnold is in high spirits. He sends the young lieutenant, Aaron Burr, with two Indians, to Montreal, to in-

Colonel Arnold Sends Aaron Burr, with Two Indians, to Montreal.

form General Montgomery (who has reached that place from Lake Champlain) of his arrival.

It is a snowy morning when the little army marches out from the woods and makes its appearance at the little French village at Point Levi, opposite Quebec. The sentinels on the walls of Quebec look across the river and see the line of men, and give the alarm. Lieutenant-governor Cramahe has heard that Arnold was on the way, for the man who was sent by Arnold to inform the French that he was coming has proved a traitor, and the lieutenant-governor has seized all the boats. The frigate *Lizard* and another war-ship are swinging at their moorings in the river. A furious storm is raging. The wind is cold and raw. There is Quebec; but with no boats Colonel Arnold and his brave men might as well be at Boston.

Still, there are boats to be had, and before night the French and Indians furnish him with thirty-six birch canoes. Night comes, and before morning six hundred of the little band are landed in Wolfe's Ravine, the spot where General Wolfe landed in '59. The crews of the war-ships have been on the watch, but in the darkness the canoes have glided backward and forward landing the men. Day dawns, and one hundred and fifty are forced to remain at Point Levi.

General Guy Carleton was at Montreal, and Colonel M'Lane commanded the troops in Quebec. He had eighteen hundred men under arms, not more than five hundred of whom could be depended upon. The people of Quebec were favorably disposed toward the Americans, and Colonel Arnold expected that the moment he made an attack the inhabitants would open the gates. The little army climbed the bluff and stood upon the Plains of Abraham; but Arnold had no cannon. The people upon the walls gazed at the Americans, but did not open the gates. Arnold saw that he must wait for General Montgomery. The next day Dodifer found himself marching away from Quebec, up the north bank of the St. Lawrence. The troops marched twenty miles, and learned that General Carleton had just gone down the river with his troops, that he had evacuated Montreal, and that General Montgomery was close at hand.

Joyful news! Happy day! Montgomery arrives with provisions and clothing, but he has only five hundred men, and some of those are on the sick-list. Together, he and Arnold have less than one thousand effective men. Montgomery has brought several cannon, and the troops march back to the city.

The cannon are only small field-pieces, and will be of little account against the solid walls, but they drag them through the snow. It is hard work, and Montgomery's men are as weak as those who have toiled through the wilderness. The small-pox breaks out, and the men begin to die. Montgomery is commander-in-chief, and resolves to attack the city at once. He is a brave man. He was born in Ireland, 1737, and is thirty-eight years old. He was with Wolfe in the battle on the Plains of Abraham, and now he is here upon the same spot to wrench the place from the grasp of England. Every body loves him. He knows all about the city, and plans the attack. He decides to leave Major Brown and Major Livingstone with two hundred men to make a feint from the Plains of Abraham, west of the city. Arnold is to attack on the north side, while Montgomery himself, with the rest of the troops, will creep along the narrow cart-path under the rocky bluff of Cape Diamond, and attack on the south side.

It was a desperate undertaking which Montgomery had in hand. The stone walls surrounding the city only came to the edge of the bluff, but a post fence, fifteen feet high, ran down the precipice to the river. The posts were spiked and bolted together. Beyond the fence was a block-house, fifty feet square, of solid timber walls, with loop-holes for musketry, and four cannon loaded with grape-shot, pointing their muzzles to sweep the road. Montgomery must saw away the posts, rush up the cart-way, and take the block-house.

It was past midnight, the last night of the year. Dodifer was asleep, wrapped in his blanket. He had made a shelter of pine boughs, but the wind whirled through it, and was drifting the snow over him. He was dreaming of home and the warm fireside there. He was getting ready to sit down to a nice supper, when Captain Dearborn touched his shoulder.

"Fall in, my boy," said the captain.

He arose, shook the snow from his blanket, wrapped it round him, and shouldered his gun. It was dark, and snowing. The wind whirled the snow in drifts. He was nearly frozen. His teeth chattered. He had no overcoat or mittens, but took his place in the line. He could barely see his comrades, moving like shadows, through the gloom.

Montgomery and his men go down the steep bank to the river-side, and creep along under the rocky cliff, the wind whirling the snow in their faces, and the river filled with floating ice sweeping past them. They come to the post-fence. Montgomery takes a saw, and with his own hands saws off several of the posts. The British sentinels in the block-house look out into the storm, and see the dark forms rushing through the opening.

"Come on!" It is Montgomery's last command—his last words. From loop-hole and port-hole there are blinding flashes. A storm more terrible than the whirling snow sweeps through the air. Grape and solid shot crash against the rocks and into the columns of men. Montgomery falls, both of his aids fall, several soldiers fall, pouring out their warm blood upon the drifting snow. The soldiers flee back to Wolfe's Ravine.

Dodifer and his comrades meanwhile are marching through the deep snow-drifts to the north side of the city. The line is formed in the darkness. They rush up a narrow street. Muskets flash and cannon blaze before them. He sees Colonel Arnold fall, shot through the knee. Captain Lamb has a part of his face torn away. Men fall, but the column does not retreat. The men composing it have not endured the hardships of the wilderness to run at the first fire, nor the first disaster. Colonel Arnold is carried back to camp, but under their captains the men fight on. Dodifer shelters himself in a door-way, takes aim at the flashes on the walls. Bullets whiz past him, or strike into the sides of the buildings around him. Solid shot sweep down the street, but he and his comrades brave the blinding snow and the storm of lead and iron. For more than an hour they continue the contest. Suddenly a gate opens, and the

British rush out. Before he is aware of it, their retreat is cut off. They might continue the fight and die there, but it would be throwing away their lives. They lay down their guns and give themselves up. One hundred and sixty have been killed or wounded. All their toiling, suffering, and privation have ended in failure. Dodifer finds himself at day-break locked into a building inside the garrison; but General Carleton is a humane man, and they suffer no cruel treatment at his hands.

Colonel Arnold, with the few men left, retreated three miles, established a camp, and waited for re-enforcements from Montreal. The small-pox raged in the camp. The men had little to eat, and were disheartened. It was midwinter, and the snow was deep. General Carleton might have captured all of them, but he knew that disease was thinning the ranks; he had nothing to fear from Arnold, and he might as well let time do its certain work.

While lying there, the troops were astonished one morning to see a woman come into camp, the wife of private Warner. They had seen their comrade sitting by a tree in the wilderness, unable to move on, and his wife, with his knapsack on her back and his gun on her shoulder, trying to help him to his feet. They had thought of them as dead; but there was the brave-hearted woman. She had sat by the side of her husband while the column passed on. She heard the sound of their retreating footsteps, and their voices growing fainter in the distance. She sat there through the day, through the night; sat till to sit longer was to die by his side. He still breathed—the fire was feebly burning—might burn a day or two longer. Should she go and live, or remain and die. The last kiss was given, the last look taken, and then, alone, day after day, she traveled, following the trail, digging roots from beneath the snow, and eating them, reaching the French settlement at last.

Spring came. General Wooster, who had been at Montreal during the winter, arrived with re-enforcements; but before he could accomplish any thing, some troops arrived from England to re-enforce General Carleton, and General Wooster was obliged to retreat.

Months passed, but there came at length an exchange of prisoners and Dodifer was glad to set his face once more toward home. Yet his sufferings, hardships, and privations had not abated his love for liberty, nor his determination to do what he could to secure the liberties of the country.

Chapter 6
FORT SULLIVAN

ALL of the thirteen colonies had revolted. The people of Charleston, South Carolina, were as rebellious as the people of Boston. They had seized all the cannon, muskets, and powder they could lay their hands on, and had every reason to expect that the king and the ministry would strike a blow at them.

In December, 1775, Lord North, Lord Germain, and Lord Dartmouth, sitting in the king's chamber, in London, decided to chastise the people of Charleston. They sent word to Governor Dunmore, in Virginia, that an expedition would be fitted out for that purpose. Governor Dunmore sent word to Governor Eden, who was Governor of Maryland, residing at Annapolis. The ship with Governor Dunmore's letter sailed from Norfolk up the Chesapeake Bay, but it so happened that Captain James Barron, commanding an American vessel in the Chesapeake, captured the vessel, and the plan of the ministers was made known to the inhabitants of Charleston. This was in April, 1776. The people of Charleston were for the most part Whigs; but up in the interior of the State the Tories were in the majority. The ministers concluded that if Charleston were taken possession of, and the royal standard raised, the whole State would once more acknowledge allegiance to the king.

To protect the city, Colonel William Moultrie was directed to build a fort on Sullivan's Island, in the harbor. The island is about three miles long, but not more than half a mile wide; and it was believed that a fort erected there would prevent the war-ships from coming up to the town. There were plenty of palmetto-trees on the island, and a large number of negroes were set to work cutting them down, and hauling them to the lower end of the island.

The engineers laid up the logs, one upon another, in two lines, sixteen feet apart, with cross-logs binding them firmly together, and filled the space between with sand, making the wall of the fort sixteen feet high, with embrasures for cannon. Thirty-one guns were mounted; nine of them were twenty-six-pounders, six were eighteen-pounders, the rest smaller. Only twenty-two of the thirty-one could be of much service. Another work, called Fort Johnson, was erected between Sullivan's Island and Charleston; so if a fleet were to pass Fort Sullivan it would have to take the fire of Fort Johnson and its twenty guns.

On the main-land, west of the fort, at Haddrell's Point, two batteries of nine guns were erected to prevent the fleet from getting into a cove, and firing at the rear of the fort, where no guns were in position.

On the 31st of May, the people living on the sea-coast, twenty miles north of Charleston, saw a fleet of more than fifty vessels sailing into a harbor by Dewee's Island, and dropping anchor. Word was sent to Charleston. So, then, the blow which had been anticipated was about to be struck.

General Washington sent General Lee to take command of the troops in Charleston. He arrived on the 3rd of June; went down and visited the fort; saw that it was not finished on the south-west side. He shook his head.

"The ships will take position out there," he said, pointing to the south-west, "and will make it a perfect slaughter-pen. Do you think you can defend it, Colonel Moultrie?"

"Yes, sir, I think I can."

Colonel Moultrie was a cool-headed, good-natured man, and had not the least doubt of his ability to hold the fort.

While Lee and Moultrie were talking, the fleet made its appearance off the bar. It was commanded by Sir Peter Parker. Governor Campbell, who had been governor of the State, was on board; also Sir Henry Clinton, with three thousand troops. Wind and tide were favorable, and thirty-six of the vessels succeeded in crossing the bar before the tide ebbed. One of the ships, the *Prince of Piedmont,* loaded with provisions, got among the breakers and was wrecked.

The People Saw a Fleet of More Than Fifty Vessels Sail up the Harbor.

The next day a boat with a white flag came in from the fleet, but a sentinel down by the shore fired at it, doing what he had no business to do. The boat started back and would not return, although an officer waved his handkerchief to call it back. Colonel Moultrie sent a boat out to Sir Peter Parker with an apology. The sentinel had fired without orders, and if another flag were to be sent, it would be properly received. Sir Henry Clinton and Sir Peter Parker accepted the apology; and Sir Henry being commander of the land-forces, and authorized to re-establish the government, sent a proclamation to the Committee of Safety, ordering all the subjects of the king to lay down their arms and acknowledge his authority. The Committee of Safety read it, laid it aside, and went on with their work getting the troops ready.

Although the ships crossed the bar during the first week in June, the British were so slow in their movements that they were not ready to make an attack till the 28th. General Lee and the people of Charleston were much obliged to them for waiting so long. Troops from Virginia and North Carolina, as well as those from South Carolina, had time to reach Charleston.

Sir Henry landed troops on Long Island, and marched them to its farther end, opposite the upper part of Sullivan's Island; took all the ships' boats up there into a cove, intending to cross to Sullivan's Island, disperse the American troops under Colonel Thompson, and march down and attack the fort in the rear, while the fleet attacked in front. Together, the army and fleet would make themselves masters of the island.

Colonel Moultrie had four hundred and thirty-five men. He had only five thousand four hundred pounds of powder—enough for twenty-six rounds to each cannon; but he resolved to make it last as long as possible.

Beautiful the morning of Friday, June 28th. A few light, fleecy clouds dot the horizon. Colonel Moultrie is riding up toward the north end of the island to see the troops under Colonel Thompson, when he discovers that the ships are spreading their top-sails and raising their anchors. The tide is coming in, the wind favorable, and the ships, one after another, are moving up the harbor. Over on Long Island drums are beating, and the regiments forming. He gallops back beneath the palmetto-trees to the fort.

"Beat the long roll!" The drums beat and the soldiers take their places beside the guns, seize their rammers and sponges, and are ready to defend the flag floating from the staff at the south-eastern bastion—a blue flag, with a crescent moon in the upper corner.

Sir Peter Parker has a powerful fleet: the *Bristol*, fifty guns; *Experiment*, fifty guns; *Active*, twenty-eight guns; *Solebay*, twenty-eight guns; *Actæon*, twenty-eight guns; *Siren*, twenty-eight guns; *Sphinx*, twenty-eight guns; *Ranger*, twenty-eight guns; *Friendship*, twenty-two guns; one bomb-vessel.

In all, there are two hundred and ninety guns, besides the

mortars for firing bombs. Proudly the ships sail up the bay—their sails filled, their flags waving, the water rippling against their sides. The drums have beaten to arms, and on the decks are the sailors, ready to open fire whenever the word is given.

In Charleston the roofs are covered with men, women, and children. They cluster in the belfries of the churches, gazing at the fleet, hoping that the garrison in the fort will be able to defend it, yet, after what General Lee has said, fearing the worst.

Half-past ten. The bomb-boat has dropped anchor more than a mile away. There is a puff of smoke on her decks. A deep, heavy roar rolls up the harbor, and a shell thirteen inches in diameter rises in the air, leaving a thin white trail to mark its course. Up, up, up it rises, sails away, describing a beautiful curve, and falls slowly, then faster, and still faster, and strikes upon the magazine at the north-west angle of the fort. It explodes, whirls up a column of sand, but no one is harmed.

The *Active* leads the fleet. She swings around the northern end of the sandy reef, called the Lower Middle Ground, followed by the *Bristol, Experiment,* and *Solebay.* They come close to the fort. Sir Peter will make quick work of it. The fight may be sharp, but it shall be decisive. He will knock that cob-house affair of logs to pieces in a few minutes. Down go the anchors, with spring-ropes on the cables to keep the ships broadside to the fort. He will soon have one hundred and fifty cannon pouring a continuous fire upon it.

As the anchors go down, the twenty-six and eighteen pounders open fire, and the ships send back a reply from all the guns on the starboard side. The roar of the cannonade jars the windows in Charleston. The sailors on the ships work with a will, determined to send the shot thick and fast into the fort, and make it so hot that the rebels will be astounded. In a few minutes they will see a white flag hung out, or else the Americans will be fleeing in consternation over the bridge of boats west of the fort to the main-land. One hundred and fifty guns are thundering on one side, and less than thirty on the other. The fire of the one hundred and fifty is concentrated, while the fire of the fort is distributed. Surely it can not take the fleet many minutes to silence every gun in the fort. Rapid the fire from the ships, slow that of the fort. The shot from the ships strike into the palmetto logs; but the wood is soft and spongy, and no splinters fly. Shells from the mortar-boat descend into the area and blow up cart-loads of sand, but do little harm. Not so the fire from the fort: the twenty-six-pound shot crash through the sides of the ships, splinter the masts, and make terrible havoc on the decks.

Twelve o'clock. The white flag is not yet flung out. Slowly and steadily the twenty-six-pounders reply to the fire of the fleet.

"Move down and take position south-west of the fort," is the signal which Sir Peter makes to three of the ships. He has discovered that the fort is weak on that side. Once there, the heavy guns of the fort will not reach the ships, and the platform inside the fort, on which the guns are mounted, may be raked from end to end. But the tide is ebbing, and the *Actæon*, *Siren*, and *Sphinx* get aground. The *Sphinx* loses her bowsprit, but, with the *Siren*, manages to get into deep water once more, while the *Actæon* remains firmly fixed on the shoal. If they had gone in on the flood-tide, they would have made it uncomfortable for the men in the fort; but now it is too late.

The bomb-ship has thrown sixty shells; but it is too far away, and the heavy charges have shattered the bed-plates of the mortars, and the firing ceases.

While this is going on around the fort, Sir Henry Clinton is embarking his troops in boats to cross to the upper end of Sullivan's Island. The boats, with field-pieces on board, glide over the water, and approach the island; but Colonel Thompson is ready for them. He opens with his eighteen-pounders, and they pull back to Long Island. Sir Henry sees that he can not hope to get a foothold till the ships have silenced the fort.

Sir Peter Parker and Governor Campbell are on board the *Bristol*, directly in front of the fort.

"Take good aim. Mind the big ships, and don't waste your powder," is Colonel Moultrie's order, as he passes from gun to gun; and the twenty-six-pounders, aimed accurately and fired deliberately, make fearful havoc on the *Bristol*. Men go down in groups, torn and mangled by the shot and splinters. A shot cuts the spring-rope of the *Bristol*, the ship swings with the tide, and the cannon-balls sweep the deck from end to end.

"Give it to her! Now is the time! She can't bring a gun to bear!" is the cry in the fort. But the ship swings back again, and the fight goes on.

"Fire once in ten minutes!" Colonel Moultrie is obliged to issue the order, for there are only a few cartridges left.

"When your powder is gone, spike your guns, and retreat," is General Lee's order, brought by Major Boyd. Colonel Moultrie has no thought of retreating. Oh, for more powder! The cartridges are almost gone.

"Stop firing!"

Colonel Moultrie will wait a while. Perhaps the ships will try to get nearer; and then, with the few remaining cartridges, he will bore them through and through.

"The rebels have done firing," says a sailor on the *Bristol* to his comrade.

"Glad am I, for we have had a terrible drubbing," the comrade replies.

But the rebels are not done firing.

"I send you five hundred pounds of powder," is the note which a messenger brings from Governor Rutledge. "Don't make too free use of your cannon; keep cool, and do mischief."

Oh yes, Colonel Moultrie will keep cool; but he will let Sir Peter Parker know that they are still alive inside the fort, and the cannon thunder once more.

So the rebels are at it again! Sir Peter will see about it, and the ships pour all together their broadsides upon the little fortress, which shakes beneath the shock. A ball enters an embrasure, and strikes down nearly every man at a gun; another ball chips a great piece from the muzzle of an eighteen-pounder; another cuts the flag-staff, and the blue banner, with the crescent moon, falls into the ditch outside the fort. There are sad hearts in Charleston now. So the fort has surrendered! Not yet.

Out from an embrasure leaps Sergeant Jasper—out where the

SERGEANT JASPER PICKS UP THE FLAG AND PLANTS IT ON THE
BASTION.

cannon-balls are flying. He picks up the flag, ties it to the rammer of a cannon, mounts the parapet, and plants it on the bastion. The balls are whirling past him; they strike around him; but not till it is firmly planted will he stir from the spot.

Oh, Sergeant Jasper! unknown by the world till now, this act of yours shall send your name down to the advancing ages!

Surrendered! No. The cannon still are flaming, and the thousands on the roofs in Charleston take heart once more.

The sun goes down. The cannon still are roaring. Through the evening those who still gaze seaward from the steeples see the flashes, and hear the roar of battle.

Eleven o'clock. The tide is flooding the marshes, and on the incoming flood the ships slip their cables and creep away. Terrible the scene on the *Bristol*. The decks are slippery with blood. There are mangled corpses lying amidst the dismantled can-

"Fight on, Boys! Don't Let Liberty Die with Me."

non. The cockpit is crowded with wounded. There are great rents in the sides of the ship, and the carpenters are at work plugging the holes. The mizzenmast is gone, the mainmast shattered, the rigging cut to pieces, the sails rent. The captain has lost his left arm. A cannon-ball has carried away the seat of Sir Peter's breeches, and a splinter has wounded him in the thigh. Forty of the crew have been killed, and seventy-one wounded. The *Experiment* is almost as badly damaged. The decks are crimsoned with the blood of more than eighty killed and wounded. The *Actæon* is still aground. Two hundred and twenty-five in all have been killed or maimed, while in the fort ten only have been killed, and twenty-two wounded. Noble the death of Sergeant M'Daniel.

"Fight on, boys! Don't let liberty die with me!" were his last words.

The morning dawns. The *Actæon* is still firmly fixed on the sand-bar. The crew have been stripping her during the night. They fire a few guns, set the ship on fire, and take to their boats. Out go Jacob Mulligan and a party in three boats. They climb the sides of the burning ship, aim the guns at the fleet, and fire them once more, seize the bell and the flag, which the crew left flying, and hasten away. The flames reach the magazine, and the *Actæon* goes up into the air, masts, spars, planks, knees, braces, cannon—all in a sulphurous, flaming cloud, to rain down, a mass of ruins, into the sea. Charleston shakes beneath the explosion, and those who look seaward behold a great cloud like a huge umbrella hanging over the harbor, while beneath it, floating serenely in the morning air, is the blue banner, with its crescent moon, still waving where Sergeant Jasper planted it.

Baffled and defeated, Sir Peter Parker and Sir Henry Clinton re-embark their troops, and sail away to New York; and for two years the people of Charleston have rest from war.

Chapter 7
BATTLE of LONG ISLAND

IN January, while General Washington was waiting at Cambridge for General Knox to arrive with the cannon from Ticonderoga, his thoughts were turned to New York. He learned that Sir Henry Clinton was to be sent somewhere with a portion of the fleet. Where but to New York would he go? New York was the largest town in America, with twenty thousand inhabitants. It was a central point, and had a good harbor. By taking possession of it, the war-ships could go up the Hudson and cut off communication between New England and the other colonies. There were a great many Tories in New York, on Long Island, and in New Jersey. The moment the British arrived, they would side with the king.

Something must be done, and that quickly, to prevent the British from getting possession. He would send a man who would act with energy, General Charles Lee. He was an old soldier—a Welshman, who was commissioned ensign by George II. when he was a boy. He had fought in Europe, was well educated, could speak all the languages of Europe, and the Mohawk besides; for in '55 he came to America with his regiment, and was stationed at "Schenectada," as he wrote to his sister. The Mohawks liked him, and chose him to be one of their chiefs, and called him Boiling Water. He was with young Lord Howe at Ticonderoga, and was well acquainted with General Howe.

General Washington had no troops to spare; but Governor Trumbull, in Connecticut, was ready to aid in the matter, and the Connecticut patriots were ready to place themselves under General Lee.

The New York Committee of Safety heard that General Lee was on his way with twelve hundred troops. The Committee of Safety were a timid set of men. They were afraid it would be impolitic to take military possession of New York. They had sent to the West Indies for powder, and if General Lee were to take possession of the town, the *Asia*, a sixty-four-gun ship, and the *Duchess of Gordon*, a smaller vessel in the harbor, might fire on the vessels when they arrived. They requested General Lee to remain in Connecticut a little while.

But General Lee had no time to wait. Sir Henry Clinton had sailed for Boston, and the Connecticut troops started. General Lee was down with rheumatism, and could not ride his horse, nor bear the jolting of a carriage, and the soldiers carried him on a litter. He was none too soon, for on the very day the troops crossed the Harlem River at King's Bridge, and entered New York, Sir Henry Clinton, with several ships, was sailing up the harbor.

The Committee of Safety in New York were in great trepidation. Between General Lee on the one hand, and General Clinton on the other, they feared the town would be destroyed: they hoped General Lee would not do anything to provoke the British. "Boiling Water" boiled over at that.

"If the ships of war are quiet," he said, "I shall be quiet; but I declare solemnly that if they make a pretext of my presence to fire on the town, the first house set in flames by the guns shall be the funeral pile of some of their best friends."

That frightened the Tories, who hastened to see General Clinton. They were glad to hear from him that he did not intend to attack the town, and they were glad to see the ships sail away southward a day or two later.

Whither Sir Henry had gone was soon understood from the

letter which Captain James Barron captured in the *Chesapeake*. The fleet was on its way to Charleston, and General Washington sent General Lee to meet Sir Henry there. We have already seen how Sir Peter Parker was defeated at Fort Sullivan, and how Sir Henry Clinton accomplished nothing.

As soon as General Howe sailed from Boston for Halifax, General Washington sent a portion of the army to New York, for he very well knew that the British felt humiliated, and that neither General Howe, nor the king, the minister, nor the people of England would sit down quietly after being driven out of Boston.

Soon word came that the king had hired thousands of soldiers of the Landgrave of Hesse to aid in putting down the Americans, and that great fleets were fitting out in England, and that by midsummer a great blow would be struck somewhere, and in all probability at New York.

While Dodifer was making his way home from Canada, and while Nicholas was waiting for his wound to heal, Elijah and Esek were marching from Boston to New York. On a pleasant afternoon in April, they crossed King's Bridge over the Harlem River, marched down the Boston road, as it was called, and went into camp close by the town.

On the 29th of June, General Howe, with a great fleet of vessels, entered the harbor; and a few days later another fleet arrived from England with the Hessians. And, still later, a third fleet, under Sir Peter Parker with Sir Henry Clinton, arrived from the South. General Howe found himself at the head of nearly thirty thousand men. On the 8th of July he landed nine thousand men on Staten Island. The British soldiers spread their tents on the green slopes of Staten Island, washed their clothes in the clear running brooks, glad to stretch their legs on land after a long sea-voyage.

The 9th of July came. Important news was brought by a post rider from Philadelphia that Congress, on the 4th, had signed one of the most important papers the world had ever seen, declaring the colonies free and independent of Great

Britain forever. Elijah's regiment was encamped on the "Common," the place now occupied by the City Hall. During the afternoon the colonel received orders to have his men paraded at six o'clock that evening. The hour came, and with it a general beating of drums in all the regiments. The brigade to which his regiment belonged was drawn up in a hollow square. General Washington, whose headquarters were down at Bowling Green, came riding up Broadway with his staff. The

One of His Aids Reads the Declaration of Independence.

soldiers presented arms, the guns gave a salute, and Washington sat upon his horse, while one of his aids in a voice so loud and clear, that not only the soldiers, but the great crowd of citizens around, could hear, read the Declaration of Independence. When the reading was finished, the soldiers and people hurraed, and the citizens, fired up by what they had heard, started off upon the run down Broadway toward Bowling Green.

"Pull it down!" they cried. They ran to the statue of the king on horseback, which stood in the centre of the Green, erected in 1770. Some of the people ran for a ladder, others for ropes. A man climbed the ladder and fastened the ropes to the statue.

"Down with it!" they cried; and men and boys and soldiers —every body who could get hold of a rope—pulled, and over it went, with a thud, to the ground. It was of lead, and gilded.

"It will make a lot of bullets," said the people; and, sure

enough, it was melted into bullets, which a few days later were fired at the king's troops.

General Washington saw that General Howe probably intended to land on Long Island, and several thousand troops were sent across Brooklyn ferry.

Elijah and Dodifer, and the other soldiers, marched past the Fly Market in Maiden Lane, stepped into the boats, were rowed across the river, and landed at the ferry stairs on the Brooklyn side. They climbed the stairs and formed in line in front of the ferry tavern, which stood on the east side of the road, kept by Captain Waldron, who owned the ferry. Captain Waldron was a patriot, ready to fight for his country. Just beyond the tavern was another large stone house, with a beautiful garden behind it, owned by John Rapalje, a bitter Tory.

The troops marched out to the fortifications which General Greene had been erecting. General Greene had constructed a formidable line of intrenchments. Over on the marsh at Wallabout Bay (the present Navy Yard) he dug a ditch, from tidewater to a spring on the edge of the marsh, at the junction of Flushing Avenue and Portland Street. From the spring a line of earth-works was carried to the top of a hill on John Cowenhaven's farm, where a strong fort was erected (Washington Park). It was named Fort Putnam.

From the fort the line of intrenchments was carried in a zigzag course south, to another small fort (corner of De Kalb Avenue and Hudson Street), and from there across the Jamaica turnpike (Fulton Avenue), to Mr. Freeck's mill-pond at the head of Gowanus Creek.

Inside of this line were several forts. One at Red Hook, one on a conical hill, which was called the "Corkscrew" fort, because the trench wound around it spirally.

The troops did not halt in the intrenchments, but marched out the Jamaica turnpike, past a little old Dutch church, and went into camp upon the hills.

One day Elijah went out with a party to get some fresh beef from some of the farmers. They were instructed to take the cattle that belonged to the Tories. The party took a road which led down toward the Narrows, passing a house where a Tory by the name of Cortelyou lived. It was an old stone and brick house. On one end of it Elijah saw the figures 1699, the year in which it was built. He passed on to Gravesend Bay, and had a good view of the British fleet at anchor. From there he turned north-east, and went by a winding road to the hamlet of Flatlands. He might have turned north-west there and gone to Flatbush, about two miles distant, and thence kept right on in the same direction by a narrow road called Martenses Lane, to their camp; but instead of that he went north-east, and came round through the hills by the Jamaica turnpike, driving in a herd of cattle.

The last of the British army arrived on the 13th of July, but General Howe seemed to be undecided what to do. One day the great fleet sailed up the bay, as if General Howe intended to push up the Hudson and land north of the city, which he could have done; but after the fleet had spread its sails, making the harbor white with canvas, the vessels dropped back to their anchorage.

On another day two ships sailed up the Hudson, paying no attention to the American cannon in a battery at Red Hook, which opened fire. The ships were two miles away, and no harm was done. The ships went up to Haverstraw to land some arms for the Tories; but they quickly returned, for the Americans had a lot of fire-ships ready to let loose.

All the while General Howe had his spies in General Washington's camp finding out the strength of the army, and how the fortifications were defended.

Every day the Americans were making the works stronger. General Greene worked so hard that he was taken down with a fever, and General Putnam was appointed to the command.

On the night of the 27th of August, Elijah was out on picket at Gravesend Bay. Early in the evening he could hear a commotion on ship-board, and on Staten Island. Before sunrise all the drums were beating, and bugles were playing. When the sun rose he could see the sailors shaking out the sails of the ships, and raising the anchors. Boats were plying here and there. About nine o'clock the whole fleet were under way, and soon after the bay was covered with boats putting out for Staten Island, filled with troops. There were thirty-seven men-of-war, and more than four hundred transport ships, besides the boats. The war-ships stood in toward Gravesend Bay, opened their port-holes, ran out their guns, opened fire, and threw shot and shell on shore. It was the most magnificent spectacle he had ever seen.

Colonel Howard was commanding the Americans along the shore. He sent messengers to General Putnam, with information that the British were landing; and as their boats reached the shore he fell back toward Brooklyn, with his riflemen and pickets.

General Howe planned so well that by noon he had fifteen thousand men and forty pieces of cannon on shore.

General Howe commanded in person. He was a great favorite with the king. He was an affable gentleman, but he loved good dinners and good wine. He was fond of gambling, and sometimes played cards all night.

Sir Henry Clinton, Earl Percy, Earl Cornwallis, Sir William Erskine, and General Grant were with him, all able officers, who had been in battle. Earl Percy was the officer who went out from Boston to Lexington with re-enforcements, and saved Colonel Smith and Major Pitcairn from being cut off by the minute-men. Sir Henry Clinton was the officer who had hastened from Copp's Hill to Charlestown, to help Howe at the Battle of Bunker Hill. He was smarting under the repulse he and Sir Peter Parker had met with at Charleston, South Carolina. Cornwallis had been fighting in Europe, and so had Sir William Erskine and General Grant. The last named officer was a great gourmand. He could eat as much as two or three ordinary men. He thought so much of his victuals, that he used to have his cook sleep in his tent, so that he could tell him in the night what to get for breakfast.

Besides these there was the Hessian General De Heister, a fat old man who had been sea-sick all the way over. He was a great smoker, having used up all his tobacco long before the voyage was finished, and was out of sorts with himself and every body else. Several days before the fleet reached the harbor, Sir George Collier went on board of De Heister's ship with a package of tobacco. The old general filled his long-stemmed pipe, took a few whiffs, and felt so much better that he set the band to playing, and drank several bottles of wine to the health of George III., the Landgrave of Hesse, and the success of the expedition.

As soon as the British troops landed, they marched to Flatlands, while Count Donop, with a party of Hessians, took possession of Flatbush. Colonel Hand, with three hundred Pennsylvania riflemen, were in that village. The riflemen had heard a great deal about the Hessians—how terrible they were in battle. They were tall and ferocious-looking with their bushy mustaches, which they blacked every morning with their boot-blacking. They wore tall caps with bright brass plates in front. They plastered their hair with tallow mixed with flour, wore it long, braided it into a cue, which hung down their backs like a whip-lash. Their uniform was a blue coat, yellow vest and breeches, and black gaiters.

The Grenadiers of Anspach wore towering black caps. The Waldeckers wore cocked hats edged with yellow scollops.

Colonel Hand did not believe all that he had heard about the Hessians. He withdrew into the woods with his riflemen, but took a look now and then from behind the trees to see what they were up to, and resolved to give the fellows who blacked their mustaches with a shoe-brush a stirring-up.

The next morning at day-break the riflemen crept down close to the village and fired upon the pickets. The Hessian sentinels fired in return, the drums beat, and the sleepy soldiers came tumbling out from their tents in a hurry. The riflemen began to pick them off; but Count Donop had six cannon, which opened fire, and the riflemen were driven. General Sullivan sent a cannon down to Colonel Hand, and at noon, while some of the Hessian officers were sitting down to dinner in Mr. Axtel's house, Sullivan's artillery fired a shot through it which sent them out-of-doors in a hurry. Then in the afternoon the riflemen crept up once more and poured in volley after volley upon the Hessians and drove them. The fight became quite hot. The riflemen, from behind the trees, picked off the Hessians very fast. The Hessians did not understand such fighting. They could see only an enemy here and there, skulking behind a tree or wall. They could see flashes, puffs of smoke, and then came the bullets, and somebody was sure to be killed or wounded.

Some of the Hessians ran into Judge Leffert's house, to fire from the windows upon the Americans, but Sullivan's artillerymen sent solid shot through the house. Some of the riflemen crept up and set it on fire, and the Hessians had to leave.

Count Donop opened with all his guns, and the battle raged more fiercely. Three more houses were burned, besides haystacks and barns.

The next day, the 25th, Sullivan's men opened fire again, and harassed the

The Riflemen, from Behind the Trees, Picked Off the Hessians Very Fast.

Hessians exceedingly. One British officer was killed, and the rifleman who shot him found his pockets well filled with gold. A Hessian officer also was killed, besides several soldiers; but though the Hessians fired many times, not an American was injured, and the riflemen began to think that the Hessians were not so terrible after all.

A little after midnight on the morning of the 26th, the riflemen made another attack, creeping up close to the Hessians before opening fire. The Hessians were utterly disgusted with such fighting. What was the use in fighting at midnight? And who wanted to be routed up from sleep to fight an enemy whom they could not see even in the day-time? They made such complaint that Cornwallis sent some British to do picket duty.

On the afternoon of the 26th, the riflemen attacked again, now vigorously, their enemy; and as General Howe was not ready to fight a battle, Count Donop was ordered to fall back upon the main body, and to Flatlands. The riflemen took possession of Flatbush. General Howe had a grand plan and an excellent one, as we shall see.

The Americans on Long Island numbered about five thousand. Very few of the soldiers had ever been in battle. General Howe had an army of seventeen thousand of the best troops in the world.

The right of the American line was commanded by Lord Stirling. Colonel Atlee, with about two hundred Pennsylvanians, was south of Gowanus Bay, close down to the shore (near Twenty-third Street). Then came the Delaware troops under Colonel Hazlet, and the Maryland regiment under Colonel Smallwood. Then three regiments were extended east toward Flatbush—in all about eleven hundred men.

Behind Stirling's position toward the ferry was Gowanus Creek and a wide marsh (all the space between Court Street and Fifth Avenue), with only one bridge across the creek near a mill owned by Mr. Brower.

General Sullivan commanded the left. He had only four regiments: Colonel Williams's, Colonel Parsons's, Colonel Miles's, and Colonel Hand's riflemen. Colonel Miles held the extreme left, and it was supposed that he would keep pickets out on the Jamaica road. But the Jamaica pass was a good way from him, and no one expected that the British would come from that quarter. General Putnam was sure that Howe would attack in front of Stirling and Sullivan. The Jamaica road was like the back door to a house. Stirling and Sullivan were guarding the front and side doors, while the back door was left wide open, which was a great mistake.

Such is the position of the American lines on the evening of the 26th of August.

Howe has formed his plan.   He leaves General Grant, with two brigades of British, about two thousand men and ten cannon, in front of General Stirling. He leaves De Heister, with all the Hessians (eight thousand), in front of Sullivan, and starts at nine o'clock with Cornwallis, Clinton, and Percy, for a long night march.   He moves east toward Jamaica.   He has eight thousand men, and a great train of artillery. He leaves his tents standing, so that in the morning, Sullivan and Stirling, looking through the trees, will see that the British army is still there.   He sends out men to seize all the inhabitants on his line of march, so that no one shall give information of his movement.

At two o'clock in the morning, Cornwallis arrived at Mr. Howard's tavern (corner of Broadway and Brooklyn turnpike).   The tavern-keeper has a son, William, fourteen years old.

"Can You Pilot Me to Jamaica Pass, My Lad?"

"Can you pilot me to Jamaica pass, my lad?" Cornwallis asks.   William knows every inch of the ground, and leads Cornwallis across the fields and up a narrow path through the hills.   Cornwallis is surprised to find no Americans in the pass. Before day-break he is through the back door, and halts for breakfast.

Just about the time that Cornwallis started for Howard's

tavern, some of Colonel Atlee's pickets, down on the seashore, by Gowanus Bay, discern some British in a melon-patch, and fire upon them. Soon after two hundred of Grant's men advance upon Colonel Atlee; but the Pennsylvanians drive them back. The volleys of musketry roll over the hills, waking up the Americans.

General Putnam is in the saddle. He is confident that when the day breaks Howe will attack with his whole force Stirling and Sullivan. General Washington is at Brooklyn, looking after things there.

General Stirling forms his line near the Red Lion tavern, and along what is now the western boundary of Greenwood Cemetery. A regiment of riflemen, under Colonel Kichline, comes to re-enforce Stirling. Just at day-break, while Cornwallis is up at Jamaica Pass, seven miles away, eating breakfast, the firing begins.

General Grant sends forward several regiments to begin the contest. He has no intention of pushing things just yet. He is only attracting attention, while Howe, with Clinton and Percy and Cornwallis, gets into position. But Stirling orders up two cannon, under Captain Carpenter, which are put in a favorable position, and the riflemen, from behind trees and fences, make it so hot for Grant that he is obliged to fall back, and Stirling's men take courage. Little do they know of what is going on at Jamaica!

And now the Hessians, under De Heister, march up Martenses Lane, and come into position in front of Sullivan.

The fleet has weighed anchor, and Admiral Howe is trying to sail up the bay to silence the American batteries at Red Hook, and be ready to pour a shower of shot and shell upon the rear of the Americans; but the wind is contrary, and the *Roebuck* is the only vessel that has succeeded in getting near enough to open fire.

Nine o'clock comes. The battle thus far has been only a skirmish. There are some American pickets at Bedford. They can hear the roar of the cannonade and the rattle of musketry in the south. They are two miles from the scene. But what is this which they discover? A long column of bright-red uniforms—thousands of bayonets gleaming in the sun—a great park of artillery rapidly advancing along the Jamaica road. They spring to their arms. There comes a rattling fire. The British unlimber their cannon, and the deep, heavy roar rolls away.

General Sullivan hears it. What is the meaning of it? De Heister and Grant hear it, and comprehend it. There is a quick movement in the Hessian and British lines, and the battle begins in earnest. Two thousand troops hasten on shore from the fleet to re-enforce General Grant, making fully nineteen thousand British to attack five thousand Americans.

A severe conflict is going on between Sullivan's men and the Hessians, but the enemy is in Sullivan's rear.

"Retreat!" is the order which runs along the line, and the men turn their backs to the Hessians, and make their way upon the run through the woods. Suddenly they find themselves face to face with the British, under Cornwallis, Clinton, and Percy.

An enemy in front—an enemy in rear. Cornwallis's troops received them with a volley. The slaughter had begun. The Hessians charge with bayonet. Some of Miles's and Parsons's men throw down their guns and beg for mercy; but the Hessians plunge their bayonets into them, paying no heed to their cries. Others, seeing that no quarter is given, resolve to sell their lives as dearly as possible, shooting their assailants and using the butts of their guns in defense.

In Sullivan's ranks is John Callender, of Massachusetts. He commanded the artillery at Bunker Hill, and was accused of being a coward, and his command was taken from him. But he is a patriot, and is in the ranks. He sees a lieutenant commanding a battery fall, and the gunners begin to leave their guns. "Stop!" he shouts. It is the voice of one accustomed to be obeyed, and the gunners return. He opens fire, and holds the position till the British sweep up the hill. The other soldiers flee, but he will not. He is ramming home a charge, when a bayonet is leveled at his breast. A British officer admires his heroism, and will not let him be harmed. He is a prisoner, and when at last he is exchanged, General Washington sends for him, to take by the hand one so brave and true.

Sullivan is taken prisoner, and so are many of his men. Others flee toward Freeck's Mill.

General Grant has heard Cornwallis's guns, and now, with four thousand men, attacks Stirling, driving him toward the creek. The fight goes on in the woods and fields, and by Cortelyou's house. Cornwallis's men take possession of it. The Maryland regiment, Colonel Smallwood's, comes through the woods to make its way to the bridge by the mill, but Cornwallis has cut off the retreat. The Marylanders are brave men. They are only four hundred. Two thousand British confront them. Cornwallis's cannon plow through their ranks.

"Close up!" shouts General Stirling, and the regiment—alone now, without any supports—is to attack four times its number, and succeeds in driving Cornwallis's front line back to Cortelyou's house. A shower bursts upon the Marylanders from the windows. Two cannon blaze upon them. They are driven, but, rallying once more, they pour in a deadly fire, and shoot the British artillery-men. For a half-hour the battle rages around the house till two hundred and fifty of the four hundred have fallen, and then Stirling surrenders his sword.

The remaining Americans are rushing toward the mill, the only place by which they can retreat. Stirling is taken prisoner. Some of Smallwood's men gain the mill; but Cornwallis has planted his cannon to sweep the road, and the balls come through the ranks. Some of Stirling's men, cut off from the bridge, retreat across the marsh, and leap into the creek to swim to the other shore. Some sink to rise no more. Some are shot by the brutal Hessians and equally blood-thirsty British, as they struggle in the water. Others, who fall upon their knees, are bayoneted without mercy. The water is crimson with their blood.

The British officers gloat over the massacre. One, after the battle, writes home to his friends about it:

"The Hessians and our brave Highlanders gave no quarter, and it was a fine sight to see with what alacrity they dispatched

FOR A HALF-HOUR THE BATTLE RAGES AROUND CORTELYOU'S
HOUSE.

the rebels with their bayonets after we had surrounded them, so that they could not resist. We took care to tell the Hessians that the rebels had resolved to give no quarter to them in particular, which made them fight desperately, and put all to death who fell into their hands."

General Washington is up in one of the forts, and the tears roll down his cheeks as he sees the slaughter; but he is powerless to save them. Before noon the battle is over; and from fifteen hundred to two thousand Americans have been killed, wounded, or taken prisoners. The British have lost between three and four hundred.

With bullets falling around them, Elijah and Esek made their way across the creek by the mill, and reached the intrenchments.

If General Howe had attacked the intrenchments at once, quite likely he would have taken them and the whole of the American troops on the island; but he allowed his troops to rest, resolving to begin a regular siege, and so lost a golden opportunity.

Elijah and Esek lay all night within musket-shot of the British. They could hear the British soldiers at work with axes and shovels, and knew that they were erecting batteries.

A thick fog had settled over the island. Day dawned, but the fog remained. General Washington called a council of his officers, and it was decided to evacuate the island. All day long the troops lay in the intrenchments, but when night came there was a busy scene at Brooklyn ferry.

One of the American regiments was from Marblehead, in Massachusetts, and the men composing it were fishermen. Every man knew how to pull an oar. The Marbleheaders were more at home on the sea than on the land. The regiment was commanded by Colonel Glover, and General Washington selected him as the fittest person in the army to superintend the ferrying, and he did it nobly.

Elijah and Esek were asleep when their captain touched them. "Get up!" he said, in a whisper. "Don't speak; make no noise."

They took their places in the ranks, and the regiment

marched away to the ferry so silently that the British heard nothing of the movement.

Boat after boat was filled and sent away in the fog and darkness, landing the troops in New York, then returning for more. From midnight till morning the fishermen plied their oars. When the morning dawned, the fog lifted, and the sun rose bright and clear. The British were ready to open fire on Fort Putnam, but found it deserted. General Clinton ordered out the cavalry to pursue the fleeing Americans. The troops dashed down to the ferry, but General Washington had just left, and his army was safely landed in New York. General Howe thought that he had Washington in a trap, but found himself mistaken, and was greatly mortified when he found that the whole army had escaped.

Chapter 8
THE EVACUATION OF NEW YORK AND BATTLE AT HARLEM

THE next day, after the troops retreated from Brooklyn, some of the ships of the British fleet sailed up the harbor and dropped anchor within cannon-shot of the city. In the night one ship passed into the East River, while a portion of the fleet sailed around Long Island and came up the Sound. It was very plain that General Howe intended to move the army from Long Island across to New York, and, by taking possession of the region north and east of the city, capture the American army.

General Washington wanted to find out exactly what Howe intended to do, and Captain Nathan Hale, of Connecticut, went over to Long Island to learn what he could of Howe's intentions. While he was gone, General Washington made preparations for leaving the city. The Marbleheaders were kept at work ferrying the sick in the hospitals across the Hudson to New Jersey, and in transporting the supplies up the river to Dobb's Ferry.

On the night of the 14th of September, ten war-ships moved up and dropped anchor in Kip's Bay. Mr. Jacobus Kip lived in an old-fashioned Dutch house, built of bricks made in Holland and brought to America, because the old Dutch burghers thought that there was no clay in America suitable to be made into bricks. The house stood a short distance from the water, and had curiously shaped windows in the roof, and a weather-cock above the ridge-pole.

Several regiments of Americans, under Colonel Parsons and Colonel Fellows, were stationed along the shore to prevent the British from landing at Kip's; but soon after day-break the ships ran out their guns and began to fire. The shot came crashing through the trees, and some of the soldiers, who never had been under fire, were greatly frightened. They started to run; but the officers stopped them, and they curled down behind the intrenchments.

Esek and Elijah saw a great fleet of boats start from the Long Island shore filled with troops—four thousand or more—under Sir Henry Clinton. They pulled past the ships, which were roaring all the while. Before the first boat reached the shore some of the Americans started to run.

"Stop, you cowards!" shouted Colonel Parsons.

"Come back!" cried Colonel Fellows; but a panic had seized the militia, and the officers might as well have tried to stop the wind. Esek and Elijah, and a few who had been in battle, fired a volley, and then, with the officers, retreated.

As they fell back they saw General Washington trying to stop the fugitives. He shouted to them, but they paid no heed to him. He was so mortified and angry that he drew his sword and started alone across the field toward the British, who were landing and forming. His bravery had gotten the better of his judgment. One of his aids seized his horse by the bit. Not till then did Washington see how foolish it would be for him to rush upon the enemy alone.

Elijah heard a tramping of feet, and saw the fishermen of Marblehead, who had finished their work on the river, and were once more in the field. They had braved the ocean all their lives, and were not frightened now in the presence of the British. Elijah and Esek, and the other cool-headed soldiers, faced about and poured in such a fire that the British, who had started in pursuit, came to a halt.

All this time General Putnam was in the city with four thousand men, ignorant of what was going on at Kip's. General Clinton had landed two miles in his rear, and was ready to move westward to the Hudson. It was only a mile that he would have to march. General Washington sent a messenger to Putnam. "Evacuate immediately," was the order.

The only way of escape left open was up the shore of the Hudson, along cart-paths, for the British were already in possession of the Boston road.

General Putnam did not know the way, but, fortunately, he had a young officer for an aid who knew every path and by-way —the officer whose acquaintance Dodifer made in the wilderness on the march to Quebec—Aaron Burr. General Putnam started.

There was one brigade (Colonel Silliman's) in a little fort which the Americans had named Bunker Hill (corner of Broadway and Grand Street). Major Burr rode up to it.

"What are you lingering here for? Why don't you retreat?" he shouted.

"We cannot retreat. The British have possession of the road! We will stay here and hold the fort," said General Knox.

"You can't hold it ten minutes. You have no water, no provisions. There is no place where the troops can be sheltered from the bombs. The British will throw in shells and make it a slaughter-pen," said Burr.

"It will be madness to attempt to retreat," Knox replied.

"I can guide you. I know every cow-path."

They trusted him, and went upon the run, down through the fields to the Hudson, past Mr. De Lancey's house, then through woods, along narrow paths, and so escaped.

Just about the time that General Putnam started, General Howe and General Clinton, having compelled Washington to retreat, rode west half way to the Hudson, and drew up at the house of Mr. Murray. It was a delightful mansion, with a lawn and graveled walks in front, a green-house, and rustic seats. Mrs. Murray received them courteously, and it occurred to her that if she could entertain them a while it might be of some service to General Washington. She invited them in, told the servants to prepare a lunch, and entertained them so charmingly that they forgot all about affairs outside. She kept them fully two hours; and while they were sipping Mrs. Murray's wine, and listening to her engaging conversation, General Putnam, with his four thousand men, was slipping past them not a half mile away.

General Howe was greatly chagrined when he learned that

She Kept Them Fully Two Hours.

Putnam had escaped, but set up his head-quarters at Mr. Beekman's fine old mansion.

General Washington had retreated toward King's Bridge, and was quartered in a house owned by an old acquaintance (Major Morris) who had served with him under General Braddock. Major Morris had sided with the king, and was absent from home with his beautiful wife, *née* Phillipse, whom General Washington once met at the house of Colonel Beverly Robinson, on the banks of the Hudson, near West Point, in 1756. Mrs. Morris was Mrs. Robinson's sister, who, as Miss Phillipse, had so charmed the rich young planter from Virginia that he asked her to become Mrs. Washington; but she declined the offer, and married Major Morris, and now Washington was occupying her house.

The next morning, the British light-infantry, under General Leslie, advanced toward Harlem through a narrow path, which was guarded by Colonel Knowlton, of Connecticut, the brave

WITHOUT JUDGE OR JURY, COURT OR TRIAL, HE WAS TAKEN INTO
THE ORCHARD AND HANGED.

officer who had fought so nobly at Bunker Hill; and by Major Leitch, of Virginia, who had three companies from Colonel Weeden's regiment.

At the first volley of the light-infantry Major Leitch fell, with three bullets through his body; and a moment later Colonel Knowlton was shot through the head. This was a sad loss, for he was one of the ablest officers in the army. General Washington wrote this in regard to him: "He would have been an honor to any country."

Colonel Griffith a n d Colonel Richardson, commanding two Maryland regiments, hastened to re-enforce those already engaged. The light-infantry had come out into a field, and the Marylanders and Connecticut men opened such a vigorous fire that they fled to the shelter of the woods.

If He Saw a Prisoner Eating His Dinner, He Would Kick the Dish from His Hands.

General Washington feared that Howe had all his army drawn up behind the hills (now in Central Park), and did not dare to follow up the advantage. The Americans lost only a few killed and wounded, while the light-infantry lost more than one hundred.

While this was going on, Captain Hale was returning from Long Island. He had been through the British camp, but was recognized by a Tory who knew him, and, having a grudge against him, had him arrested. He was brought over to General Howe's head-quarters, at Mr. Beekman's house, and turned over to the provost-marshal, Cunningham, a brutal Irishman, who had charge of the prisoners. He was so brutal that, if he saw a prisoner eating his dinner, he improved the opportunity to kick the dish from his hands. No scene of suffering moved him, and many Whigs were hanged under his command.

Captain Hale was shut up in Mr. Beekman's green-house. Sentinels, with loaded muskets, paced the graveled walk through the night. In the morning Captain Hale was told that he was to be hanged. No trial was granted him. He asked for a Bible, that he might read some of its comforting words before being executed; but Cunningham would not permit him to have one. He asked that a clergyman might be permitted to pray with him; but this Cunningham would not grant. He had written some letters to his mother and sisters; but these the unfeeling wretch tore to pieces. Without judge or jury, court or trial, on a bright September morning, he was taken into the orchard and hanged. There was no quivering of the lip, no blanching of his cheek, as he stood beneath the tree. "I only regret that I have but one life to give to my country," he said. They were his last words.

General Howe, in the flush of his success, ignored the usages of war—to try men by court-martial before hanging them. He decreed that the young patriot should die the death of a dog, without trial of any kind. It was an unworthy, ungracious act; and it came back to trouble him, as we shall see by-and-by.

Chapter 9
BATTLE OF WHITE PLAINS

WASHINGTON was in a strong position, and Howe did not dare to attack him in front: he would get in his rear. He embarked his army in boats, sailed east through Hell Gate, sixteen miles to Throck's Neck, a point of land owned by Mr. Throckmorton.

Washington sent General Heath with Colonel Hand and Colonel Prescott, to defend a bridge over a causeway. Heath took up the planks, planted his cannon to sweep the causeway, and Howe had to re-embark once more, and go farther east to Pell's Neck, where a body of Hessians had landed. When Howe reached that place he found General Sullivan confronting him, and the fishermen of Marblehead, under Colonel Glover; but the British greatly outnumbered the Americans, and Howe was able to push inland to the hills south of New Rochelle. The country was thickly covered with woods; but Howe found a small house in which he established his headquarters.

The next day seventy-two ships sailed up the Sound, bringing ten thousand Hessians, two hundred British, and two thousand horses, besides an immense amount of supplies. General Howe had left several thousand troops in New York; but this arrival gave him an army of thirty thousand in the field, well supplied; while Washington could number only nineteen thousand, many of whom were farmers who had hastened in to serve a few days.

Washington saw that Howe intended to get in his rear and

sweep in the whole army, as a fisherman incloses a school of fish in a seine; but he had no intention of being caught.

On the 21st of October the army moved from Harlem north, in four divisions, commanded by Sullivan, Lee, Heath, and Lincoln.

There was a small fort on the bank of the Hudson called Fort Washington, and another fort opposite on the west bank, called Fort Lee. They were erected to prevent the British fleet from going up the Hudson. General Washington wanted to evacuate Fort Washington, but Congress thought it ought to be held, and, out of deference to the wishes of that body, he left Colonel Magaw with two thousand men to hold it.

A little river called the Bronx rises among the hills fourteen miles north of New Rochelle, runs to the Sound parallel with the Hudson, four miles from it. Howe was east of the Bronx, while Washington was between the Bronx and the Hudson. Washington made a rapid march and reached White Plains on the night of the 21st of October, and established his head-quarters in Mr. Miller's house.

No use for Howe to attempt to inclose him now. Washington was beyond the sweep of the net.

Elijah and Esek camped in a corn-field. While sitting by their camp-fire, a young captain of artillery came out and sat down by it to warm himself. He had two cannon in the woods near by, placed so as to sweep the British if they should attempt to cross the Bronx at the foot of the hill below them. There was something about the officer that attracted Elijah's attention. He was very polite and well-informed. Elijah learned that his name was Alexander Hamilton, and that he was born in the West Indies. Little did he imagine what a career Captain Hamilton would have—that he would become Washington's most intimate friend, and be known as one of the ablest writers and most accomplished orators of the age; that he would finally be shot in a duel, across the Hudson, by the young officer who had piloted General Putnam out of New York—Aaron Burr.

General M'Dougall commanded the troops on the hill. The

WHILE SITTING AT THEIR CAMP-FIRE, A YOUNG CAPTAIN CAME
TO WARM HIMSELF.

next morning, the 28th of October, General Howe brought up twenty cannon, and began to throw shot and shell across the Bronx. Captain Hamilton made no reply. Soon the British under Sir Henry Clinton, and the Hessians under De Heister, who had the left of the line, moved down from the hill to cross the little stream. The pioneers, with axes and fence-rails, came in advance to build a bridge. Captain Hamilton opened with his two guns. He had the exact range, and sent his shot right down into the Hessian ranks. The fire was so destructive that the Hessians fled in confusion; but General Leslie, with a British brigade, and a brigade of Hessians, under Colonel Rall, crossed where they were sheltered from Captain Hamilton's guns. They came upon M'Dougall's right wing, south-west of the hill, and the battle began. M'Dougall's men had made breastworks of the corn-stalks, piling them against a fence, and were well protected. General Leslie attempted to charge up the hill; but Colonel Smallwood, with the Maryland troops who had fought so gallantly at Cortelyou's house, and had escaped by swimming Gowanus Creek, cut them down, and drove them in confusion back to the shelter of a hill. For more than an hour they held the ground against four times their number.

General Howe had two hundred and fifty cavalry, which went out through the fields and woods toward the Hudson, making a wide sweep. They were followed by Colonel Rall. After marching west, they turned north, and came upon some militia companies on M'Dougall's right. The militia fired once and then ran, and the troopers and Hessians attacked Smallwood on his right flank, and so forced him to retreat to the main line, which Washington had established on the hills a mile in the rear of Chatterton Hill.

When M'Dougall began to retreat, General Putnam, with several regiments, started out from the main line, and M'Dougall's men retreated through the advancing ranks. The Hessians were following, thinking they had won the victory, but suddenly found themselves face to face with Putnam. They saw a flash, heard a roar, and then came the storm of leaden rain.

General Howe came up, looked at Washington's position,

and concluded that it would not do to attack him in front. He had lost three hundred men, and did not care to march directly against the strong intrenchments.

Although he had ten thousand more troops than Washington, he halted, and sent for Lord Percy to come from New York with four thousand men. Percy arrived on the 30th of October. Everybody expected that there would be a great battle the next day; but at midnight a terrible storm arose, which lasted all the next day, damaging the ammunition of both armies. General Washington was not satisfied with his position, for he saw that Howe, by marching east, might get in his rear. There was a much stronger position three miles farther north, where the hills were high and steep, and where the Croton River would prevent Howe from getting in his rear. He had constructed strong intrenchments on these hills, and, just before day-break, while the storm was still raging, the army moved silently away.

Howe was greatly surprised when he found the Americans had retreated. He advanced with his army; but when he saw Washington's cannon planted on hills one hundred feet high, and that there was no opportunity to get in his rear, he was greatly perplexed. He had expected to capture the army on Long Island; was confident of hemming the Americans in New York; was sure of sweeping them in by the movement to New Rochelle, and here he was, completely baffled. Winter was coming on. What should he do? There were Fort Washington and Fort Lee; he would turn his attention to those fortifications, and, instead of attacking Washington, moved his army toward New York.

What should Washington do? More than half of his army were of the militia, who had come out to serve a few days; their time had expired, and they went home. He saw that Howe would probably invade New Jersey, and, leaving General Putnam, with a portion of the army, to guard the Highlands, crossed the Hudson, and encamped in the rear of Fort Lee.

General Howe invested Fort Washington. Colonel Magaw made a brave defense, but a hopeless one. In a few days he was forced to surrender, and the soldiers, who might have been saved if Congress had but allowed Washington to manage affairs, were taken to New York and put into the prison-ship *Jersey*, where they suffered the most inhuman treatment, and where they nearly all sickened and died.

General Washington stood on the Palisades, at Fort Lee, and saw how bravely the fort was defended. There were tears on his cheeks as he saw the flag hauled down and the garrison march out as prisoners, going to their terrible fate; but he was powerless to aid them.

Howe, having captured Fort Washington, s e n t Cornwallis with six thousand troops across the Hudson in boats to take F o r t Lee. Cornwallis crossed from Fort Washington, landing at the foot of the Palisades. A British engineer drew a picture of the landing, which shows how the Palisades looked, and how the army climbed the steep bluff. The soldiers tugged at the cannon and got them to the top;

A British Engineer Drew a Picture of the Landing.

the army formed to make the attack, but there was no one in the fort to oppose Cornwallis. The place was of no value to the Americans, now that Fort Washington had been captured, and the garrison was retreating to Hackensack to join Washington. If Cornwallis had pushed on, he might have scattered Washington's little army, for it numbered only four thousand now; but he was well satisfied with what had been accomplished. He waited two days, and so missed a great opportunity.

Chapter 10
LAKE CHAMPLAIN

WHEN spring opened and the ice went out of the St. Lawrence, a fleet of vessels sailed up the river to Quebec with re-enforcements, under General Burgoyne, for Sir Guy Carleton. There were only a few American troops in Canada, under General Wooster. Generals Arnold and Sullivan were with Wooster, but General Carleton had much the larger army. He advanced to Montreal, then to St. Johns—the American generals retreating before him; and in June there was not an American soldier in Canada. The last week in May, General Burgoyne and General Carleton moved from Montreal to St. Johns. The Americans shipped their supplies and cannon on boats, and sent them up the river to Lake Champlain. The last boat put off. General Arnold and Major Wilkinson, his aid, rode out two miles toward Montreal, saw the British rapidly approaching, rode back, shot their horses to prevent them from falling into the hands of the British, jumped into a canoe, paddled south, and overtook the retreating boats. All the toiling through the wilderness, all the hardships at Quebec, had ended in failure. Carleton had no boats to pursue the Americans, who retreated to Crown Point and Ticonderoga; but they very well knew that he would soon have a fleet of vessels on the lake, for seven hundred British went to work cutting down trees and hewing timber. Congress decided that a fleet must be built to hold the lake, and ship-carpenters were soon on their way from Rhode Island, Massachusetts, and New Hampshire to Ticonderoga. They felled the trees on the shores of the lake, hewed the timbers, floated them to Ticonderoga, and by September had quite a fleet of vessels —three schooners, two sloops, three galleys, eight gondolas, and twenty-one gun-boats. One of the schooners carried twelve guns, the other two eight. One of the sloops carried twelve, and the others eight guns. The gondolas carried three guns, and the gun-boats one gun each.

General Carleton had one very powerful vessel, the *Thunderer*—a flat-bottomed craft, carrying eighteen guns, six of them twenty-four-pounders. The *Inflexible* carried eighteen guns, the *Carleton* twelve, the *Loyal Consort* seven, the schooner *Maria* fourteen guns. Besides these, General Carleton had twenty-one gun-boats, each carrying one gun. His fleet was much more powerful than the American fleet commanded by General Arnold. Captain Pringle commanded it, and one of his officers was young Edward Pellew, who afterward became one of the great naval commanders of England, known as Admiral Viscount Exmouth.

About ten miles south of Plattsburg, near the western shore of the lake, is Valcour Island. Between this island and the New York shore, Arnold was lying with all his fleet on the 11th of October. It was a dangerous position, for the British fleet could sail south, past Valcour, and cut off his retreat to Ticonderoga. Many of Arnold's men never had sighted a cannon, very few had ever loaded one; while Carleton had old artillery-men. He had seven hundred men, and Arnold less than five hundred. Carleton had experienced seamen, while many of Arnold's men did not know the difference between the foresail and the mainsail.

It is early in the morning, when Carleton's fleet is seen under full sail, coming round a wooded point of land called Cumberland Head, forming Plattsburg Bay. The wind is favorable, and all sails are spread to the breeze. It is the largest fleet ever seen on the lake. General Arnold orders the *Royal Savage,* of twelve guns, one of his largest vessels, and three galleys, to get under way, advance, and engage the enemy. Arnold is a gen-

eral, not an admiral. In manœuvring troops, he sends out skirmishers, and so will he begin this battle on the water. An
admiral would bring all of his vessels into action at once, if
possible.

In attempting to approach the British, the *Royal Savage* runs
aground. So firmly is the vessel grounded that it will be impossible to get her off, and the crew leap into the water, or push off
in boats to the other ships,
and this ship is set on fire.
Thus, at the outset, Arnold
loses one of his largest
ships, and all his personal
baggage, which is on board,
though he himself is on
board the *Congress*.

The Deck Is Slippery with Blood.

It is twelve o'clock when
the British fleet, having
sailed past the island, approaches the American
fleet, and the battle begins.
The British gunboats are
within musket-shot, but the
Thunderer has not been
able to beat up against the
wind. All through the af-
ternoon, from twelve till
five, the unequal contest
rages. The vessels are at
anchor. The British do
not come to close quarters, but, having experienced gunners,
take position and send the shot into the American vessels. The
rigging is cut to pieces. Two shots go through the mainmast
of the *Congress*. Twelve times that vessel is struck—seven
of the shot going below the waterline. The deck is slippery with
blood. The slaughter is fearful. But brave men are on board.
They know very little about naval warfare, and Arnold himself
has to sight most of the guns.

The *Washington* galley is shattered to pieces—the captain and sailing-master wounded, the lieutenant killed. All the officers on one of the gondolas are killed or wounded. Another gondola is so riddled with solid shot, that it sinks soon after the engagement. Sixty have been killed and wounded. On the British side forty have fallen, but the vessels are very little injured.

Night closes upon the scene, with the British fleet anchored in a line from the island to the main-land. The wind is blowing from the north, cold and raw. The Americans can not beat up against it, and go round between the island and Cumberland Head, and so escape. In the morning Carleton will finish the work, sinking every vessel.

It was a sad plight in which the Americans found themselves. The vessels were leaking badly; their ammunition was nearly gone; the *Royal Savage* was lost; one of the gondolas sunk; the *Lady Washington* was a wreck; sixty men had fallen. What was to be done?

As the last rays of twilight faded away, General Arnold took particular notice of the position of the British vessels. If possible, the fleet must escape to Crown Point. There was no moon, no stars, and dark clouds were rolling from the north. The wind was blowing briskly. At a signal, one by one, the vessels slipped away, sailing past the British so quietly that no sentinel pacing the decks discerned the white sails in the darkness. The *Congress* was the last to run the gantlet.

Morning dawned, and the British, all ready to blow the American vessels out of the water, were surprised to see the entire fleet ten miles away. Up came the anchors. Quickly were the sails shaken to the wind, and the fleet went gayly up the lake before the wind. The *Congress* and some of the other vessels were leaking so badly that Arnold was obliged to drop anchor while the carpenters tried to stop the leaks. The wind died away, and the lake became calm; but, though smooth, nothing could keep two of the gondolas from sinking.

The wind changed to the south, and neither of the fleets

could make much progress against it, and night shut in once more. Carleton had not overtaken his prey.

The morning of the 13th dawned. The *Congress, Lady Washington,* and four of the gondolas had made little progress, while the rest of the fleet was well on its way to Crown Point. The British were hastening on. The *Lady Washington* was overhauled and obliged to surrender. On came the British fleet —a ship of eighteen guns, another of fourteen, another of twelve—all pouring their broadsides into the *Congress* and one of the galleys. The fire was returned. With all sail set, the pursuers and pursued pressed on; but the wind was light, and very little headway was made. For four hours the battle went on, till the American vessels were nothing but wrecks—sails rent, sides stove in, water pouring into the holds, yet the men on board will not surrender. They run the vessels into a creek on the east side of the lake. The vessels ground. "Set them on fire!" Arnold shouts from the deck of the *Congress*. "Leap ashore with your muskets!" are his orders to the marines.

The men, holding their muskets over their heads to keep them from being wet, jump into the water, wade to the shore, ready to open fire upon the British.

Up from the decks roll the flames. Wreaths of fire curl around the masts. The sails are broad sheets of flame. When every man has left the fleet, Arnold lets himself into the water by a rope, and wades to the shore. The British are close upon him. The soldiers on the nearest ship open fire; but from the alders and beneath the pines the rifles are cracking, and they continue to crack till the ships are all aflame. Then, helping on the wounded, the crews make their way to Crown Point, just in time to escape the Indians whom Carleton has landed to intercept them.

The fleet was destroyed, but not captured, and the country rang in praise of the men who had fought so bravely against a superior foe.

General Carleton had driven the Americans out of Canada, had attached the Indians to the cause of the king; but he was not strong enough to attack Ticonderoga, and returned to Mon-

"LEAP ASHORE WITH YOUR MUSKETS!" SHOUTS ARNOLD.

treal; while General Burgoyne, with great plans for the future, hastened to England to make them known to the ministers and the king.

There being no further need for an army at Ticonderoga, all except three or four regiments were dismissed, or else went south under General Sullivan, to join General Washington; but before they arrived General Washington was retreating before Cornwallis across New Jersey, as we shall see.

ENERAL HOWE, having secured New York, began to make preparations to take Philadelphia. Congress was in session there, in Independence Hall, and had declared America to be independent of Great Britain. He would see about that. He would chase Washington through New Jersey as a hound chases a fox, scatter the last remnant of the rebel army, seize the members of Congress, and send them to England to be hanged as traitors. A division of the army was placed under Cornwallis, who was instructed to pursue Washington.

Washington had less than three thousand men. It was a weary march to Elijah and Esek across the marshes from Hackensack to Newark, and from there to New Brunswick. Their hearts sunk at New Brunswick when the New Jersey and Maryland troops, whose time had expired, left camp and started for home. The army numbered only seventeen hundred, after their departure.

From New Brunswick they marched to Princeton, with Cornwallis pressing hard after them. From Princeton they hastened to Trenton over the frozen roads, with Cornwallis marching faster than ever. They were hastening to the Delaware. If they could but reach Trenton, where a large number of boats had been collected—if they could have an hour or two there, they would be safe. They reached the river; sent over the cannon first, then the baggage. Regiment after regiment crossed; and just as the last reached the Pennsylvania bank, Cornwallis marched into Trenton, his drums beating and colors flying.

Cornwallis was baffled. The river could not be forded. He had no boats, and must wait till it was frozen before seizing his prey. General Howe issued a proclamation, offering pardon to all who would lay down their arms and own allegiance to the king. A great many people who had favored Congress flocked to Cornwallis's camp, and swore fealty to the king. Half of the people in New Jersey were Tories, and Washington k n e w n o t whom to trust.

The little army was disheartened to learn that General Lee, who had returned from Charleston, had been captured. He was marching from the Highlands of the Hudson toward the Delaware with a division of the army. General Sullivan was with him. Lee was ambitious,

General Howe Issued a Proclamation
Offering Pardon.

and wanted to be commander-in-chief, and, though ordered to join Washington, was meditating a disobedience of his orders. His troops were at Morristown. He left them under Sullivan, and rode down to Basking Ridge, a few miles, to pass the night in his own house, and was surprised the next morning to find the house surrounded by British dragoons. The Tories had given them information.

In his dressing-gown and slippers, bare-headed, with nothing but a blanket to protect him from the cold, he was taken to New York. Perhaps, instead of being a loss, his capture was a gain, for Sullivan, with the troops, hastened on, and crossed the river at M'Conkey's Ferry, twelve miles above Trenton. A bridge now spans the river there, but then there was no bridge all the way from the mountains to Delaware Bay.

Although Cornwallis had not been able to capture Washington, General Howe was well satisfied with what had been accomplished. He had gained possession of New York, scattered the American army, driven Washington beyond the Delaware, and could write home to the ministers that the people were becoming loyal, and that the rebellion would soon be crushed. He was well situated in New York, gave grand dinners, drank his wine, enjoyed his evenings in playing cards, and looked forward to an agreeable winter.

General Cornwallis was well satisfied with the part he had performed. He had captured Fort Washington, chased Washington across the Delaware, and was going home to England to enjoy the honors which the king would confer upon him. He left Colonel Rall, with fifteen hundred Hessians and two hundred British cavalry, at Trenton; stationed Count Donop eight miles farther down the river, at Bordentown; and sent another party eight miles south of Bordentown, to Burlington; and another party ten miles from Burlington, to Mount Holly. He left some troops at Princeton, and made his grand supply of stores at New Brunswick. By dividing the army into detachments, the troops could obtain forage and fresh provisions. He held Washington and his little force in contempt. The American army had dwindled from twenty thousand, at White Plains on the 28th of October, to less than two thousand in December.

But Congress had made a patriotic appeal to the country, promising to give each officer and soldier a liberal bounty of land, and the militia of Pennsylvania were coming into camp. Two thousand came, under General Cadwalader and General Ewing, and took post at Bristol, between Trenton and Philadelphia.

Elijah and Esek could look across the river, at Trenton, and see the Hessians on parade, or roaming through the village. The Hessians enjoyed themselves. At night they plundered pig-pens and hen-roosts, and made themselves at home in the kitchens. They insulted the girls, and felt that they were conquerors.

General Washington saw that Cornwallis had made a mistake. in the military game: he had spread his troops out too much.

He resolved to take advantage of it, and laid his plan. He had about twenty-five hundred men opposite Trenton, and twenty cannon. The boats in which he had crossed the river had been taken up stream to M'Conkey's Ferry, and were safely moored on the Pennsylvania side. Generals Cadwalader and Ewing, at Bristol, also had some boats. He would send the two thousand men there across the river to attack Count Donop at Bordentown. Such a movement would prevent Donop from helping Rall at Trenton.

Roaming Through the Village, the Hessians Enjoyed Themselves.

With his twenty-five hundred, with Greene, Sullivan, and Knox to aid him, Washington resolved to make a night march up the river to M'Conkey's, cross there, divide his army, and make a rapid march to Trenton in two divisions—one on the river road, and the other by the road leading through the village of Pennington. He would knock at the front door and back door at the same instant, surprise the Hessians, get them between two fires, cut off their retreat, and capture the whole force.

General Washington thought that Christmas-night would be the best time to make the attack, for the Hessians kept Christmas, and would drink a great deal of beer, and be boozy before morning.

General Putnam was in Philadelphia; and, to help the plan on, two days before Christmas, sent Colonel Griffith, with four hundred and fifty militia, across the river to march toward Mount Holly, but to make no attack upon the British there. If they advanced, he was to retreat. Colonel Griffith crossed the river, and Count Donop started south from Bordentown with all his troops.

Christmas came. The wind was raw, the ground frozen and covered with snow. Elijah and Esek sat around their camp-fire, thinking of the folks at home, and the comfort by the fires in the old kitchens. They had been fighting for liberty a year and a half, and now the prospect was gloomier than ever before. In a few days the river would be frozen over, for it was now filled with floating ice, and then the British could cross anywhere, and the little army would be scattered to the winds.

Night came. The wind was east, and the cold, gray clouds came rolling in from the sea, bringing darkness at an early hour.

"Fall into line, boys!" said the captain of their company. The soldiers wondered what was going on, but the regiments all paraded. There was no beating of drums, but silently they moved away, marching up the road leading to M'Conkey's.

They reached the ferry, and found the Marblehead men there, in the boats, ready to pull at the oars. They were the men for the hour—as they were at Brooklyn.

The artillery-men led the horses into the flat-bottomed boats, and held them by the bit, while the soldiers wheeled the cannon on board, and the boats pushed out into the stream. The current was strong, and the great cakes of ice whirled against the boats and ground their sides. It was slow work, cold work, hard work. Elijah and Esek stood at the bow of one of the boats, with poles to push the ice away. They had no mittens, nor had any of the soldiers, nor the rowers. The water froze upon the oars. They thrashed their hands till the blood oozed from under their finger-nails. The current carried them down stream. The night was dark, but they pulled and pushed, and reached the shore, and lifted the cannon up the bank; then the boats, pulled by the ever faithful fishermen, pushed off in the darkness for another load.

General Washington stood upon the Pennsylvania shore, wrapped in his cloak, directing affairs; while General Knox, on the New Jersey side, shouted to the men to be quick in getting the cannon up the bank. From seven in the evening till four in the morning the boatmen pulled at the oars, and the soldiers stood shivering upon the bank. Many of them had no overcoats, some no blankets; some had no shoes, but stood in the snow with old rags around their feet.

They Are Hungry and Weary, but On They Go.

The wind was blowing more keenly from the east, and the snow-flakes began to fall. Some of the soldiers curled down under the bank to keep themselves warm; some stamped their feet and thrashed their hands, waiting through the gloomy night.

The last boat came, bringing General Washington. He took

General Greene, General Stirling, General Mercer, and General Stevens, and started, with about half the troops, down the Pentonville road. Esek was with this division. General Sullivan, with the rest of the troops, started down the river road, to knock at the front door, while General Washington was approaching the back door. General Sullivan had half of the artillery. Elijah was with this division.

They move rapidly, for the cocks are crowing in the barns, and they have fully seven miles to march, and it will be daylight before they reach Trenton. They fear that the plan will fail. Oh, the dreariness of the night! So cold, so dark; the wind cutting like a knife, the snow falling in their faces, their clothes frozen, the crust cutting through the rags bound around their feet. They leave their blood-stains on the snow; they stagger and stumble over the uneven ground. They are hungry and weary, but on they go—tramp, tramp, tramp! For what? To secure their liberties and the liberties of those who may live when they are dead. Dead! For this night's work they shall live forever.

In Trenton the Hessians are asleep, or else singing songs and drinking their last mugs of beer. Colonel Rall is at Mr. Abraham Hunt's. Mr. Hunt is a Quaker—some say that he is a patriot, others that he is a Tory. At any rate, he has invited Colonel Rall and his officers to take Christmas supper with him, and they are there, having a merry time, smoking their pipes, drinking wine, and playing cards, with an old negro to wait upon them.

It is not quite day-break, but a Tory has discovered the approach of the Americans, and has sent a man upon the run to Trenton. The messenger, out of breath, brings a note to Colonel Rall. The old negro guards the door.

"I must see Colonel Rall," says the messenger.

"The gen'men can't be disturbed, sah," the negro replies.

"Then give that to him, quick!"

"Oh yes, sah."

The negro enters the parlor; but Colonel Rall is dealing the

COLONEL RALL HEARS THE DRUM-BEAT, THE CARDS DROP FROM HIS HANDS.

cards, and can not look at it at that moment. The candles have burned low. There are bottles and glasses upon the table. The officers are puffing their pipes. Colonel Rall puts the note in his pocket. He will examine his hand before reading it. The destiny of a nation has been thrown into the game, but Colonel Rall does not know it. His own life is at stake, but he does not dream of it.

A Hessian picket sees something moving along the road in the dim gray of the morning. Men on horseback and on foot appear. He hears the heavy rumbling of wheels, and the tramp of the army. He fires his gun, and the report goes out over the snow-clad hills and the half-frozen waters of the dark rolling rivers.

"Forward!" It is General Sullivan who shouts it. The soldiers break into a run. The artillery-men whip up their horses. The cannon rumble heavily over the frozen ground. Elijah can hear a hubbub in the village. The Hessian pickets are shouting to one another, and running here and there. They hear a drum beating the long roll, and can see soldiers forming in the street.

"Unlimber!" shout the artillery-men. The cannon are wheeled into position, a cartridge is rammed home; there is a flash, a roar that awakens every sleeper in Trenton.

Colonel Rall hears the drum-beat, the cards drop from his hands—the game unfinished. The deep thunder of that gun, jarring the windows and shaking the earth, brings home to his intellect, beclouded with wine, some sense of the greater game now beginning. The cards, the empty wine-bottles, the half-filled glasses, the pipes and tobacco are still upon the table; the candles are burning low in their sockets. Colonel Rall is leaping into his saddle. Too late! Sullivan has knocked at one door; Washington is about to knock at the other.

The column under Washington is coming down the Penton-ville road. It reaches a farm-house, where a farmer is chopping wood.

"Can you tell me where the Hessian pickets are?" Washington asks.

The chopper hesitates.

"It is General Washington wno asks you," says the aid at Washington's side.

A gleam of joy lights up the chopper's face as he points to the spot.

And now comes the roar of a cannon. Joyful, soul-thrilling sound! Sullivan is there! "Forward!"

Out from the road, over the fields sweep the shivering men. Shivering no longer now, for that deep and heavy roar has warmed them. There it is again! They hear the rattling of muskets. Moments are ages now.

A little stream, called the Assanpink, comes down through the town, and empties into the Delaware. There is a bridge across the stream, and a mill-dam. Sullivan has seized the bridge. No escape for the Hessians in that direction; and now Washington is coming down from the northwest, in their rear. It is scarcely five minutes after Sullivan begins the attack before the troops under Washington, Greene, and Stirling make their appearance.

Captain Forrest wheels six cannon into position, to send his shot down King Street. While he is doing it, the Hessians bring two guns into the street. The gunners are ramming down the cartridges, the match-man is lighting his port-fire, but before he can touch them off a company of brave men, under Captain William A. Washington, of Colonel Mercer's regiment of Virginians, dash up the street, drive the Hessians from their guns, and capture them. In this company is a young lieutenant, James Monroe, destined to be President of the country for whose redemption he is fighting.

Sullivan is pressing nearer, driving the Hessians over against Washington, and Washington is driving them back again. Colonel Rall is riding here and there shouting to them; but the men, just aroused from sleep, know not which way to turn.

The British cavalry have saddled their horses, but are in confusion. They ride up the Assanpink to a ford above the mill-pond, spur their horses across the stream, and flee toward Bordentown. Colonel Rall falls from his horse mortally wounded.

All is confusion now. Some of the Hessians throw down their arms, while others flee toward Princeton; but Washington has not come so far to leave the Princeton road open for their escape. Colonel Hand and his riflemen, who gave the Hessians such a stirring-up at Flatbush, is there. Surrounded; no chance to escape; the bewildered, panic-stricken men who have not had time to blacken their whiskers with their shoe-brushes this morning rush back to the village, throw down their guns, fall on their knees, hold up their hands, and make doleful cries.

So Stirling's men, and Sullivan's, pleaded for life at Brooklyn; but the Hessians and British drove the bayonet home, and crimsoned the ground with blood, and thought it pleasant work and a pretty sight to see the life-blood flow. Little did they think, then, that the time would come when the begging for life would be on the other side. But it has come. Oh, life is so dear, so sweet, now!

Kindness is better than brutality, forgiveness more noble than revenge. No bayonet is plunged remorselessly into the hearts of unresisting foes. Humanity triumphs on this glorious morning. One thousand prisoners are captured, with six cannon, a thousand muskets, and all the baggage. It is the work of twenty minutes.

Washington, in the kindness of his heart, visits the dying Hessian colonel, and does what he can to soothe his last moments on earth.

Cadwalader and Ewing have not been able to cross the river at Bordentown, and it will not be wise for Washington to remain on the New Jersey side. Back to the ferry with the prisoners, with six cannon, with tents and supplies, moves the victorious army. Last night the cause of liberty was dark and gloomy; but now the future is radiant with hope.

Little do those patriots, toiling through the snow, know what they have done for the world. Coming centuries alone will reveal the worth of their morning's work.

Chapter 12
PRINCETON

ENERAL CORNWALLIS was in New York. He had his trunk packed ready to sail for England, when a messenger arrived with the news that General Washington had crossed the Delaware and swooped up one thousand men! General Cornwallis was astonished, and so was General Howe. They had not supposed such a thing possible. The Yankee army had dwindled to a handful of poor, half-starved men—a rabble of wretches destitute of every thing, and yet they had crossed the Delaware and captured a thousand of the best German troops under an old and experienced commander! Such audacity was amazing. It must be punished, and General Cornwallis mounted his horse, and rode with all haste to Newark, and on to New Brunswick and Princeton, gathering up the troops in those places to chastise the Yankee general.

The news of the success at Trenton filled the country with enthusiasm. The Whigs rejoiced. The Tories did not know what to think of it. Those who had made up their minds to take the oath of loyalty to the king concluded to wait a little and see what would happen next. The Whigs, who had been desponding, plucked up courage. The militia began to flock into Washington's head-quarters. Congress, sitting in Baltimore, invested Washington with full powers, for six months, to raise and muster into service sixteen battalions of infantry, if he should need so many, and three thousand cavalry. That was well for Congress to do; but how would the men be paid? Some of the soldiers' time had expired, and Washington had no money to pay them. There was a noble man in Philadelphia, Robert Morris, who had spent a great deal of money for the cause. The next day after the victory at Trenton he sent Washington all the hard money he could lay his hands on—four hundred and ten Spanish dollars, two English crowns, half a French crown, and ten and a half English shillings! That was all; and yet so firm was the faith of Washington, that he promised each soldier ten dollars bounty, in hard money, if he would stay six weeks longer! He wrote to Morris what he had promised. It would take fifty thousand. Mr. Morris had no money, but he had a Quaker friend in Philadelphia who had the cash. Mr. Morris called upon him. "What security canst thee give, Robert?" the Quaker asked.

"My note and my honor."

"Thee shall have the money, Robert," and the next day a messenger came with the fifty thousand dollars, with this note:

"I was up early this morning to dispatch a supply of fifty thousand dollars to your excellency. It gives me great pleasure that you have engaged the troops to continue; and if further occasional supplies of money are necessary, you may depend on my exertions, either in a public or private capacity."

No wonder Washington felt encouraged upon receiving such a note! The very next day he crossed the Delaware to Trenton with his army. He had about five thousand men; but half of the number had never been under arms before.

On the morning of the 2d of January, 1777, Cornwallis was at Princeton. He had gathered up eight thousand soldiers, and more were close at hand—ten thousand in all—and he would quickly put an end to the rebellion. He started for Trenton, marching south, crossing a stone bridge three miles out of Trenton, by Mr. Worth's mill. He reached the little village of Maidenhead by noon, and left General Leslie there with three thousand, and pressed on with the other five; before night he would scatter the rebel army to the winds.

General Washington knew that Cornwallis was on his way, and sent General Fermoy and General Stevens, with Captain Forest's battery of six guns, Colonel Hand's riflemen, and Colonel Scott's regiment of Virginians, to skirmish with the British, while he placed the main army on the south side of the Assanpink.

A Citizen Came Riding Down the Road, Pursued by a Hessian Dragoon.

General Fermoy w e n t out about five miles. Soon a citizen came riding down the road, pursued by a Hessian dragoon, with his sword flashing in the air. One of the riflemen raised his rifle, there was a crack, and the Hessian tumbled to the ground. Soon the British skirmishers made their appearance, but a volley stopped them. Other British came up, and Fermoy retreated two miles to a little rivulet. There he formed his men in the thick wood on both sides of the road. Forrest planted his cannon to sweep the road. Cornwallis came on; but his skirmishers were shot down. Cornwallis thought that Washington was intending to offer him battle there, and formed his army on both sides of the road, planted his cannon, and commenced firing.

The troops under General Fermoy held their ground manfully. They kept up a rattling fire, and it took Cornwallis more than two hours to drive them out of the woods. Fermoy retreated nearer the town. Washington and Greene rode out and thanked the men for what they had done. Greene stayed to take command of the troops, while Washington rode back to Trenton. He had resolved to use the Assanpink for a line of defense. There was only one bridge by the mill across the Assanpink; but the stream could be forded between the bridge and the Delaware, and above the mill-pond there was also a ford. He placed General St. Clair, with two guns and several regiments, to guard the upper fords, and stationed General Knox with his cannon to sweep the bridge.

The bank of the Assanpink was high, and the soldiers were hard at work with spades, digging ditches and throwing up embankments. There were two breastworks, one above the other. Colonel Hitchcock, with some Massachusetts and Rhode Island troops, was over in Trenton. General Washington sat on his horse and directed the troops as they filed past him across the bridge. Cornwallis was pressing hard upon Greene, and the troops were coming down through the streets of Trenton upon the run.

"Take position in that field instantly," said Washington to Colonel Hitchcock, as his troops came upon the bridge. The cannoneers stood by their guns with lighted port-fires ready for the British.

Cornwallis formed his men in two columns, one to rush upon the bridge, the other to attack the upper ford.

It was not wise generalship, but the British commander was burning to take revenge upon Washington for the disaster of Christmas night, and he wanted to chastise him upon the spot.

The troops come down the street upon the run. Washington, Knox, and Greene are upon the bank. The infantry are behind the banks of earth, with their muskets cocked. The cannon are loaded with grape and solid shot. The match-men are waving their port-fires, to keep them burning. The British reach the bridge. The cannon blaze, the river-side is a sheet of flame, and the head of the column goes down in an instant. The British flee up King Street, beyond the reach of the murderous fire.

The officers swear at them—strike them with their swords. "What! be driven by such a miserable rabble of countrymen, with old firelocks? For shame! Charge, and scatter them as you would a flock of sheep!"

Once more the British run down the street to the bridge. Washington and Greene and Knox, the cannoneers, the infantry —all stand calmly waiting. Again the roar, again the discomfiture. No troops can stand such a concentrated fire. The British flee, and a wild hurra goes up from the Americans. Cornwallis hears it, and it inflames him. The bridge must be carried. A third time the soldiers are driven to the attack, but are scattered by the stream of death thrown across the bridge.

Not willing to give up the contest so, Cornwallis looks around to see what he can do next. There are the fords above the millpond. He will cross there, and attack Washington's right flank. But the men under St. Clair are ready for him. The British march in splendid order almost to the bank, down which they go upon the run; but, from up stream and down stream, from every bush, from every fence, from cannon and muskets, a pitiless storm bursts upon them. They fall as the leaves drop from the maples in the autumn. The water is crimsoned with blood. They flee, discomfited, up the bank, and the midwinter darkness settles over the scene.

Sir William Erskine wanted Cornwallis to march up the Assanpink to a higher ford, cross the stream with most of the army, leaving the artillery and a few troops to keep Washington from crossing the bridge, and come down the other side of the Assanpink and attack Washington in the rear; but it was almost dark, the troops were tired, and Cornwallis concluded to wait till morning.

"Washington will be off somewhere else before morning," said Erskine.

"That fox can't escape me: I'll catch him in the morning," said Cornwallis.

Both armies kindled their bivouac-fires and cooked their suppers, separated only by the little stream. It had been a disastrous beginning for Cornwallis, who had lost one hundred and fifty men, while Washington had lost very few. But Washington was anxious about the morrow. While the soldiers were cooking their suppers, he called his generals together, to consult as to what was best to be done. Should they fight a battle there in the morning? If so, what were the chances? They had only five thousand men, and half of these were raw troops, just arrived—militia; few of them had ever been in battle. Cornwallis had as large a force, and his troops were nearly all British —the best in the service. The chances were that the Americans would be defeated. Could he retreat down the Delaware to Bordentown, and cross the river with all his baggage and cannon, before Cornwallis could overtake him? Doubtful. All the officers said so.

But there was another move that could be made. Cornwallis had just come from Princeton. He had left a body of troops there, while at New Brunswick there was a large supply for the British army. Why not steal away during the night along the road leading through the little village of Sandtown, march to Princeton, capture every thing there, then push on to New Brunswick and seize the supplies? It was a bold plan.

"We can't get the artillery through the mud," said General Knox.

"We can send the baggage to Bordentown, and have it ferried across the river before Cornwallis can overtake it," said Washington.

The council decided that on account of the mud the plan could not be carried out.

The day had been calm, not a breath of air had stirred the twigs of the leafless trees; but now there came a gust of wind from the north-west, sweeping through the trees and rattling the windows.

"It is going to be colder," said the officers.

The soldiers, sitting by their bivouac-fires, drew their blankets around them.

"We shall have a cold night," said Elijah to Esek.

"We'll keep up a good fire," said Esek, as he pulled the rails from a fence, and built a rousing fire. The ground was stiffening fast, and would be frozen solid before morning.

"We will go to Princeton," said General Washington, breaking up the council.

An officer came down the line, and in a whisper ordered the soldiers to fall in. The artillery-men harnessed their horses and started away, followed by the soldiers. A man from each company was left to keep the fires burning. Elijah was selected, for one, to stay behind. He pulled the rails from the fences, and heaped them upon the fires to let the British know that their antagonists were keeping themselves warm.

Elijah Was Selected to Keep the Fires Burning.

The baggage-wagons, instead of following the army toward Princeton, turned off in the opposite direction toward Burlington. As soon as the baggage-men were beyond hearing of the British, they whipped up their horses, determined to reach Burlington and get the wagons ferried across the river before Cornwallis could overtake them.

It was about midnight when the army started. Washington took a road leading through the little hamlet called Sandtown, north-east from Trenton. It was nearly four o'clock when Elijah and his fellow fire-tenders put their last armful of rails upon the fires, took their muskets, and started up the same road to overtake the army.

Beyond Sandtown was a new road, cut through the woods to Princeton. It was only half finished. There were stumps and logs in it; but Washington chose to take it, for on the direct road, at Maidenhead, were some British troops, under General Leslie, whom he wished to avoid; but it was slow getting-on.

The morning dawned clear and beautiful. Washington was approaching Princeton. Just at that moment Lieutenant-colonel Mawhood, with the Seventeenth, Fortieth, and Fifty-fifth regiments, which were on their way to re-enforce Cornwallis, and which had halted at Princeton the night before, started from Princeton for Trenton. Mawhood was on the old road, while Washington was on the new road. Mawhood was marching south, and Washington north. The Fifty-fifth regiment was in Princeton; the other two had advanced to the bridge by Mr. Worth's mill.

General Washington directed General Mercer, with three hundred and fifty men, mostly young men from Philadelphia, to file through the fields and take possession of the bridge, and to intercept any fugitives that might fly that way to join Cornwallis.

Mawhood, with the Seventeenth, had crossed it, and a few minutes later would have been out of sight; but it so happened that Mawhood, looking eastward, saw the troops of Mercer coming through the fields toward the bridge. Mercer saw Mawhood's troops at the same moment. Mawhood faced his men about, recrossed the bridge, and started to gain possession of a hill east of the road near a house occupied by Mr. William Clark. Mercer's men crouched down behind a rail-fence, and, as Mawhood advanced, fired a volley. The British returned it, and after two or three volleys, with a hurra, charged across the field.

Mercer's troops had no bayonets; besides, the British outnumbered them two to one; and the Americans broke and fled in confusion. General Mercer's horse was wounded at the first fire, and he fought on foot. He tried in vain to rally his men. While attempting it, a British soldier knocked him down with the butt of his gun. The soldier saw that he was a general, and thought that he had captured Washington.

"The rebel general is taken," he shouted. Other soldiers rushed up.

"Call for quarter, you rebel!" they shouted, with oaths.

"I am not a rebel," Mercer replied, still grasping his sword. He made a fatal mistake in the excitement of the moment, and, stunned as he was, perhaps did not know what he was about. He struck at them with his sword, and they plunged their bayonets into his body, and left him mortally wounded.

Mawhood was rushing after the fleeing troops, but suddenly found himself confronted by Washington's whole force. The column has been marching north, but now it turns from the road into the fields to the west.

Captain Moulder commands a battery. His men are from Philadelphia—ship-riggers, quick and active. They see the British.

"Unlimber!" shouts Moulder, and the men wheel the cannon in a twinkling.

Mawhood sees the cannon. He is flushed with the success of the morning.

"Take the rebel guns!" he shouts.

The British rush upon the cannon. "Hurra!" they shout, as if the victory were already won, and the cannon theirs.

The cannon blaze, and there are wide gaps in the advancing ranks. Upon the run, to support Captain Moulder, came the Rhode Island troops, under Colonel Hitchcock, pouring in a volley. The ship-riggers have rammed home another cartridge of grape, and the cannon blaze once more, and the British, astounded by the sudden appearance of Washington's whole force, flee in confusion, throwing away their guns. They rush for the bridge and cross it, fleeing toward Trenton.

Washington sends Major Kelley, with a company, to destroy the bridge, and pushes on to Princeton; but, just before reaching the village, he encounters the Fifty-fifth regiment. The officer commanding the regiment has heard the firing, and is hastening to aid Mawhood. He turns about, retreats to Princeton, and takes possession of the college—a large stone building. The soldiers fire from the windows upon the Americans. General Knox plants his cannon, to riddle it with solid shot.

The first ball crashes into the chapel, and makes a hole

"THE REBEL GENERAL IS TAKEN," HE SHOUTED.

through the portrait of King George II. The Americans rush up and batter down the door. "Surrender!" they shout, and the British throw down their guns and give themselves up as prisoners. It has been a disastrous morning to Lord Cornwallis. He has lost altogether about four hundred men.

To go back a little—to the moment when Mawhood is rushing upon Captain Moulder's guns. Cornwallis is getting ready to move up the west side of the Assanpink at Trenton, cross the stream, march through the woods, and come down the other side and attack Washington, whose camp-fires have been burning brightly through the night; but they are getting low just now, at day-break. His own soldiers are kindling theirs to cook their breakfasts. After breakfast he will begin the march to catch the "fox," as he calls General Washington.

There does not seem to be much stir in the American camp. The sentinels are not on their posts. Has Washington taken a new position? Whither can he have gone? Down the river to Bordentown? Possibly.

Cornwallis hears a heavy rumbling far away in the north. "Can it be thunder?" Impossible, for it is midwinter, and there is not a cloud in the sky. Sir William Erskine comprehends it.

"It is Washington! He is at New Brunswick. He has out-generaled us."

Gradually Cornwallis comprehends it. He is astounded. Yesterday he toiled all day through the mud to catch the fox before he could get across the Delaware; but the fox is in his rear, committing terrible havoc. The drums beat; officers give hasty orders, and do a deal of swearing; the troops take a quick-step; and the outwitted general, with his five thousand men, starts for Princeton over the deep-rutted road along which he toiled yesterday to Trenton.

They meet Mawhood's straggling troops, and learn of the disaster of the morning. They rush on to Worth's: Major Kelley and his men are hacking away with their axes upon the bridge. Cornwallis mistrusts that Washington, with his army, is in the woods on the north side of the stream, and moves cautiously. He unlimbers his cannon and opens fire. Major

Kelley sends the last timber down stream, and then retreats. Cornwallis can not wait to have the bridge rebuilt. He is in great haste to get at Washington. "Plunge in!" he shouts, and the soldiers rush into the stream. It is a foolish order for Lord Cornwallis to give, for nothing is gained by it. The wintry air is biting cold, and in five minutes the soldiers' clothes are frozen; and they are so chilled that they could not fight if there were any fighting to be done. The soldiers are across, but the cannon are not, and the army must wait, after all, till the bridge is rebuilt. An hour is lost.

Across at last. Cornwallis moves on toward Princeton. Surely he will find Washington there. He sends out his cavalry to reconnoitre. The troopers approach the town. A cannon-shot comes whizzing over their heads, and the report goes rolling over the hills to Worth's. Cornwallis is delighted to hear it. Now he will give Washington a good drubbing for outgeneraling him. The cavalry reconnoitre a long while. They can see the intrenchments and the cannon behind it. They form to attack it. With a whoop and a hurra they rush forward, and find nobody there! The single cannon stands there— a British gun which Washington had captured, but which he could not take away. An American soldier lingering in Princeton had determined to have some fun, and had sent the shot toward the advancing troopers, and then had fled; but he had detained Cornwallis another hour.

Precious hours to Washington! He is pushing north-west— not toward New Brunswick. It is a great temptation to move on to that town, and seize all the British stores; but his troops are nearly worn out. They have been without sleep for thirty-six hours, have eaten nothing since their supper on the Assanpink, have fought two battles, and made a rapid night-march over the frozen ground. They have no overcoats; some have no shoes, and are marching with rags bound around their feet. Cornwallis will soon be upon him, with his whole army. Tempting the prize, but too great the risk. Prudence will be valor now. He turns north-west, and marches eighteen miles from Princeton to the town of Pluckemin, before halting.

It is a weary march. The soldiers are foot-sore, hungry, exhausted. Some drop from the ranks, and fall asleep in a moment upon the frozen ground. Mile after mile they drag themselves along. Some are dressed in rags, but the people are kind to them. Little children give them bread, glad to do so much for those who have fought so bravely, and receive in return a kind "God bless you!"

Washington breaks down the bridges behind him. At midnight he allows the troops to halt. A great day's march they have made—a great day's work have they done for liberty!

Cornwallis arrives at Princeton, finds Washington gone, fears that he is at New Brunswick, and hastens on. He finds his supplies are safe; but he is chagrined at being so completely outgeneraled.

Washington moves north to Morristown, and there, amidst the hills, where nearly all the people are patriots, builds log-huts,

Little Children Gave Them Bread.

and goes into winter-quarters; while Cornwallis and Howe, who begin to respect *Mister* Washington, as they have called him, gather in their scattered detachments to New Brunswick and New York, and settle down for the winter. General Howe likes good dinners and good wines and a game of cards. He will let the troops rest till winter is over; but when summer comes, he will speedily crush the rebellion.

Chapter 13
TICONDEROGA
and HUBBARDTON

ENERAL BURGOYNE, in October, 1776, after the destruction of the American flotilla on Lake Champlain, hastened to England. He had thought out a plan by which the rebellion could be crushed, and laid it before Lord North and Lord Germaine. It was to send a large army to Canada, and thence through Lake Champlain to Ticonderoga, capture that place, and push on to the Hudson. At the same time another army was to ascend the Hudson from New York; they would meet at Albany. These movements would sever New England from the other colonies; it would be like cutting the head from the body. New England started the rebellion, and if it were separated from the other colonies, the rebellion would soon come to an end.

The ministry and the king favored the plan; it was reasonable; the invading armies could go almost the entire distance by water; there would be only a short march from Lake Champlain to the Hudson; Canada was loyal, and all the horses, wagons, and forage necessary could be obtained at Quebec and Montreal. More, the Canadians would enlist, and the Indians. It was an excellent plan, the ministers thought; and they began at once to make preparations, and appointed General Burgoyne commander of the expedition.

In April, 1777, as soon as the ice was out of the St. Lawrence, a great fleet sailed up that noble river to Quebec, and from there to Montreal. General Burgoyne sent out runners to all the Indian tribes, to have the warriors come and join their great father, the king, in putting down the Boston men, as the Indians called the Americans. He bought horses, oats, and other supplies, and set the Canadian carpenters to making boats, carts, and wagons at St. Johns. The Indians gathered there, set up their wigwams on the bank of the river, or slept at night under their birch canoes.

One feature of Burgoyne's plan was to have a portion of his army go up the St. Lawrence to Lake Ontario, across the lake to Oswego, up the Oswego River to the Mohawk, take Fort Schuyler on that stream, and then go down the Mohawk and meet him and the army from New York at Albany.

Such a movement would secure all the Indians of western New York to the king. They would be at home, on their own ground, and would soon drive all the Whigs out of the Mohawk Valley. Many Tories lived there. Sir John Johnson, from Johnstown; Colonel Butler and a great many other Tories, who had fled from their homes, would go with the expedition, and enlist all the friends of the king in the Mohawk Valley.

This expedition was commanded by Colonel St. Leger. He had some British troops, a regiment of Canadians, commanded by Sir John Johnson, which wore a uniform trimmed with green, and so the troops were called the "Johnson Greens." There was another regiment, under Colonel Butler; and the Indians, with Thayendanegea, or "Bundle of Sticks," at their head. In all, St. Leger had about two thousand men. The expedition started from Montreal.

Having sent Colonel St. Leger away, Burgoyne came from St. Johns to the island Aux Noix, where he issued a pompous address to the army.

"This army must not retreat," he said. Great generals are just as ready to retreat as to advance, if they see that victory lies in that direction. King Alfred, Frederick the Great, Napoleon, Wellington, Washington, and a great many other generals have known how to retreat. None of them ever made such an address to their armies.

Burgoyne's boats were ready, his provisions on board; and the first week in June, the great army, numbering between nine and ten thousand, with a great park of artillery, sailed from the island into Lake Champlain, moving south to Crown Point. Arriving there, four hundred Indians joined the army, with war-paint on their faces, and eagles' feathers in their hair, ready to steal out into the country and tomahawk the peaceful inhabitants.

Four Hundred Indians Joined the Army.

On the 21st of June, Burgoyne gave them a great feast on the shore of the lake near Crown Point. He was dressed in his showy uniform, and so were all his officers. The Indians painted their faces, and rigged themselves out in all their finery. General Burgoyne made a grand speech.

"Go," said he, "in the might of your valor and your cause. Strike at the common enemies of Great Britain and America; disturbers of public order, peace, and happiness; destroyers of commerce and parricides of state. I positively forbid bloodshed when you are not opposed in arms. Aged women and children and prisoners must be held sacred from the knife and hatchet, even in time of conflict. You shall be paid for the prisoners you take, but you will be called to account for scalps. You will be allowed to take the scalps of the dead, when killed by you in opposition; but on no account or pretense are they to be taken from the wounded, or even the dying."

General Burgoyne might as well have addressed a pack of

wolves. When the news reached England that Burgoyne had employed the Indians, Edmund Burke made a speech in regard to it in Parliament. He said:

"Suppose there was a riot on Tower Hill. What would the keeper of his majesty's lions do? Would he not fling open the doors of the wild beasts, and address them thus, 'My gentle lions, my humane bears, my tender-hearted hyenas, go forth! but I exhort you, as you are Christians and members of civilized society, to take care and not hurt any man, woman, or child'? "

Mr. Burke supposed that General Burgoyne had employed the Indians of his own accord, and did not know that Lord North and Lord Germaine had especially instructed him to employ the savages. Lord North was present, and laughed till the tears ran down his cheeks, while Mr. Burke pictured the scene, laying all the blame on Burgoyne.

An old chief, with his face covered with war-paint, replied to Burgoyne:

"We receive you as our father, for when you speak we hear the voice of our Great Father beyond the great waters. Our hatchets are sharpened on our affections. We promise obedience."

It was all very fair for the old chief to promise it; but the people in Vermont, who had fought the Indians twenty years before, knew how little reliance could be placed on such promises; and many of them packed up their goods and started, with their families, to cross the Green Mountains to the Connecticut Valley.

Soldiers were wanted to stop Burgoyne, and Dodifer buckled on his knapsack once more, shouldered his gun, and marched to Ticonderoga, on Lake Champlain. He had stopped a night there, on his return from Canada.

The fort stands at the outlet of Lake George. The French built a fortification there in 1775, and called it Fort Carillon; but the Indians called the place Cheonderoga, meaning *sounding waters,* which soon became Ticonderoga.

A great deal of fighting had been done in the region from 1755 to '59. Putnam, Stark, and a great many others who were now fighting the British, had fought the French and Indians there. General Howe's brother had been killed there. Many of the British officers now fighting the Americans had fought there side by side with Putnam and Stark. General Amherst took it from the French in '59, and the English had made it a strong fortification. Ethan Allen, with a company of Green Mountain Boys, had seized it on the 10th of May, 1775, astonishing the British officers in command by demanding the surrender in the name of "Congress and the Great Jehovah." General Knox had dragged a large number of the cannon to Boston in February, '76, and Dodifer had rammed home many a ball into the eighteen-pounders on Winter Hill. But now other cannon were mounted on the parapets, and General St. Clair, who was in command, was making preparations to give Burgoyne a warm reception. He had about two thousand five hundred men; but about nine hundred soldiers from New Hampshire and Massachusetts came to aid him, making his force three thousand four hundred. St. Clair was confident that Burgoyne would not be able to take the fort. He built a great boom of timber across the narrow path of the lake, opposite the fort, and erected another fort on a high hill, called Mount Independence, on the Vermont side. It was called Mount Independence, from the fact that the Declaration of Independence was read to the soldiers on the top of the mountain in '76, the soldiers having swung their hats and cheered lustily at the conclusion of the reading.

Dodifer was once more with the army at Ticonderoga. He was a sergeant now, and went out with a scouting-party one day toward Chimney Point, opposite Crown Point, to see what Burgoyne was doing. He came across a Tory who was distributing a proclamation to the people. General Burgoyne had written it at Montreal. It was a printed document, and General Burgoyne expected that it would strike terror to the hearts of the people in the New Hampshire Grants, as Vermont was then called. The soldiers gathered round while Dodifer read it. Thus it began:

THE SOLDIERS GATHERED ROUND WHILE DODIFER READ IT.

"By John Burgoyne, Esquire, Lieutenant-general of His Majesty's Forces in America, Colonel of the Queen's Regiment of Light Dragoons, Governor of Fort William, in North Britain; one of the Commons of Great Britain in Parliament, and Commanding an Army and Fleet employed on an Expedition from Canada."

"Any more titles?" a soldier asked.

The proclamation described the army, how powerful it was, and magnified the number of Indians. General Burgoyne said:

"I have but to give stretch to the Indian forces under my direction—and they amount to thousands—to overtake the hardened enemies of America."

The proclamation threatened terrible consequences upon all who would not submit. The soldiers were not in the least frightened by the proclamation, but took the Tory to the fort a prisoner.

On the 1st of July Burgoyne was ready to move. The Indians went through the woods along the western shore of the lake toward the fort, while the British and Hessians, about eight thousand, embarked once more, and sailed up the lake.

The American soldiers, from the top of Mount Independence, could see far down the lake. They beheld the boats, one after another, come round a point of land in grand procession. There were so many boats that the lake seemed black with them. The bright uniforms, the flags, the forest of bayonets gleaming in the sun, the dipping of the oars, made it a grand spectacle.

The British landed on the New York side north of the fort, pitched their tents, and advanced and took possession of the road leading to Lake George. Lieutenant Twiss, the chief-engineer of Burgoyne's army, looked at Mount Defiance. He saw that it was much higher than Ticonderoga, and, although the mountain was steep and rugged, he thought that cannon might be dragged to the top. General Fraser set his soldiers to work during the night, and before morning they had a path to the top; but when the sun rose they quit work, and lay still in the woods through the day. The next night the soldiers were at it again, and, under the light of the full moon, dragged several cannon to the top, and placed them in position to pour a fire down into the fort.

It was Dodifer's turn to stand guard on that night. The moon was full, and its beautiful light fell upon the mountain and reflected its shadows from the lake. The air was calm; not a ripple disturbed the water.

In the fort every thing was hushed in silence. All except the sentinels were asleep. Dodifer could hear confused noises from the British camp, and wondered what was going on. The morning dawned, and as the light streamed up the east he saw that the top of Mount Defiance was swarming with British troops. General St. Clair came out from his quarters and beheld the scene with amazement. He saw that, having neglected to fortify that point, the fort was of no account. He must evacuate it at once. But as the British could see all that was going on in the fort, he could make no movement till night.

General Fraser was not quite ready to open fire, and the day passed quietly; but when night came every body was astir in the fort. All hands were set to work loading bateaux with provisions and ammunition. St. Clair had two hundred bateaux, besides some armed galleys. The boats, as fast as loaded, started up the lake toward Skenesborough (Whitehall). To make the British think that he was going to stand a siege, General St. Clair ordered the cannon to open fire upon Mount Defiance.

Dodifer laid down his musket, and helped load and fire the great thirty-two-pounder. They elevated the muzzle of the gun so as to send the ball plump upon the top of the mountain. That made it easy loading.

Dodifer rammed home the cartridge, then a soldier put the heavy thirty-two-pound ball into the muzzle of the gun, and Dodifer pushed it down with the rammer. While he was doing this another soldier primed the gun: then all stood back while one touched it off. The gun-carriage would almost leap from the ground, and the report went rolling up and down the lake and out over the hills, and then as they listened they could hear the ball crash against the rocks, or tear its way through the trees, making it decidedly uncomfortable to the British on the mountain.

The soldiers in the fort packed their knapsacks with provisions, and their cartridge-boxes with powder. It was about three o'clock when they left the fort and crossed the bridge to the Vermont side.

As Dodifer crossed the bridge he could see signs of approaching day. General St. Clair had given strict orders against setting any of the buildings on fire; but suddenly the top of Independence was all ablaze. General Fermoy, in command there, disobeyed the order, and set the barracks on fire. The British on Mount Defiance could see all that was going on; their drums beat the long roll, and the British and Hessians sprung to their arms to be ready to make pursuit.

It was nearly four o'clock when Dodifer, who was in the rearguard, under Colonel Francis, started from the foot of Mount Independence. The army was retreating to Castleton, in Vermont. Besides his gun, Dodifer had cartridge-box and bullet-pouch filled with powder and balls, and his knapsack with provisions. He had his blanket—in all nearly sixty pounds, that he staggered under. All day long, through the hot midsummer sun, he marched, reaching Hubbardton, eighteen miles from Ticonderoga, at night.

Every body was in motion in General Burgoyne's army. Some of the soldiers rushed into the fort, others went to work with axes cutting away the bridge and the boom, and long before noon the British gun-boats were past the obstruction, and, with all sail spread, were hastening to capture the bateaux of General St. Clair. Before night the gun-boats came up with them near Skenesborough. The crews, seeing the British boats close upon them, ran them ashore, set them on fire, and fled to Fort Edward.

So the fortress, which every body supposed would be an insuperable barrier to Burgoyne, had fallen in a night, and there was nothing to hinder his advance to Albany, except a few hundred troops under General Schuyler at Fort Edward.

The news was carried by messengers to Boston, New York,

and Philadelphia. Every body was astounded. General Washington was at Philadelphia, watching General Howe. This was what he wrote to General Schuyler:

"The evacuation of Ticonderoga is an event of chagrin and surprise not apprehended, nor within the compass of my reasoning."

When the evacuation took place, the people of New England were turning out by the thousand to oppose Burgoyne. Some companies were almost at Ticonderoga; but now they turned sadly about and marched home. It was a disheartening day that 5th of July, 1777.

But there was more disheartening news for the country to hear. Colonel Francis, with his own Massachusetts regiment, Colonel Seth Warner's regiment of Green Mountain Boys, and Colonel Hale's New Hampshire regiment, spent their first night at Hubbardton. Dodifer had not slept a wink for forty-eight hours. He eat his supper, spread his blanket under a tree in a wheat-field, and soon was sound asleep, with his knapsack for a pillow. Colonel Francis did not know that General Fraser, with a portion of the British troops, and General Reidesel, with the Hessians, were in pursuit of him. Quite likely he thought that Burgoyne would take his whole army by water to Skenesborough. But there were a large number of Tories from Skenesborough, and the towns in New York and Vermont, with General Burgoyne. Major Skene himself, who lived at Skenesborough, had joined Burgoyne, and was giving all the information possible, and doing what he could to help Burgoyne conquer his fellow-countrymen. Some of the Tories who knew all the roads were acting as guides to General Fraser, who marched late into the night. General Fraser was informed that the rearguard, under Colonel Francis, had halted at Hubbardton, and laid his plans to surprise and capture it. With the light-infantry he pressed on till he was within three miles of Hubbardton, when he halted and allowed his men to rest till three o'clock, and then started again.

It was sunrise on the morning of the 6th of August. The drummer had beaten the reveille, and the American soldiers had risen from their beds on the ground. Some were folding up their blankets, some washing their faces in a little brook. Others were kindling fires to cook their breakfast and light their pipes. Dodifer was getting ready to eat breakfast, when there was the crack of a gun, fired by one of the pickets. Then another and another. A picket suddenly discovered a red-coat standing on a big rock, and looking around to see what he could discover. The picket fired at him, and the soldier rolled from the rock, a dead man; but behind him were other British soldiers, and now it was discovered that General Fraser, with the light-infantry, was upon them.

A Picket Suddenly Discovered a Red-coat on a Big Rock.

Dodifer quit his breakfast, seized his gun, and every body else did the same. "Fall in!" shouted Colonel Francis, and in a moment the soldiers fell into line. Colonel Francis had about thirteen hundred men; but some were sick, others were stragglers that had been picked up on the way. General Fraser had about eight hundred of the best soldiers in Burgoyne's army, and General Reidesel was coming with as many Hessians.

General Fraser was forming his lines to make an attack; but Colonel Francis did not wait for him. He marched through the wheat-field, and fell upon the British. The fight began along a little brook, partly in the field and partly in the woods. Colonel Francis was a brave officer, and so was Colonel Warner, and they commanded brave men. The men in Warner's regiment were fighting for their homes, for many of them lived in that region.

General Fraser was also a brave officer, the ablest in Burgoyne's army—abler than Burgoyne himself. In all England there were no better soldiers than those with him at that moment. They were under excellent discipline; but they found their match in the undisciplined troops in front of them.

Colonel Francis advanced boldly to meet the British, and in a few moments there was a terrific fire. Dodifer saw a battalion or red-coats come out from the woods. The rays of the rising sun fell in their faces, and were reflected from their bright buckles, gun-barrels, and bayonets. Beyond the red uniforms was a dark background of shadows under the tall forest-trees. He took deliberate aim, as did his comrades, and many a British soldier fell under their withering fire. For nearly an hour the fight raged, when the British gave way, and the Americans were masters of the field; but only for a moment, for just then the Hessian drum-beat was heard, and General Reidesel appeared, with his banners waving in the morning air. He quickly formed his men, and the British, who had retreated, now came back to renew the battle.

The Tories with General Fraser told him that the only road by which the Americans could retreat was one leading south-west to Skenesborough. He at once sent the Earl of Balcarris, with the grenadiers, to take possession of it, and to fall upon the left flank of the Americans. At the same time General Reidesel attacked the right flank.

It is possible that the Americans would have remained masters of the field even now, had not the stragglers and the men in Colonel Hale's regiment retreated when they saw the British in possession of the road. A panic seized them, and they fled up a steep hill-side into the woods. Many were so frightened that they threw away their guns and every thing else.

Dodifer saw the grenadiers come up the road, to attack Colonels Francis and Warner in the rear. At the same moment the Hessians came down upon the right, and Fraser, with the light-infantry, charged in front. He saw Colonel Francis fall mortally wounded. The line gave way as a dam breaks in a freshet, and every body ran. Dodifer was too old a soldier to throw away his gun or knapsack, or any thing else, till obliged to. He had not toiled through the woods to Quebec for nothing. He had no intention of throwing away his dinner. He made his way up the steep hill-side, with the bullets whistling about him and the British in pursuit, but, with the others, made his way through the woods, and reached Rutland.

It was a terrible blow. More than one hundred had been killed and wounded, some had been taken prisoners—in all, more than three hundred were lost. The little army was scattered and disheartened.

But General Fraser had not won his victory without loss. Nearly two hundred British and Hessians had been killed or wounded in the short but desperate battle.

Chapter 14
FORT SCHUYLER

NICHOLAS DOLOFF was on the march once more. Men were needed to check Burgoyne, and he shouldered his gun and started. He marched to Albany, where the troops were gathering under General Schuyler.

He found that Albany was a queer old town. It was settled by the Dutch. Many of the houses were built of brick, which they had brought from Holland. The buildings stood with their gables toward the street.

The old Dutch burghers took life easy, smoking their pipes and drinking beer, and talking with their friends. In the warm summer evenings the round-faced Dutch girls used to sit beneath the porches of the queer old houses, and chat with the young mynheers of the town.

Troops were wanted to drive back Colonel St. Leger at Fort Schuyler up the Mohawk. During the French and Indian war it was called Fort Stanwix; but it had been changed to Schuyler in honor of General Schuyler, who lived at Albany, and who was in command of the Northern Military Department, doing what he could to stop Burgoyne.

Nicholas and his fellow-soldiers were marching to stop Colonel St. Leger, whom Burgoyne had sent from Montreal up the St. Lawrence and through Lake Ontario to Oswego. St. Leger was to attack Fort Schuyler, and then sweep down the valley of the Mohawk, and join him at Albany. It would not be a difficult journey for St. Leger, for he could take all his cannon and supplies by water up the Oswego River, through Oneida Lake, almost to the fort. When he had captured the fort, he could drag his boats a short distance to the Mohawk, and descend that stream to Albany.

Colonel St. Leger was accompanied by Sir John Johnson, son of Sir William Johnson, who defeated Dieskau at Lake George in 1755, whose home was at Johnson Hall, in the valley of the Mohawk. Sir John had fled to Canada in 1776, and had enlisted a regiment of Canadians and Tory Americans, who wore coats trimmed with green, and so were called "Johnson Greens."

Another officer with Colonel St. Leger was Colonel John Butler, who had enlisted a regiment of Tories, most of them citizens of the Mohawk Valley, who had fled to Canada. Another Tory officer was Colonel Daniel Clous, a son of Sir William Johnson, but whose mother was an Indian.

Besides these, Colonel St. Leger had the Mohawk chief, Joseph Brant, whose Indian name was Thayendanegea, and whose mother Sir William took for one of his wives. (Thayendanegea means, in English, "Bundle of Sticks.") He had been educated by Rev. Mr. Wheelock, at Lebanon, Connecticut, who taught Indian children, and who started Dartmouth College, in New Hampshire, as an Indian school. The young chief could speak good English, and had been trying to educate his tribe. He had accepted the Christian religion, and was a missionary interpreter to the good Mr. Kirkland, who preached in a little meeting-house near Johnson Hall; but Sir John had espoused the king's side in the war, and it was quite natural that Bundle of Sticks should take the same side. More, he had been to England, and had been made much of by Sir John's friends in high life. Bundle of Sticks had influenced the Indians, and all the tribes, except the Oneidas, had agreed to take the war-path against the "Boston men," as they called the Americans.

St. Leger had in all seventeen hundred men, with several cannon, and an abundant supply of provisions. A great many of his soldiers had their homes in the vicinity of Fort Schuyler, and they were going to fight their old neighbors and friends.

The first night after leaving Albany, Nicholas and his fellow-soldiers camped at Schenectady; the second night they reached Johnson Hall, the house built by Sir William, and where he used to entertain the Indian chiefs and distribute trinkets to the braves and squaws, and from which Sir John had fled the year before. The house was built in 1760. It was sixty feet long and forty feet wide, and two stories high. The walls were thick, and there were loop holes around the eaves through which it would be easy to fire upon an enemy outside. There were two stone buildings near by, with loop-holes in the walls. Although the Indians were friendly to Sir William, he had taken the precaution to make his buildings forts, for there was no knowing what might happen. Sir John had fled from the place the year before with Brant and Colonel John Butler, and Walter Butler, a son of John, who lived in a small house down the valley.

The next day, Nicholas passed the church in which Mr. Kirkland preached, and where Bundle of Sticks used to listen to his sermons and interpret them to the Indians. After passing the meeting-house, they came to a large brick house, the residence of General Herkimer, who welcomed them heartily. They found the militia of the country, nearly eight hundred in number, quartered there, for the citizens knew that St. Leger was on his way, and would soon be in the valley, and they had turned out to defend their homes. We shall hear more about his neighbors by-and-by.

Beyond General Herkimer's the soldiers came to a place called Little Falls, where the river has worn a narrow channel through a great ridge of rocks, over which it leaps, whirls, and tumbles in a frightful manner. The baggage of the regiment and a lot of supplies for Fort Schuyler had been taken along in boats; but here the soldiers had to unload them, carry them past the falls, and reload them.

The next camping-place was at "German Flats," settled by Germans in 1720, where there was a stone meeting-house. The next day they halted at a place called Oriskany, where a little creek joined the Mohawk, and where the road ran through a ravine, once a causeway made of logs, a place which we shall visit again farther on.

Just before sunset, Nicholas looked across a field and saw the fort which he had come to defend situated opposite a bend in the river. The gates opened, and he and his fellow-soldiers marched in, glad to be at their journey's end. The soldiers in the fort set up a shout of joy; for that very afternoon, the 2d of August, Bundle of Sticks and his Indians, and Lieutenant Bird with a British flag, the advance column of St. Leger's army, had made their appearance, and St. Leger was not far off. At that very moment they could hear the British drums, and in a short time the redcoats and Hessians, and the Johnson Greens and Tories, were seen coming across the plain north-west of the fort.

Colonel Gansevoort Makes a Flag.

Colonel Gansevoort commanded the fort, and had a brave officer with him, Colonel Willett, and about one thousand men. They had provisions enough for six weeks, and plenty of ammunition for the muskets, but lacked cannon-balls. He saw that the fort was strong, and was confident that St. Leger never could make much impression on the thick earth embankments. He felt very sure that they could successfully defend it.

Colonel Gansevoort had no flag, but soon contrived to make one by cutting up some shirts for the white stripes, and some flannel for the red stripes. He lacked the blue for the field of stars, but Captain Swartwout had a blue cloak.

"Here, take it," said the captain.

Colonel Gansevoort accepted it, cut out a large square piece, sewed the stars and stripes to it, nailed the flag to a pole, and raised it above the fort, and was ready for St. Leger.

That officer had marched up in grand style from Lake Oneida. He gave the Indians, under Brant, the post of honor, with the British flag at their head. Then came sixty Tory sharp-shooters, led by Captain Watts; then Colonel John Butler with his Tories, and Sir John Johnson with the Johnson Greens; and then the Eighth and Thirty-fourth British regiments, and the Hessians, followed by the artillery and baggage. His drums were beating and colors flying. Perhaps he thought to frighten the Americans; but they were not so easily frightened.

A British officer with a white flag approached the fort. Colonel Gansevoort sent out an officer to see what he wanted, and found that he had brought a proclamation very much like the one which Burgoyne had sent out from Lake Champlain, offering clemency to all who would lay down their arms, but declaring terrible vengeance upon all who would not. The soldiers read the proclamation, and laughed at it.

The next morning, St. Leger got his artillery into position, and began to cannonade the fort. The balls struck into the earth-walls, some flew over the fort, but no soldier was harmed. During the day the Indians crept up through the grass, on their hands and knees, and wounded two or three men; but Nicholas and his comrades soon stopped that fun. They kept close watch through the loop-holes, and a half-dozen fired as soon as they saw the flash of an Indian's gun, and the savages went back quicker than they came.

While this was going on, Colonel Gansevoort sent word to General Herkimer that the attack had begun. General Herkimer marched the next day, the 5th of August, with his eight hundred men. The messengers started back to the fort with the news that Herkimer was coming. Herkimer reached Oriskany, eight miles from the fort, before noon, and halted. He was a prudent man. He thought that if St. Leger knew he was on his way, the British commander might get between him and the fort, and attack him at a disadvantage. He had sent word to Gansevoort to fire three guns the moment the messenger arrived, and he halted to hear the guns, for then Gansevoort would act in concert with him. If St. Leger left to attack him, Gansevoort would make a sortie on St. Leger.

But the officers and men were impatient of the delay; they wanted to push on. Colonel Cox and Colonel Paris urged him to hasten forward. They accused him of being a coward. That was hard to bear.

"I am placed over you as a father and guardian, and shall not lead you into difficulties from which I may not be able to extricate you," Herkimer replied.

That did not satisfy the impatient men.

"You are a Tory," said Cox.

That was a sharp sting. Cox and his fellow-colonels were next in command, and Herkimer saw that to delay any longer would have a disastrous effect upon the men.

"March on!" he shouted.

Well would it have been for Colonel Cox and many of the impatient men if they had heeded the wise plan of General Herkimer.

"If we are attacked," said he, "you who accuse me of being a coward will be the first to run."

The column moved on. General Herkimer made a mistake in not sending pickets in advance, and we shall soon see what happened for want of such prudence. The men marched without order, not dreaming that they might be attacked.

The Tories with St. Leger knew that Herkimer was on his way, and St. Leger sent Bundle of Sticks, Butler, and Captain Watts, with about twelve hundred men, to surprise him. Nicholas, from the parapet of the fort, saw the Indians and Tories move down the river, and wondered where they were going. The messenger sent by Herkimer had not then arrived. It was noon when he came. He had taken a roundabout course to elude the Indians.

"Fire three cannon as quick as you can, for Herkimer is on

the march, and will cut his way through. He wants a sortie made from the fort at once," said the messenger.

The soldiers gave a hurra. All hands were ready to go. But a dark cloud had been rising in the west, and the lightnings were flashing and thunder rolling, and the rain soon fell in torrents. When the shower was over the gates opened, and Colonel Willett, with two hundred and fifty men and a cannon, started out, moved rapidly across the field, and made a furious attack upon the Johnson Greens, the British, and the Hessians. The attack was so sudden, so unexpected and furious, that the enemy fled in all directions. Nicholas and his comrades gave a hurra, and rushed into the Tory camp. Sir John Johnson tried for a moment to rally his men, but soon found that he must take to his heels, or be captured. He had no time to put on his coat. Nicholas and his comrades seized all the plunder that was visible, then rushed upon the Indian camp, set fire to the wigwams, and chased the Indians into the woods. In a few minutes, before St. Leger could get his troops under arms, they had seized twenty-one wagon-loads of clothing, provisions, and ammunition—taken five British standards, all of Sir John's baggage, his writing-desk and papers, and were back in the fort again without losing a man. They raised the standard on the parapet beneath the stars and stripes, so that St. Leger could see them, and hurraed louder than ever.

General Herkimer had reached the ravine at Oriskany. His men were crossing the causeway. Just at that place the road ran nearly south, and there was a hill covered with beeches and maples on the west side. The soldiers were marching without any order, never mistrusting that the hill was swarming with Tories and Indians. Suddenly there was a wild yell, the rattle of guns, and the balls came pouring down upon them. Colonel Cox, who had charged Herkimer with being a coward and a Tory, fell dead. The column was thrown into confusion. It was a terrible moment. Men were falling, but no one was to be seen. The yells came from all quarters, the bullets also. Those in the rear fled in an instant toward Fort Herkimer, leaving their comrades to fight the battle alone.

"ONE FIRE AND THE OTHER KEEP WATCH," SAID HERKIMER.

A moment later, Herkimer, who was on horseback, received a ball through one of his legs. He was taken from his horse.

"Take off the saddle," he said.

A soldier took it off, and placed it on the ground under a tree. The brave man sat down in it.

"Now, fight!" he said, and encouraged his men, telling them to get behind the trees. They were surrounded, and could not escape. They saw the Indians scalping the dead, recognized some of their old neighbors among the Tories, and resolved to fight to the bitter end. They saw the brave old man whom they had accused of being a coward, with his leg shattered and bleeding, take out his tinder-box, light his pipe, and commence smoking as calmly as if sitting beneath the porch of his old home. That put them to the blush. They plucked up heart, loaded their guns, took deliberate aim, and picked off the Indians and Tories as if they were so many wolves and foxes.

While the battle had been going on, deep and heavy thunder had been rolling overhead, and the rain began to fall. Neither party could load their guns while it was raining. During the shower Herkimer re-arranged his men. He formed them in a circle, told them to take their stand behind the large trees— two men to a tree. He had noticed that the Indians, after a soldier had fired, would rush up with their hatchets, and kill him while he was reloading his gun.

"One fire, and the other keep watch," said Herkimer.

The battle began again. The Indians tried their old game.

A soldier fired. An Indian rushed forward to bury his hatchet in the soldier's skull, but the next moment fell headlong with a bullet through his own skull.

The Tory leader thought he could capture Herkimer by stratagem. He sent one of his companies to the rear, told the men to turn their coats inside out to hide the green facings, and come as Americans from the fort to aid Herkimer.

Soon there was a cry among the Tories that the Americans from the fort were close at hand. The turn-coats came down the road, breaking through the Tory lines. They were close upon Herkimer, when Captain Gardiner recognized an old Tory neighbor, and the Americans poured a volley into the ranks of their pretended friends. So that game could not be played. More than half of Herkimer's men were killed or wounded; but still they fought on, never thinking of giving in. They had picked off nearly one hundred Indians. The Indians wanted to take scalps, but could not get up to the wounded without themselves being shot. Suddenly a panic seized them.

"Oonah! oonah!" was the cry which the Americans heard, and in an instant the Indians were gone. The panic seized the Tories, and they too fled, leaving their killed and wounded. More than two hundred of the Indians and Tories had fallen, and more than four hundred of the Americans. The brave general was carried down the river to his own home, where he died a few days later. He had fought one of the bravest battles of the war, and was victor.

The Tories and Indians made their way back to camp to find that their baggage was inside the fort. It was not comforting to think that they had been defeated, and had lost their baggage while absent.

The next morning a British officer approached the fort with a flag, having a letter for Colonel Gansevoort, written by Lieutenant-colonel Billings and Major Frey, who had been captured at Oriskany, in which they urged Colonel Gansevoort to surrender, for General Herkimer had been utterly defeated. Colonel Gansevoort had no idea of surrendering, and a few days later learned that the officers had to choose between writing the letter and being shot.

The officer demanded the surrender of the fort.

"Tell Colonel St. Leger," said Gansevoort, "that I do not accept a verbal summons to surrender."

The next morning, Colonel John Butler and two British officers appeared before the fort with a flag. Nicholas went out with an officer to see what they wanted.

"We have a letter to deliver to Colonel Gansevoort, and wish to be admitted to the fort," said Butler.

"Blindfold them, and admit them," said Gansevoort.

The officers were blindfolded. They were taken into Colonel

Gansevoort's dining-room; but before they entered, Gansevoort had the blinds closed so they could not get a sight of any thing outside. Candles were lighted, and the bandages taken from their eyes. Nicholas stood guard at the door and heard all that was said.

Major Ancram, the British officer, addressed Colonel Gansevoort.

Colonel St. Leger wished to avoid further bloodshed, and the only salvation of the garrison was an immediate surrender on the honorable terms which St. Leger would offer. The Indians were eager to march down the valley and massacre the inhabitants, and could not be restrained unless the fort was surrendered. There was no relief for the garrison, for Herkimer had been defeated, and General Burgoyne was at Albany. Colonel Gansevoort and Colonel Willett were satisfied that the speech was all a lie. If Herkimer had been defeated and Burgoyne was at Albany, why the persistent attempts to obtain a surrender without attempting a siege? The threat to let the Indians loose aroused the ire of all the officers. Colonel Gansevoort deputed Colonel Willett to reply to Major Ancram. Willett looked him in the eye and said:

"Do I understand you, sir, to say that you came from a British colonel who is in command of the army that invests this fort? By your uniform you appear to be a British officer. You come to the commander of this fort to inform him that if he does not deliver up the garrison, Colonel St. Leger will send his Indians to murder our women and children. You will please reflect, sir, that their blood will be on your heads, not on ours. We are doing our duty. The garrison is committed to our charge, and we will take care of it. I consider the message you have brought a degrading one for a British officer to send, and by no means reputable for a British officer to carry. For my own part, before I would consent to deliver this garrison to such a murdering set as your army, by your own account, consists of, I would suffer my body to be filled with splinters and set on fire, as you know has at times been practiced by such hordes of women and children killers as belong to your army."

The officer hung his head in shame. He and Butler were blindfolded once more, and they were led out of the fort. They had seen nothing, nor had they learned any thing, except that they had a plucky garrison to conquer.

St. Leger placed his sentinels around the fort so that no one could get in or out, and began to dig trenches. He must approach it by a regular siege.

Colonel Gansevoort wished to communicate the situation of affairs to Colonel Schuyler at Albany. Who would run the risk of getting through St. Leger's lines?

"I will," said Colonel Willett.

"So will I," said Captain Stockwell.

They waited till ten o'clock at night. It was pitch-dark and raining when they started. They crept on their hands and knees through the tall grass in the meadow, crossed the river on a log, and made their way past the sentinels. A dog barked, and they found that they were close to an Indian camp. They did not dare to move—did not know which way was north, which south. From eleven o'clock till almost day-break they stood there, not daring to move. Joyful sight! The clouds broke in the east, and they saw the bright morning-star gleaming above the horizon. Stealthily they crept along. They heard the gurgling of the water in the river, went down to it, and waded in the stream, so that the Indians could not track them. They reached a settlement, obtained horses, and rode as fast as they could to Albany.

General Arnold was there, and started at once with Colonel Learned's brigade of Massachusetts troops. The troops reached Little Falls. There they found some Tory prisoners, who had been captured at Oriskany. One was Yost Schuyler, a nephew of General Herkimer. The citizens had tried him by court-martial, and condemned him to be hanged; and now his mother came to Arnold begging that he would spare her son's life.

"I can not interfere," said Arnold; and the poor woman, almost distracted, pleaded still harder.

Arnold thought he could use Yost to great advantage.

"I will spare him on one condition," said Arnold; "that he

shall go to St. Leger, and tell him that a great army is on its way to relieve the fort; and I will hold his brother in prison as a hostage for the faithful performance of the service."

The brother was put into prison, and Yost was glad enough to start on such an errand. A friendly Oneida went with him to aid him. Yost hung up his coat, and had the soldiers fire several bullets through it. He put it on and started. He reached Bundle of Sticks's camp, and ran into it out of breath. The Indians were at the moment consulting the Great Spirit through their medicine-man.

"T h e Americans are coming," said Yost.

"How many?" the Indians asked.

He pointed to the leaves on the trees and to the holes in his coat. All of those bullets the Americans had fired at him. Just then the friendly Oneida came upon the run, and two more that he had picked up, and they pointed to the leaves on the trees.

He Pointed to the Leaves on the Trees.

"Burgoyne is cut to pieces," said one of them to the assembled Indians, telling a big lie.

The chiefs ran to St. Leger with the news, and said that they were going home. They would not stay and be killed. St. Leger made great promises to induce them to stay, offered them all the rum they could drink, but they would not touch it.

"You said there would be no fighting for Indians—that we might look on and see white men fight; but our braves have been killed. We will not stay."

They were gone. The Tories became panic-stricken, and fled. St. Leger went. The Tories threw away their arms and knapsacks, and every thing else, in their haste; and the Indians who had carried the news picked up the plunder, and kept crying that the Americans were coming, and frightened the Tories almost out of their wits.

Yost ran a little way with the rest, then turned about, came back to the fort, and told Colonel Gansevoort what had happened, and the garrison rushed out, followed the fugitives, overtook them at Oneida, killed some, captured others, burned their boats, and dispersed the motley crew who had lost every thing, and returned to the fort laden with the spoils of victory.

Chapter 15
BENNINGTON

TICONDEROGA was taken; St. Clair's army scattered; Burgoyne was pushing on to the Hudson; General Howe, with a great army, was menacing Philadelphia; Colonel St. Leger, at Fort Schuyler, was ready to sweep down the Mohawk; the Indians were killing and scalping, and the people were flying in terror before them.

The days were dark and gloomy, for Great Britain was putting forth all her forces.

The people of Vermont left their wheat-fields, their homes, packed up what goods they could, and moved into New Hampshire and Massachusetts. Some of the citizens of Albany fled into the country.

"We are greatly burdened with people who have fled from the New Hampshire Grants," wrote the good minister of Stockbridge, Massachusetts, "almost down to the Connecticut line."

"The disaster at Ticonderoga has given our cause a dark and gloomy aspect," wrote Dr. Thacher in his journal.

"Nothing since the war began has created such dissatisfaction," said the *Boston Gazette*.

In a week an army of nearly five thousand had been dispersed, and there was only a handful of men on the Hudson to oppose Burgoyne, and these were retreating to Albany. Tents were gone, provisions gone, guns gone, courage gone, and an exultant enemy getting ready to move on and desolate the country.

No wonder that General Burgoyne felt well. He sat down

and wrote a letter to Lord George Germain, and this was what he wrote:

"As things have turned out, were I at liberty to march in force immediately by my left instead of my right, I should have little doubt of subduing before winter the provinces where the rebellion originated."

The ministers at London had directed him to march to Albany, so that he could not turn aside as he wished and march to Boston. He must go on; but he thought it would be an easy matter to march across the country to Boston. He perhaps thought differently a few days later, as we shall see.

Dodifer marched from Rutland to Bennington. There he learned that the Indians were killing and scalping the inhabitants at Fort Edward; that a beautiful girl, Jane M'Crea, had been killed and scalped. Her brother was a Whig; but she had a lover, David Jones, who was a Tory, and had joined Burgoyne, who had given him a lieutenant's commission. The news of her death was a terrible blow to Lieutenant Jones. It is said that no smile ever was seen upon his face afterward; that the gray hair came, and that he grew old while yet young in years.

On the same day that the Indians killed Jane M'Crea, they also killed and scalped a farmer, John Allen, who lived on the banks of the Hudson, his wife, and two children.

So many had been killed and scalped, that General Gates, who took command of the Northern army, wrote a letter to Burgoyne, remonstrating, in the name of humanity, against his permitting the Indians to kill the unoffending inhabitants:

"Upward of one hundred men, women, and children have perished by the hands of the ruffians to whom, it is asserted, you have paid the price of blood," wrote General Gates.

But Burgoyne could not control his "gentle hyenas," as Mr. Burke called them. To kill and scalp was the Indian's mode of warfare.

Though the prospect was so gloomy, the people had no intention of giving up the contest. The Vermont Committee of Safety, at Manchester, sent a messenger to New Hampshire.

THE MURDER OF JANE M'CREA.

The New Hampshire Assembly came together on the 17th of July, at Exeter. What to do they did not know. It was no use to wait for Congress to act, for that body was in session at Baltimore. The State must defend itself. There was no money in the treasury to pay troops or to purchase provisions. They might issue bills of credit, but who would take them? They might promise to pay, but who would furnish beef, pork, and flour on their promises?

The farmers sat in silence. Then up rose John Langdon, who kept a store in Portsmouth, down by the sea. It was a short speech that he made. This is what he said:

"I have three thousand dollars in hard money; I will pledge my plate for as much more; I have seventy hogsheads of Tobago rum, which shall be sold for as much as it will bring: these are at the service of the State. If we succeed in defending our homes and firesides, I may be remunerated; if we do not, the property is of no value to me. Our old friend Stark, who did so nobly at Bunker Hill, may be safely intrusted with the enterprise, and we will check the progress of Burgoyne."

Glorious John Langdon!

The farmers listened to it. They were thrilled by it. With so much hard cash to start with, and so much rum that they could sell, they could go ahead.

Before night the militia of the State was all reorganized, and messengers were riding on fast horses to all the towns in the Merrimac Valley, with orders to colonels and captains to march at once. One messenger rode westward to Derryfield with a general's commission in his pocket for Colonel John Stark, Dodifer's and Elijah's colonel at Bunker Hill, to take command of all the troops, and to do what he could to stop Burgoyne.

A great day's work that, as we shall see. Before the week was through, the men composing Colonel Stickney's, Nichols's, and Hobart's regiments, twenty-five companies in all, were on the march. Colonel Stickney had 602 men; Colonel Nichols, 594; and Colonel Hobart, 448; in all, 1644. Each man packed his knapsack, left his grain, ripe for the sickle, and started.

They all flocked to Charlestown, on the Connecticut River. General Stark was there. Some of the men he set to work running bullets. He had only one pair of molds; but those were kept in use day and night. He wanted lead, and some of the farmers brought the clock-weights, some their pewter spoons and porringers, to be melted.

General Stark found an old cannon at Charlestown; it was rusty and not mounted; but he obtained a pair of cart-wheels, placed it on the axle, and sent it over the Green Mountains. In some places where the hills were too steep for the horses to drag it, the soldiers laid down their guns, lifted the wheels, and tugged at the ropes.

Enoch Had No Coat, but His Mother Soon Made One for Him.

Old men sixty and seventy years of age turned out, and boys of fifteen. Dodifer was surprised to see his younger brother, Enoch, come into camp. He was only fifteen. When the call came for troops, Enoch had no coat, for the family had hard work to get bread enough to eat, to say nothing of clothes. But his mother soon had a coat for him. She took a meal bag, cut a hole for his head, two holes for his arms, cut off a pair of her stockings, sewed them on for sleeves, and with his knapsack and gun he joined the brave men who were determined to do what they could in defense of their country. They stopped wherever night overtook them, kindled a bivouac fire, ate their supper, and lay down to sleep beneath the trees.

General Stark arrived at Bennington on the 6th of August.

The next day General Lincoln came from General Schuyler, who was at Saratoga, ordering General Stark to march at once to that place; but General Stark was under orders from the State of New Hampshire, with liberty to act according to his own judgment.

Schuyler wanted to get an army in front of Burgoyne. General Stark thought that he could attack him to good advantage on the flank and rear, and would not go.

Burgoyne had reached the Hudson, but before he could move on he must have a supply of provisions sent forward from Lake Champlain. He must have horses, oxen, and wagons. He wanted to mount the Hessian dragoons, so that they could sweep over the country, and bring in cattle. Fortunately for him, the Americans had a lot of flour, beef, pork, cattle, horses, and wagons, at Bennington, which had been collected for his special purpose. He would send a party to seize them, and then march to Charlestown, down the Connecticut to Brattleboro', then turn west and join him again, while Sir Henry Clinton would come up from New York, and Colonel St. Leger would come down from Albany. It would be a grand move and a joyful meeting, for by that time the rebellion would be pretty effectually crushed.

Burgoyne sent Colonel Baume, a Hessian officer, with General Reidesel's dismounted dragoons, a company of sharpshooters, the best marksmen of Fraser's division, a battalion of Tories from Vermont and New York, under Colonel Peters; a part of a Canadian regiment; the Hessian artillery, with two cannon; fifty chasseurs; and one hundred and fifty Indians—in all, between seven and eight hundred men.

On the 13th of August, Baume reached Cambridge, twelve miles west of Bennington, where he surprised fifteen Americans and captured five of them, besides some cattle, which he sent to Burgoyne, with the information that there were eighteen hundred Americans at Bennington, who, he supposed, would retire on his approach.

General Stark did not know that Baume was so near him, for the men who had escaped from Cambridge, when they came into Bennington, said that they had seen only some Tories and Indians. General Stark would not have the Tories and Indians prowling about the country in that way, and sent Lieutenant-colonel Gregg, with two hundred men of Colonel Nichols's regiment, down to stop the plunderers.

Dodifer was one of the party. It was early in the morning when they started. They marched down the valley of a little river called the Walloomscoick.

Mr. Van Schaick had a mill on the river, and a bridge crossed the stream close by the mill. Dodifer had crossed the river, and was pushing on, when he saw an Indian down the road in the bushes. The next moment a bullet came whizzing through the air. He sent one in the other direction, and a moment later the guns were cracking all around him and the bullets flying. The two parties had come into collision. Colonel Gregg ordered his men to retreat across the bridge, and then, seeing a great body of the enemy down the road, told the men to break down the bridge.

Some of the soldiers ran into the mill, and fired from the windows; others outside fired from behind trees. Dodifer and some others threw the planks of the bridge into the river, and began to cut the stringers; but before they had finished, the bullets came thick and fast, and they had to run.

Colonel Gregg sent word to General Stark of what was going on, and General Stark sent a messenger northward to Manchester, twenty-six miles, for Colonel Warner's regiment to hasten to Bennington. Having done this, instead of retreating, he started with all his troops to meet Baume.

The British and Hessians were repairing the bridge, and messengers from Baume were riding to Burgoyne, with the news that he had driven the rebels, and taken several barrels of flour and some wagons.

General Stark formed his men in line of battle two miles above the mill; but it was nearly night, and he did not like the position he had chosen, and concluded to fall back to his camping-ground. It seemed to some of the soldiers like retreating; but Dodifer knew what stuff General Stark was made of, and it did not trouble him.   He felt sure there would be hot work before long.

Baume followed Stark up the valley overlooking the little river, pitched his tents, and encamped for the night, which set in dark and rainy.   The British and Hessians were in their tents; but the Americans had few tents.   General Stark had his headquarters in The Catamount tavern, so called from the figure of a catamount on the sign.   Dodifer and his brother, and a great many other soldiers, slept in the meeting-house.   Some slept in barns and sheds, or wherever they could find shelter.

In the night, Dodifer heard some soldiers tramping through the mud, and learned that they had come from Williamstown and Pittsfield and other towns in Massachusetts.   There were about one hundred, under Colonel Jacob Symonds; and Rev. Mr. Allen, of Pittsfield, came with them in his sulky.   He had been a chaplain at Ticonderoga, and could fight as well as preach.

Mr. Allen drove to the tavern, and hastened to see General Stark.

"General," he said, "the people of Berkshire have frequently been called upon to fight, but never have had a chance, and we have resolved that if you don't give us a chance now, never to turn out again."

"Do you want to go now, in the rain and darkness?" the general asked.

"No, I'm not particular about that."

"Well, if the Lord gives us sunshine once more, and I don't give you fighting enough, you needn't turn out again."

When Dodifer awoke in the morning, he saw that there was not a cloud in the sky.   The air was calm.   Not a breath of air stirred the leaves of the trees.   The ground was soaked.   There were pools of water in the road, and the grass was wet; but the sun soon dried it.

Dodifer took a stroll out to the picket-line, picking blackberries by the roadside, to take a look at the enemy.   There they were on a hill the other side of the river.   The Hessians had rekindled their camp-fires, and were cooking their breakfasts and drying their clothes. They had thrown up an intrenchment on the top of the hill. He could see the sunlight reflected from their cannon. Down by the bridge that crossed the river were two log-houses: the Canadians were there. On a little knoll nearer the east side of the Walloomscoick were the Tories, under Colonel Peters. They had thrown up intrenchments. He could see the Indians skulking about as if to get a chance to scalp a Yankee. He went back to camp, cleaned his gun, and was ready for battle.

General Baume had learned enough to make him cautious. He concluded not to move on without re-enforcements. He strengthened his intrenchments, and waited. The river near his intrenchments is so winding that it almost forms the letter S— running west, then south, then west again. The hill on which Baume was encamped is between the two bends. A small brook comes down from the north-west, and empties into the river by the upper bend. North and west of the hill was a dense forest. South of the hill were cleared fields. The road up which Baume had marched from Cambridge crossed the river at the foot of the hill, and continued east to Bennington about two miles.

Baume directed Colonel Peters and his Tories to cross the bridge and throw up intrenchments on the little knoll south of the road. He placed the Canadian troops in and around the log-houses by the bridge; the Germans and British occupied the hill, while the Indians skulked in the woods. Five hundred of Baume's men were disciplined troops.

The men and boys who had gathered at Bennington were nearly all of them farmers. They had come from the hay-fields to drive back the invader. True, they numbered eighteen hundred—one hundred and fifty from Massachusetts, a few from Vermont, and fifteen hundred from New Hampshire. Baume had eight hundred; but he was strongly intrenched, had two cannon; his troops were disciplined, and had bayonets. Military men would say that the probabilities were all in favor of a victory to Baume. But General Stark and his men had come to fight. General Stark divided his forces into three divisions—each division to attack at the same moment.

Noon.   He selects Colonel Stickney and Colonel Hobart, with two hundred men from their regiments, to attack the Tories under Colonel Peters east of the river.   He directs Colonel Herrick, with three hundred, to cross the river above the upper bend, where Baume can not see him, make a long march through the woods, go round north of the hill, and approach it from the west.   He directs Colonel Nichols to follow Colonel Herrick with two hundred men, and be ready to attack from the north.   Colonel Nichols wants more men, and General Stark sends another hundred.   That leaves about one thousand with General Stark.

We see the parties starting out.   Colonel Stickney and Colonel Hobart leave the road, go through a corn-field; and each soldier pulls off a corn tassel, and sticks it under his hat-band—not for a plume; but they are all in citizen's dress, and so are the Tories under Peters, and the tassel will enable them to distinguish friends from foes.   Colonel Stickney marches through a piece of woods, comes out into an open field in front of the Tories, to attract attention; but he will not make an attack till he hears the rattle of Herrick's guns from the west.

Three o'clock.   It has taken Herrick three hours to make his circuitous march through the woods.   Stark and Colonel Warner are sitting in their saddles, with the thousand men in line, half a mile up the river, where Baume can not see them. Nichols has reached his position in the woods north of the hill.   All are awaiting the signal.   There comes a rattle of guns from the west.   Herrick has begun the battle.   At the first volley the Indians take to their heels, through the woods, down the valley.   They have been in the woods, and have discovered that they are full of Yankees.   Yankees on the south, Yankees on the east, Yankees on the north, Yankees on the west.   They have no idea of being caught in a trap.

"Forward!"   It is General Stark who issues the order.   The one thousand men move through the woods, and come out in view of the intrenchment.   The soldiers can see it swarming with British and Hessian troops.

"Soldiers, there are the red-coats! We must beat them, or else Molly Stark will be a widow to-night," says General Stark.

Dodifer has been with General Stark behind the rail-fence at Bunker Hill, and knows that there is to be no boy's play in this battle.

"Hurra! hurra!" the soldiers shout, making the woods ring, and letting the British and Hessians know that the battle is about to begin in earnest.

They march nearer, and begin the conflict. Almost at the same instant there comes a roll from Stickney and Hobart, who are confronting the Tories, and a roar from Nichols. On all sides the battle begins. The old cannon on cart-wheels, which General Stark found at Charlestown, thunders—not hurling cannon-balls upon the intrenchments, but stones, such as the soldiers can ram into it, for Stark has no cannon-balls. The two brass field-pieces of Baume reply. The British and Hessians load and fire as fast as they can, and the hill smokes like a volcano.

Men begin to drop in the ranks; but nearer and still nearer to the intrenchments move the lines.

"Drive the Tories into the river!" is the shout which Stickney's and Hobart's men send up. They rush upon the intrenchment, pour in a volley. Hobart closes around it on one side, Stickney on the other. The struggle is short and desperate; but the Tories suddenly lose heart, and flee across the bridge. Stickney and Hobart follow, make a rush upon the Canadians in the houses, and drive them out and take possession. Some of the Tories flee down the road toward Cambridge; but most of them join Baume on the hill. Hotter grows the fight, nearer and still nearer. The battle now is on and around the hill. More deafening the roar.

Baume sees that the battle is going against him. His ammunition is failing. His men are brave. The Americans have no bayonets. He will charge upon them. The Reidesel dragoons make a rush, but are received with a volley. Dodifer fires into their faces; and, though a line of bayonets is gleaming in his face, he will not run. He seizes his gun by the barrel, and is ready to annihilate the Hessians. The dragoons waver, come to a halt, then turn and flee to their intrenchments.

"Charge! charge!" The order goes along the line. Officers shout it, soldiers shout it. With a yell, the Americans spring forward, sweep up the hill, and rush upon the intrenchments, to beat out the brains of the Hessians and British. They leap over the breastwork, seize the cannon, capture the gunners. The Hessians fall on their knees, throw down their guns, hold up their hands. Dodifer can not understand a word of their language, but knows that they are crying for quarter. Others, seeing that the battle is lost, flee down the road toward Cambridge, leaving every thing in their flight.

What a wild hurra goes up! The battle is won, and the victorious troops disperse to collect the prisoners and the booty. The regiments are all disorganized. General Stark has promised them all the plun-

"Charge! Charge!" the Order Goes Along the Line.

der, and each soldier is hunting for guns, swords, pistols, or blankets.

But suddenly they hear a drum-beat, and Lieutenant-colonel Breyman, with five hundred British, makes his appearance. He has marched twelve miles from Cambridge, has met the fugitives, gathered them up, and is hastening on with his fresh troops to retrieve the disaster.

"Fall in! fall in!" is the cry of the Americans. The lines reform. Men do not stop to find their own regiments, but fall in where they are.

On come the British, driving all before them. And now the battle rages hotter than ever. All is confusion on the American side, every thing in order on the British. Their volleys are regular, and roll like peals of thunder; while each American fights by himself. The British have two cannon. The Americans wheel the two captured from Baume into position, and fire them. Step by step Breyman advances, and the Americans fall back. Are they to lose the battle, after all?

And now Colonel Warner's regiment, the one hundred and fifty men who were at Hubbardton, make their appearance. They have marched from Manchester, twenty-five miles, have heard the roar of battle, and have come upon the run. They are burning to avenge the disaster at Hubbardton. They fall upon the British like a thunder-bolt. The red-coated line wavers, breaks, and then, seized with a panic, all who can get away, flee; those who can not, throw down their arms and give themselves up as prisoners. The escaped ones flee down the road, followed by the Americans to Van Schaick's mill. There, in the evening twilight, the pursuit ends, and the victorious soldiers return to the battle-ground and count up the spoils of victory—four cannon, nine hundred muskets, swords, and pistols, and seven hundred prisoners. Two hundred and seven British have been killed or wounded. The American loss is about one hundred.

The expedition which was to supply Burgoyne with horses, wagons, cattle, and provisions has ended in disaster. A thousand men have been lost, and horses and wagons have not been obtained. Burgoyne begins to see that it would not be so easy as he had thought to march to Boston. The farmers of New Hampshire have beaten two of his best officers in a pitched battle. Without bayonets they have charged upon intrenchments—a thing unheard of. His prospects, yesterday so bright, have all been changed. He sees that he will have trouble before reaching Albany. He writes a letter to Lord Germain. This is the beginning of disaster; he fears worse, but will try and do his duty.

More discouraging news reaches him. An Indian comes from the valley of the Mohawk. Colonel St. Leger has not been able to take Fort Schuyler, and is retreating to Canada; so he will have no help from that quarter.

Chapter 16
BRANDYWINE

ELIJAH and Esek were on the march once more. After the battle at Princeton, General Washington established his quarters at Morristown, in New Jersey. The winter had passed away, summer had come, and the army, now containing fourteen thousand men, was marching southward; for General Howe had put his army on board the ships, and General Washington concluded that he was intending to sail south, ascend the Delaware, and attack Philadelphia. Such was Howe's design, who sailed from New York on the 23d of July with eighteen thousand men. He reached Delaware Bay, and then learned that Washington had erected strong fortifications on the river. He spread his sails once more for Chesapeake Bay. It was a long voyage, and it was the 25th of August before he reached the place he had selected for landing, on the Elk River.

During these sultry days of August the army was moving south-west from Philadelphia, to meet the British. Esek was marching with his gun on his shoulder, but Elijah was on horseback. He had been appointed a captain. The first week in September the army was posted on the river Brandywine, a small stream which runs south, and empties into Delaware Bay at Wilmington.

Elijah had studied surveying a little. He was quick to see the features of a country, and so had been appointed an engineer, to select positions and lay out intrenchments.

General Washington thought that, with the Brandywine for a defense, he could hazard an attack from General Howe with a fair prospect of a victory. Howe would have to cross the stream at some ford, for there were no bridges.

Elijah rode up and down the river and saw all the fords, and took notice of the banks, the fields, roads, hills, fences, and woods, for in a battle a fence or a hill is sometimes of great value to an army.

He began at a place called Pyle's Ford, and rode up the east side of the river. General Maxwell was stationed at that ford with one thousand Pennsylvania militia. His troops were encamped on a rocky hill. The next ford, a half mile above, was Chad's, on the great road leading from Philadelphia to Wilmington.

About two miles east of the river was the house of Mr. Benjamin Ring, where Washington had his head-quarters. General Wayne commanded a brigade at Chad's Ford, and Captain Proctor, of the artillery, had his six guns planted to sweep the crossing.

A mile farther up was Brinton's Ford, and two miles above that was Jones's Ford, and seven miles above Chad's was Jefferis's Ford. About two miles north-east of Mr. Chad's house, which was near the ford on the east side, was a Quaker meeting-house, called the Birmingham meeting-house, a long, narrow, one-storied building with board blinds on the windows. General Sullivan, who was in command of the right wing, had his head-quarters near by. His troops were encamped west of the meeting-house, between it and the river. Sullivan had his own brigade, and Lord Stirling's and General Stevens's. General Conway was with Stirling's brigade. There were two French officers with General Sullivan: General De Borre, who had fought in Europe, but who had been with the army only a short time; and a young French nobleman, Lafayette, who had just arrived in America in his own vessel to aid the patriots with his fortune and his services.

Looking across the fields toward the south-east, Elijah could see a little cluster of houses called Dilworth village. Riding north from Birmingham meeting-house, he passed over a ridge of land called Osborne's Hill, and came to a little village called Sconnel, where there was another Quaker meeting-house. Turning west from Sconnel, he came to Jefferis's Ford. Mr. Emmon Jefferis lived near by in a large stone house. The merchants of Wilmington had moved their wines, sugars, and other goods to Mr. Jefferis's house for safe-keeping. It would have been better if they had moved them somewhere else, as we shall see.

Elijah's horse waded through the stream, which was only knee-deep. Reaching the west bank, he galloped south a mile and came to the west branch of the Brandywine. He crossed that at a place called Trimble's Ford, and rode south, crossing roads which led to Jones's and Brinton's Ford, and came to the great road leading to Wilmington. At the junction of the two roads was a tavern kept by Johnny Welsh, as every body called him. He called his tavern the Lancaster Hotel. From there Elijah rode east to Chad's Ford, about three miles distant.

There had been a good deal of marching and countermarching by the two armies, but General Washington had placed his troops to cover these fords, and General Howe was approaching from the west. Howe reached Johnny Welsh's tavern, and halted to see what he could do. He saw that it would cost him a good many men were he to attempt to cross at Pyle's, or Chad's, or Jones's, or Brinton's. He must find a back door somewhere, and get in through that. This was his plan: He would leave five thousand Hessians under General Knyphausen to make a feint at Pyle's and Chad's; but would go with ten thousand up the road to Trimble's Ford, cross that, move on to Jefferis's, cross that, march to the little village of Sconnel, and then come down in Sullivan's rear at Birmingham meeting-house. It would be a long march—fifteen miles—but if he could carry out his plan, it would be successful.

General Washington thought likely that Howe might be making some such movement, and directed General Sullivan to keep a sharp lookout upon all the upper fords.

The 11th of September came. The morning was foggy. Neither army could see the other—just the morning for General

Howe. About day-break, General Maxwell sent out his pickets toward Johnny Welsh's, who quickly brought back word that the Hessians were advancing toward Pyle's and Chad's Ford. The pickets fired upon each other. The Americans fell back, and Knyphausen advanced slowly. About ten o'clock the Hessians showed themselves in the fields, but did not seem inclined to advance. Maxwell concluded to invite them on, and crossed the ford. Knyphausen thought he was going to be attacked in earnest, and opened with his artillery. Proctor's guns replied. There was sharp firing of muskets, and Maxwell retreated across the ford.

All the morning General Sullivan kept a sharp lookout upon the fords. He sent Colonel Bland, with some cavalry, across the river at Jones's Ford to reconnoitre. In a short time a trooper came back, saying that Howe was marching north toward Jefferis's Ford.

General Sullivan sent Elijah with the information to General Washington. While Elijah was at Washington's head-quarters, another officer came with a dispatch from Colonel Ross, who also was out reconnoitring. He had discovered the British army marching northward toward Jefferis's Ford. Another officer came from Colonel Hazen, confirming the dispatches.

Washington saw that Howe had divided his army. He sent Elijah back to General Sullivan with instructions to cross the Brandywine at Jones's Ford, and fall upon the rear of Howe. He told General Greene to push across Chad's Ford and attack Knyphausen on his left flank, while he, with the main army and Maxwell, would cross at Bly's Ford and attack Knyphausen's right flank. Sullivan would keep Howe from returning to help Knyphausen, while Greene and himself would grind the latter to powder, and seize all of the baggage which had been left at Johnny Welsh's. They would quickly finish Knyphausen, and be ready for Howe.

It was about noon, and the troops were ready to move; but now a messenger came down from the region of Jefferis's Ford, sent by Major Spear, of the militia, who said that he had not seen any thing of Howe in that region. Another officer came to General Sullivan, who said that he had seen nothing of Howe in the vicinity of Jefferis's Ford. General Sullivan did not know what to make of it, and sent word to Washington by Elijah once more. General Washington was also unable to comprehend it. He thought perhaps Howe had made a march north to entice him across the river, and that his army was concealed in the woods above Jones's Ford.

"Tell General Sullivan to wait," was the answer Elijah carried back.

It was a great mistake which Major Spear had made. He had only been toward Jefferis's Ford, not to it, and had he gone a little nearer, he would have seen the whole British army halted beneath the trees. General Howe and General Cornwallis, and the other officers, were in Jefferis's house, having a merry time in drinking the fine old Madeira wine of the Wilmington merchants. They drank all they wanted, and took along a large quantity, and made Mr. Jefferis show them the way to Sconnel. It was Sunday, and the Quakers were holding a meeting in the meeting-house there.

Howe made a rapid march down the road to Birmingham meeting-house. A Whig farmer, Thomas Cheney, saw the British, and in an instant he was on the back of his mare, and flying like the wind down the road to let Washington know of their approach. The British skirmishers fired at him, but the balls flew wide of their aim.

Just about the same time Colonel Bland discovered the British, and sent a messenger to Sullivan that Cornwallis was advancing over Osborne's Hill.

Sullivan's troops had all been facing westward, but now he had to change front and face them north. General De Borre's brigade was stationed by Birmingham meeting-house, and from there Sullivan's line extended west nearly to the Brandywine. He had hardly changed front before the Hessians were upon him.

Mr. Samuel Jones lived in a house a short distance north of the meeting-house, and some of the Americans took position

THEY MADE MR. JEFFERIS SHOW THEM THE WAY TO SCONNEL.

197

in his orchard and garden, and, when the Hessians were near enough, opened fire.

It is the beginning of the battle. A few minutes later a terrible conflict is raging. Cornwallis has between twenty and thirty cannon. Sullivan brings his into position, the small-arms join in, and there is a great uproar. Cornwallis has twice as many soldiers as Sullivan, and the contest is unequal.

General Howe is with the troops east of the road, and is swinging them out through the fields to close in upon the men in the garden and by the meeting-house. The Hessians charge to drive them out with the bayonet, but the Americans force them back. General Sullivan sends Elijah down to tell them to hold the position, that Washington will soon be there to help them; but before Elijah reaches the spot, De Borre's men give way and flee past the meeting-house in confusion. Elijah tries to rally them, but in vain. He rides back to Sullivan, who is in the centre of the line, just in season to see the left give way before Cornwallis, who has swept around from the west. Sullivan and Lafayette try to rally their men. Elijah sees Lafayette leap from his horse, sword in hand, and discovers that the animal has been shot through one leg and can not move. Two of Sullivan's aids fall. The bullets are flying around him. The centre, under General Conway, still holds its ground; but the British are on three sides. It is useless to attempt to hold the position any longer. Of what use is the centre of a dam when both banks have been swept away? All flee across the fields and through the woods and pastures toward Dilworth.

A welcome sight greets the eyes of the fleeing soldiers. General Greene has been marching from Chad's Ford north-east upon the double-quick, and there he is near Dilworth, forming his line and rallying the fugitives. The moment that he heard Sullivan's guns, he started Weedon's brigade, and the men have made four miles in forty minutes. The soldiers are panting for breath, the sweat is pouring down their cheeks; but there they are with their artillery in position to sweep a narrow defile. Washington is riding along the line, and Greene and Washington together are bringing order out of confusion.

Cornwallis is hastening on. So rapid has been his pursuit that his lines are broken. He comes to the defile, but his troops make a sudden halt, for grape and solid shot are plowing through their ranks. He forms his lines, and advances to the attack again; but with the troops he has at hand can make no impression on that wall of men before him. He tries again and again, but his troops have had a wearisome march; they are panting with the heat. They have lost their energy, and it is a terrible fire that rolls upon them from that line of men. From three o'clock till sunset Greene and Washington hold the line, and Howe and Cornwallis can not force it.

While this is going on at Dilworth, cannon are thundering and muskets rattling at Chad's and Pyle's Ford. Knyphausen has been on the watch; he sees Greene leave suddenly. Wayne and Maxwell, with two thousand men, are left to hold the fords; but he has five thousand. He moves upon Chad's Ford, plants his artillery to cannonade the other bank. His column moves on. The soldiers go down the bank, and enter the water. Proctor's guns blaze upon them; whole platoons drop into the stream; the water is crimsoned with their blood, their bodies float down the river; but before the cannoneers can reload, a large number have gained the shelter of the eastern bank, and are ready for an attack. Wayne is waiting for them. But suddenly a messenger comes from Sullivan announcing the disaster to his troops.

No use for Wayne to remain there; to do so will be fatal. Cornwallis will soon be between him and Washington. Knyphausen is so near now that he can not withdraw Proctor's guns. He orders a retreat, leaving the cannon to the Hessians. He hastens across the field and comes up to aid Greene and Washington in keeping Cornwallis at bay. Maxwell retreats, and joins Washington.

The Sabbath sun goes down upon the battle-field. Howe has won the victory by getting in at the back door once more, and all because the men who were detailed to look after the door did not go near it to see whether or not Howe was there. They only went toward it. Had Major Spear not sent in any report, in all probability the battle would have had a far different ending, for Knyphausen would have been annihilated, had not the order which Washington had given been countermanded, and Howe might have lost his baggage before he could have retraced his steps.

Defeated once more. It was a sad night to the Americans. Twelve hundred of their number had been captured, wounded, or killed. Howe had lost eight hundred; but his army was much the larger. Washington had lost his strong position, and must retreat. During the night the army moved north-east toward Philadelphia.

The news of the battle reached the city before

The News of the Battle Reaches the City.

morning, and the people were greatly excited. Many of the Whigs packed up their goods and moved into the country. Some of the streets were almost deserted. The Tories remained, ready to welcome General Howe.

DODIFER HANSCOM was a lieutenant. He had fought bravely at Bunker Hill, at Quebec, Bennington, and Hubbardton, and was well qualified to command men. A few days after the battle at Bennington he marched south-west, and came to the Hudson River, opposite Stillwater, crossed on a floating bridge, and came to Mr. Bemis's tavern. It was a large house on the great road leading from Albany to Canada. It was a place well known; for the young people of Albany, before the war, if they took a sleigh-ride in winter, usually rode up the river to Bemis's tavern, where they were sure of having a good supper after a dance.

Between the tavern and the river there was a smooth field. Behind the house were hills covered with oaks and pines.

Dodifer found four or five thousand troops on Mr. Bemis's farm. They had just arrived from the mouth of the Mohawk, and General Gates, who had succeeded General Schuyler, was in command—a small man with a red face. He was Adjutant-general of the Continental Army; but as there was a great deal of dissatisfaction with General Schuyler, who was held responsible for the disaster at Ticonderoga, General Gates had been appointed to the command. It was hardly just to hold General Schuyler responsible for what had happened at Ticonderoga and the scattering of the army. He was a brave officer, but unfortunately situated, and the people had lost confidence in him.

Colonel Morgan Lewis, the quartermaster of the army, was laying out a camp on the beautiful interval in front of the tavern, and building an intrenchment to stop Burgoyne from coming down the road. While the soldiers were at work with picks and shovels, a young man from Poland came into camp. He had served in the armies of Poland, and had come to America to aid the patriots in preserving their liberties. He had called upon General Washington, offering his services.

"What can you do?" Washington asked.

"Try me," said the young man.

That pleased Washington, who appointed him an engineer, and here he was.

He looked at the camp and at the hills, up the river and behind the tavern.

"It vill be easy for ze enemy to fire ze cannonballs into ze camp from that hill," said the young Polander, Thaddeus Kosciuszko, pointing to a hill.

"From That Hill They Vill Be Able to See All That You Vill Be Doing."

"From that hill they vill be able to see all that you vill be doing: they vill aim ze cannon at your shoe-buckles," he said, pointing to another hill.

Colonel Lewis was astonished. He had not thought of that. He saw that the young foreigner knew more about military engineering than General Gates, or any body else in the army. But General Gates was a proud, self-conceited man, who had selected the site for the camp; and it would not do for Kosciuszko, or any body else, to inform him that Burgoyne, with his artillery, would drive the army from that position in a very few minutes. But Major Wilkinson introduced Kosciuszko to General Gates, who soon saw that the foreigner knew what he was talking about.

"You will please ride over the ground around here, examine the positions, and give Colonel Lewis the benefit of your advice," said Gates.

"If you vish ze place defended, I must know how many men you have before laying out ze vorks," said Kosciuszko.

"About five thousand."

"Very vell. Now ve vill ride and see ze ground."

Colonel Lewis rode with him up the hills and along the ravines.

"Here is ze place for ze breastvorks, and there ve vill make ze angle. Ve vill carry ze line up ze hill," said Kosciuszko, selecting the proper place for building the line of intrenchments.

The soldiers went to work under Kosciuszko's direction, and in a short time had a line of works extending from the river, up the hills, to the house of Mr. Neilson, nearly a mile.

General Glover's brigade was stationed down by the river; then came General Nixon's and General Paterson's. General Gates's head-quarters were in Mr. Chatfield's house, about three-quarters of a mile from the river. Beyond Gates's head-quarters was General Poor's brigade—three New Hampshire regiments (Colonel Cilley's, Colonel Scammell's, and Colonel Hale's), which had fought at Trenton and Princeton, and were now ready to do their best in stopping Burgoyne. Besides these, there were Colonel Van Cortlandt's and Colonel Henry Livingston's New York regiments, Colonel Cook's and Colonel Latimer's Connecticut troops, and Colonel Morgan's riflemen, and Major Dearborn's battalion of New Hampshire troops— three hundred and fifty picked men. They drilled as light-infantry, but were attached to Morgan's command; for they were nearly all armed with rifles.

A few days later, General Learned's brigade of Massachusetts troops—consisting of Bailey's, Wesson's, and Jackson's regiments, and James Livingston's New York regiment—arrived. With them came Nicholas Doloff, from Fort Schuyler.

General Arnold was in command of the left, with his headquarters near Mr. Neilson's house.

General Burgoyne, after his success at Ticonderoga and Hubbardton, had pushed on to Fort Edward. He had had a smart skirmish before reaching Fort Edward; but, having reached the Hudson, had taken things easy. He had scattered the Americans; the road was opened to Albany. He must transport boats from Lake Champlain to the Hudson, bring forward his supplies, and then he would push on.

The boats were loaded on wheels in Wood Creek, which empties into Lake Champlain, and then, with six horses in a team, drawn to the Hudson, about twenty miles. It was slow work, however, for the teamsters were in no hurry. They were getting British gold, and the longer they could work, the more money they would have. The horses had been purchased in Canada, and the Canadians had been shrewd enough to sell all their old, knock-kneed, spavined, ring-boned animals at high prices. They had come from Canada by land, along the Vermont shore, and had had no grain. In a short time they were broken down.

Burgoyne and his officers had a mountain of baggage—fine uniforms, ruffled shirts, camp equipage, and things good to eat. They must have wine at dinner; and there was so much to be transported—boats, cannon, powder, balls, tents, pots, kettles, biscuit, beef, pork, sugar, rum, rice, wine, trunks, bales, and boxes—and the teams were so poor and so few, that it was slow work.

The trouble was, Burgoyne and all his officers liked to play cards and drink wine too well, not unfrequently sitting up all night, and consequently were not fit for business in the morning. From the middle of July to the middle of September, Burgoyne was employed in getting ready to move on.

Meanwhile, the Americans were assembling. General Gates

now had eight or nine thousand men, with a line of strong fortifications in front of Burgoyne. General Stark was on his left flank. Colonel Brown, with some troops, captured three hundred British near Ticonderoga, and a vessel containing provisions and ammunition. He captured also several cannon, and made an attack upon Ticonderoga.

Burgoyne found that he must move on, and be quick about it. On the 13th of September, he built a bridge of boats, and crossed to the west bank of the Hudson. He might have gone down the east bank, but Lord North and Lord Germain had given him strict orders to go to Albany, and he was, therefore, obliged to cross the river. On the 18th, he went into camp two miles north of Mr. Neilson's house, on Mr. Freeman's farm.

There was a frost on the ground the next morning. The grass in the fields was white with it. The air was calm, and the sun shone from a cloudless sky. The blue smoke curled up from hundreds of camp-fires, and rested upon the hills.

All through the forenoon Dodifer could hear a confused sound in the British camp—the beating of drums, the rumbling of cannon-wheels and baggage-wagons. Burgoyne had a great train of artillery down by the river, under General Phillips. The Hessians, under General Reidesel, were there. The right wing was commanded by General Fraser, and was composed of the British light-infantry, the grenadiers, and the riflemen under Colonel Breyman. Fraser had also a regiment of Tories and the Indians.

General Burgoyne directed the Tories and Indians to creep up to a ravine where the American pickets were, and begin an attack, which would attract the attention of the Americans; and, while they were hastening to that point, he would make a march with the light-infantry and grenadiers west through the woods, get close up to the breastworks, fire his cannon to let Reidesel know he was ready, and then, down by the river, and up in the woods, the battle would begin in earnest.

It was a very nice plan, but the American pickets all along the line were on the lookout. At half-past eleven, those away

"IS THIS COLONEL MORGAN?" THE SERGEANT ASKS.

out on the left discovered Fraser's movement, and sent word to General Gates.

Colonel Morgan and the surgeon of Morgan's brigade are in the quartermaster's tent. Colonel Lewis, the quartermaster, has invited them in to lunch. His cook has broiled some kidneys, and peppered them hot. The quartermaster has a jug of rum. They call the jug Brown Betty, and Colonel Morgan is kissing Brown Betty's lips, when a sergeant enters the tent.

"Is this Colonel Morgan?" the sergeant asks.

"That is my name."

"I am General Arnold's orderly, and am directed to hand this to you," says the sergeant, presenting a paper.

Colonel Morgan sets the jug upon the ground, and reads the paper.

"It shall be done, or my name is not Dan," he says, bringing his big fist down upon the table, jumping from his seat, and running out.

Colonel Lewis and Dr. Potts wonder what it all means, but soon see that the paper is an order from General Arnold:

"The enemy in force is advancing to turn the left of our position. Colonel Morgan will meet him with his command, and instantly engage him," is the order.

Colonel Lewis leaps into his saddle and rides up to Morgan's quarters. He finds the regiment, between five and six hundred in all—more than half of them New Hampshire boys—ready to march; Dearborn leads off; Major Morris, of New Jersey, and Major Butler, of Pennsylvania, with their battalions, follow.

General Burgoyne has laid a very nice plan of attack. The Indians and Canadians are slowly working their way up through the woods. In a few minutes they will fall upon General Gates's left wing. The Sixty-second regiment is close behind them, and General Fraser is following. He will strike a blow which will be felt; but Colonel Morgan is going to make some alterations in Burgoyne's plan.

Dearborn forms his line, and comes up to the American pickets, who have been slowly falling back. The New Hampshire boys soon make it so hot for the savages that they flee through the woods, followed by the Canadians. Morris and Butler file into line, and Morgan moves on through Mr. Neilson's wheat-field. Mr. Neilson has girdled the great trees, and the dead trunks, blackened by fire, are standing thick in the field, in the middle of which is the Sixty-second British regiment, which numbers six hundred. The noon-day sun falls in the men's faces as they stand there looking south-west. The riflemen open fire. Each man loads and fires, taking deliberate aim at the line of red-coated men. The British see the puffs of white smoke rolling up amidst the limbless trunks, and fire rapidly, but at random, and wildly.

The riflemen charge upon the British, and drive them. They follow on, but soon come face to face with the Twentieth, Twenty-first, and Ninth regiments, the grenadiers, and eight cannon. There is a blaze of fire along the whole British line. The cannon-shot crash through the trunks of the trees, the air is filled with leaden rain; the British advance, and the riflemen, in turn, are obliged to retreat. The battle has raged scarcely twenty minutes, but during that time terrible the slaughter in the Sixty-second regiment. More than half have been killed or wounded.

Not many of the riflemen have fallen, but they are scattered in the woods. Colonel Morgan blows a whistle, and its shrill notes ring through the forest, sharp and clear, above the noise and confusion. The riflemen hear it, and flock once more around their leader.

General Burgoyne, thinking that he has put a large part of the Americans to flight, advances toward the intrenchments.

The three New Hampshire regiments, under General Poor, were behind the intrenchments by Neilson's house. They heard the volley of the riflemen, and the louder volley of the British light-infantry, and the roar of the British cannon. They could see the smoke of battle rolling above the trees. Then came the lull, and some of the riflemen were running to the intrenchments.

"Forward!" said General Poor, and Scammell's regiment

filed down a path toward the ravine. Colonel Cilley and Colonel Hale followed with their regiments.

Dodifer and Nicholas were together once more. They could hear a rattling fire down on their right toward the river; but the Tories and Canadians there were getting the worst of it, for thirteen had been killed, and thirty-five captured.

They met a rifleman who informed them that Captain Van Swearingen and Lieutenant Morris, and twenty of the riflemen had been captured; that the regiment was very much scattered, and that the British were pressing on. The next moment Dodifer and Nicholas found themselves face to face with the enemy. There were fifteen hundred Americans against three thousand British.

There were volleys on both sides. The New Hampshire men took deliberate aim, fired, and stepped behind trees while loading. The British soon found that they had a stubborn foe before them. The men who had fought at Bunker Hill, Trenton, and Princeton were not going to run at the first fire. Not an inch of ground would they yield. The battle raged furiously, the British slowly advancing, the New Hampshire boys standing their ground.

From two o'clock till four, the three New Hampshire regiments, with Dearborn's New Hampshire battalion, and the few riflemen that Morgan had called back, faced the whole of Fraser's force. They compelled the British to give way, but Fraser rallied them. The British prepared to charge bayonets.

"Charge! charge!" was the cry that ran along their lines, and the light-infantry came sweeping through the woods with a hurra; but the New Hampshire boys let them have a volley in their faces, and drove them back again.

The British officers were brave men. Several of them were earls, lords, or baronets. Their reputation was at stake. They ran along the wavering lines and rallied the men, encouraging some, swearing at others; but the men in homespun clothes, fighting in their shirt-sleeves, and some of them without shoes or stockings, born in log-cabins, and having no title of nobility, were just as brave and noble as any of the earls, lords, and members of Parliament of England. A title does not always confer nobility. Worth makes the man. The New Hampshire men had no thought of yielding the ground so long as their ammunition held out.

The eight cannon which Burgoyne has brought into position are all thundering. They add to the uproar, but do very little harm. The New Hampshire troops have no cannon; the artillery is behind the breastworks at Neilson's house. Dodifer and his comrades pick off the artillery-men one by one, and shoot the horses.

In an Instant They Are Rushing Forward up to the Muzzles of the Guns.

"Let us take the cannon!" some one says.

"Hurra!"

In an instant, almost before they know what they are about, they are rushing forward up to the muzzles of the guns. The artillery-men flee. Dodifer and Nicholas seize a gun, and begin to turn it round, but the next moment the light-infantry are sweeping down upon them. They see a line of gleaming bayonets and they in turn are obliged to run. The light-infantry follows them with a yell. That does not frighten the New Hampshire boys, but inspirits them. They turn about and meet their pursuers, and the battle goes on hotter than ever.

General Reidesel is down by the river, waiting for orders from Burgoyne. He hears the din of the conflict growing louder every moment, and fears that things are going badly. He sends an officer up to see if he is wanted, and the officer returns with a request for him to hasten up to support Burgoyne, who thinks that he is fighting nearly the whole army under Gates, whereas up to this moment only Morgan and the New Hampshire men have taken part. Reidesel starts with a portion of his men and several cannon.

The New Hampshire men have fired away nearly all of their ammunition, and there is a lull in the strife, while they fall back and wait for more powder.

It is half-past three. Burgoyne and Fraser think that they have driven the Americans, and are re-forming their lines to storm the intrenchments; but suddenly the battle begins again. Colonel Cook, with the Connecticut men, leaves the intrenchments, moves forward, and joins the New Hampshire men.

The British are on the north side of the ravine, through which flows a little brook. The Americans are on the south side, and the battle rages, now on one side and now on the other.

Half-past four. General Reidesel is coming up through the woods with one regiment, two companies, and several cannon. The Hessians come into line east of the British light-infantry. The artillery unlimber. But others besides the New Hampshire and Connecticut men are taking part in the battle now. Colonel Brooks, Colonel Learned, and Colonel Marshall, commanding three Massachusetts regiments, and Colonel Van Cortlandt, and Colonel James Livingston, with two New York regiments, are in front of Burgoyne, and the battle is terrific.

Things are going badly on the British side. The Sixty-second regiment is cut to pieces. Colonel Anstruther and Major Harnage wounded; a great many captains and lieutenants killed or wounded, and the whole force on the point of retreating. Captain Jones has lost thirty-six of his artillery-men, and has not enough left to work his guns.

During a lull in the battle, Dodifer can hear the British officers giving their orders to get ready to charge bayonets, and then the British come through the woods; but there is a ripple, a roar, like a great wave of the sea breaking upon the rocks, and the British line tumbles to pieces.

General Arnold is riding along the American lines, encouraging the soldiers, and Dodifer sees a stout man riding here and there along the British lines. He is in the thickest of the fight, encouraging and rallying the wavering troops. It is the same officer that commanded the British at Hubbardton—General Fraser. He has left his home on the banks of a beautiful lake in Scotland to win glory in America. Dodifer admires his bravery.

Six o'clock. It is sunset, on this 19th day of September. All through the afternoon the battle has raged in the fields and woods, and along the ravine. Burgoyne has not reached the American intrenchments. The Americans have not fought behind breastworks, but have met him in the fields and woods. He did not expect to encounter such stubborn resistance, and is amazed. His troops have fought bravely, but have gained no advantage. He has lost a great many men, and some of his ablest officers; and now the sun goes down, and the main body of the Americans, as twilight comes on, retire to their intrenchments, to rest till the morning. Not all go back, for through the evening small parties hang on Burgoyne's flank, creep up close to his lines, and pour in a volley now and then.

Burgoyne confidently expected in the morning to strike the American right flank such a blow that every rebel would take to his heels; but he has made no advance, and is perplexed to know what to do next. His wearied troops lie down upon the battlefield beneath the stars, with the dead and dying around them. Little sleep do they get with the rattling of wagons here and there, picking up the wounded, and the American pickets firing every few minutes.

Burgoyne tries to make himself think that he has won a victory; but there is the thought that it was his object to advance, that he has not made any progress, that the Americans are ready to dispute every inch of ground in the morning, that the object of the Americans was to stop him, and in that they have succeeded. He has lost between six and seven hundred men, and the Americans less than three hundred.

Dodifer and Nicholas lie down to sleep, quite well satisfied with what they have done. They have fought the British in the open field, and are ready to fight them again, confident that they can defeat them.

The sun rises clear on the morning of the 20th; the smoke of the battle-field hangs along the valley. Dodifer and Nicholas are ready for the battle, or would be if they only had some powder and balls. They do not know that there is very little powder in camp—not enough for another battle; but General Gates knows it. No order comes to renew the attack. Burgoyne does not care to renew it. The pickets hear a sound of axes, and soon report that Burgoyne is erecting breastworks. Instead of attacking, he is afraid of being attacked.

General Gates will wait for more powder; besides, time is his ally. Fresh troops are on their way, and Burgoyne's provisions are growing less. He, better than Burgoyne, can afford to wait.

Chapter 18
GERMANTOWN

FTER the battle of Brandywine, General Washington retreated toward Philadelphia. The army was defeated, but not discouraged, though the soldiers were in a sad plight. They had lost a great deal of baggage—tents and blankets—and they had barely food enough to last from day to day. More than a thousand were barefoot; yet in a day or two they were ready for another battle, and stood resolutely facing the British.

The two armies were twenty miles west of Philadelphia. General Howe determined, if possible, to get possession of the city by skillful manœuvring instead of fighting another battle, for, though he had won the victory at Brandywine, he had lost a great many men. To accomplish this object, he must cross the Schuylkill River. He marched north-east, as if intending to cross at Swedes' Ford and approach the city from the north.

Washington saw the movement, and crossed the Schuylkill nearer the city, to be ready to face him. But Howe, instead of crossing the river, marched up the west bank. Where was he going? It was plain enough that he was after the beef, pork, flour, and other supplies which had been collected at Reading, away up the river; and, to save them, Washington made a rapid march up the east bank.

Captain Elijah Favor had a great deal of riding to do. He was kept in advance of the army, obtaining information of Howe's movements—not an easy thing to do, for many of the people were Tories, and gave him false information. Many narrow escapes he had from capture by the Tory troopers sent out by Howe to scour the country.

But General Howe, although marching toward Reading, had no intention of going there. What were a few barrels of beef and flour in comparison with the greater prize—Philadelphia? He was marching to get Washington away from the city, and had succeeded, for the American army had passed on through Norristown to Pottstown. Howe was on the west bank of the river, opposite Pottstown. Suddenly he faced about, made a rapid march, crossed the river at Norristown, and was in possession of the prize. He had won it without fighting another battle. He encamped the army six miles out of the city, at Germantown, while Washington went into camp about twelve miles north of that place.

The British army was encamped in a delightful old town. There was a wide and level street a mile long, with houses on both sides, many of them more than one hundred years old, with porches and verandas where the German citizens were accustomed to sit in the summer evenings and smoke their long-stemmed pipes, and tell stories of the fatherland. Behind the houses were nice gardens, filled with cabbages, which they made into sourkrout.

On Sundays the people of Germantown assembled for worship in a little old meeting-house with a low roof. They were *Tunkers*—which is the German for "Dippers"—Baptists who kept the seventh day for Sunday. Some of the people were Whigs and some Tories. Judge Chew, who lived at the north end of the street in a large stone house, on the east side of the road, was a Tory. He was rich, and a judge, and rode in a coach, with a driver and footman in gold-laced cocked hats. He lived in fine style, with a retinue of servants. The grounds around the house were beautifully laid out. He had some charming daughters, and it was a delightful place for the British officers to spend an afternoon or evening.

The owner of so fine an estate—being a judge, a public man, and loyal to the king—was greatly respected by General Howe and other British officers. They took care that his property should not be destroyed, and a guard was kept about the premises. Judge Chew gave grand receptions to the officers and all the big-wigs. It was delightful to the officers, after their hardships in the field, to be invited to one of Judge Chew's entertainments, and spend the evening in the society of the agreeable young ladies of the city.

The house stood on the southern slope of a hill, called Mount Airy. From the top of the hill, a road ran south-west to the Wissahicon Creek, and across it to the Manatawny road, which runs parallel with the creek, and crosses it at its mouth. Another road, called School-house Lane, leads from the Manatawny road, below the creek, up to the Germantown road, and crosses it—running north-east. East of Germantown, it is called the Limekiln road. The market-house stands at the crossing; but east of the Limekiln road is another—the Old York road.

This is the way the British army was encamped: The right wing extended out to the York road. The Queen's Rangers, under Colonel Simcoe, were there, and south of them were the Guards. On the Limekiln road was the light-infantry, under General Grant; while along School-house Lane was the left wing, composed of Hessians, under General Knyphausen. General Howe had his head-quarters about a mile south of the market-house.

At the north end of the town, in the field opposite Judge Chew's, was the Fortieth regiment, under Colonel Musgrove. He had two cannon on the top of Mount Airy, in the road by Mr. Allen's house. The pickets were a short distance beyond.

Although General Washington had been defeated at Brandywine, although he had lost Philadelphia, he was ready to give battle any day; but General Howe seemed to be contented with what he had accomplished, and made no movement.

Washington resolved to make a night march, and fall upon Howe. He would attack at four points at the same time: sending one column, under Colonel Forman and Colonel Smallwood, down the York road, to attack the Rangers; another, under General Greene, with General Stevens and General

M'Dougall, down the Limekiln road, to attack the troops under General Grant; one, under General Armstrong, to go down the Manatawny road, cross the Wissahicon, and attack the Hessians there; while Washington himself, with Wayne, Nash, Maxwell, Sullivan, Conway, and Knox, with the artillery, would move down the main road, drive Colonel Musgrove from Mount Airy, and attack the Hessians under Knyphausen.

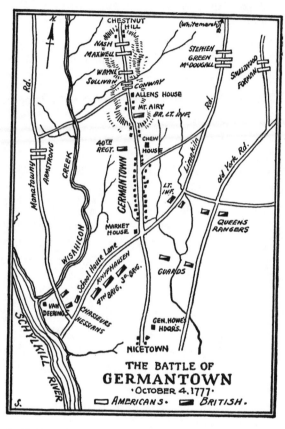

THE BATTLE OF
GERMANTOWN
·OCTOBER 4, 1777·
☐ AMERICANS· ☐ BRITISH·

The morning of the 4th of October was selected for the attack. It was seven o'clock in the evening previous when the columns started. General Washington had ordered the pickets the day before not to permit any one to pass toward the city, and no information of the movement reached General Howe.

Colonel Forman and Colonel Smallwood, having farther to march than the other columns, started first. The other columns started in order.

The night was dark, the road uneven, and the cannon rumbled heavily over the stones. Before morning, a thick fog set in, and the column made slow progress. It was a march of twelve miles, and day was breaking when General Conway's troops, who led the column commanded by Washington, came upon the British pickets north of Allen's house, who fled and gave the alarm. The British artillery-men were asleep in their tents, but sprung to their feet, lighted their port-fires, rammed home a cartridge, and fired at random into the fog.

The deep, heavy roar awoke every soldier in the British army, and in less than a minute drums were beating down in the field by Judge Chew's house, in the light-infantry camp by the market-house, in the Hessian camp south-west of the market-house; while out in the camp of the Queen's Rangers there was a quick saddling of horses. Nobody knew what was going on; but a minute later there was a roll of small-arms.

Sullivan was behind M'Dougall. His men jumped over the fence on the right-hand side of the road, dashed across a field, and came to the lane leading from Allen's house to the Schuylkill.

South of the lane, the Fortieth British regiment was encamped; and the soldiers were putting on their cartridge-boxes, and the officers buckling on their swords, when Sullivan's men fell upon them. Some were shot down at once, some fled, others returned the fire.

"To the house!" shouted Colonel Musgrove; and about half of the regiment rushed to Judge Chew's house. Its stone walls would make a fortress. The British soldiers entered the house, and poured a terrible fire from the windows upon Sullivan's men, many of whom were shot down. The other British soldiers fled through Germantown.

"Let us leave these men in the house and push on," said General Reed.

"Oh no, that will never do. We must not leave a fort with five hundred men in it in our rear," said Knox. "We will bring up the artillery and knock it to pieces."

"While doing it we shall lose the main chance," said Reed.

"We will leave it to General Conway," said Knox.

General Conway decided to wheel the artillery into position and batter the house to pieces. A messenger was sent with a

A MESSENGER WAS SENT WITH A WHITE FLAG DEMANDING THE SURRENDER OF THE HOUSE, BUT WAS KILLED BY A SHOT FROM THE WINDOWS.

white flag demanding the surrender of the house, but was killed by a shot from the windows.

"Set the house on fire," said one.

"I will do it," said Major White, one of Sullivan's aids. He was a brave man. He ran up to the house on the rear, where there were no windows, with a fire-brand, and held it against the wood-work; but a British soldier discovered what he was doing, ran down cellar, and fired out of the cellar-window, and the brave young officer fell dead, with the fire-brand in his hand.

General Wayne, with his division, had got a good distance past the house, but, finding that Sullivan and Conway had halted, came back to help capture the British. Knox wheeled his artillery into position to riddle the house with shot, and killed some of the soldiers inside, but found it no easy matter to batter down the walls. He would have to punch many a hole through the edifice before the walls would crumble.

While this was going on, General Greene was pushing down the Limekiln road. He had farther to march than Washington, and it was three-quarters of an hour after the firing of the cannon at Allen's before he fell upon the light-infantry east of the market-house. He heard the roar of battle through the fog, and knew that the British would all be under arms. He suddenly found himself face to face with a body hastening toward Chew's house, and the fight began in the orchards, fields, and gardens. There was a great deal of firing at random.

Smallwood and Forman, for some reason, failed to drive in the Tories, and so turn the right flank of the British. General Howe was surprised at the vigor of the attack; he was thinking of retreating.

Neither Washington nor Howe could see what was going on. Men got lost: Americans fell into the hands of the British, and British into the hands of the Americans. In a short time all was confusion. The soldiers fired at random; but General Greene pushed his way into Germantown, and met General Agnew, of the British troops, advancing toward Judge Chew's house. Sullivan, with Colonel Armstrong, commanding a regiment of North Carolinians, swept down toward Wissahicon Creek, and drove the British there back into Germantown; but the fog was so thick that no one could tell what was going on.

"We are surrounded," said some of the soldiers, hearing the firing at Chew's house in the rear; and the soldiers in Sullivan's division, just when victory was in their grasp, took to their heels. The officers tried to stop them, but in vain. The golden moment was lost, and the whole army retreated. They had lost one hundred and fifty-two killed, and five hundred and twenty-one wounded, besides some prisoners—nearly one thousand in all. General Howe lost about eight hundred, among them two of his best officers, General Agnew and Lieutenant-colonel Bird.

The American army did not go back to its old camp, but to Whitemarsh, six miles from Germantown. The soldiers were not discouraged, as after the battle at Brandywine, for they had attacked the British and all but defeated them.

ANTHONY'S NOSE is a mountain in the Highlands, on the east bank of the Hudson, nearly eleven hundred feet high. Its sides are steep, and white granite ledges crop out here and there, and great bowlders are scattered at its base. On the other side of the river, a little lower down, rises Dunderberg, the Thunder Mountain. Up beyond its rocky defiles, in the Catsbergs, Rip Van Winkle saw the old bowlers at play, and drank some of their schnapps, and had his twenty years of sleep, according to the old legend. These two mountains form the gate-way of the Hudson, and through it winds the noble river.

On the east bank, two miles below Anthony's Nose, the Americans erected Fort Independence, and on the west bank, opposite the Nose, Fort Clinton, and just above it Fort Montgomery. Fort Clinton required a garrison of about four hundred men, Fort Montgomery about eight hundred. A great iron chain was stretched across the river, and a boom made of logs. Above the boom were several ships. These were the defenses of the Highlands; and it was believed that the British fleet never would be able to get past them.

The month of September came, and this is the way the men stood upon the chess-board: Up at Saratoga, General Burgoyne was trying to push southward, but was confronted by General Gates. In the Highlands was General Putnam, with nearly five thousand men, many of them New England militia, with no British army in front of him nearer than New York, where Sir

Henry Clinton was in command; but he had few troops, for General Howe had sailed into Chesapeake Bay with nearly the whole army, and was moving to capture Philadelphia. General Washington was out on the Brandywine, trying to prevent him from taking that city. Washington wanted more troops; and as Sir Henry Clinton had no force that he could send up the

It Was Proved That Palmer Was a Spy.

Hudson to aid Burgoyne, he sent an order to Putnam to forward twenty-five hundred men to Philadelphia.

The troops marched south, leaving Putnam only fifteen hundred militia, besides six hundred farmers from Dutchess and Ulster counties, in New York, who came in to help garrison Fort Montgomery and Fort Clinton. There was also a small garrison in Fort Independence. General James Clinton commanded Fort Clinton; and his brother George, who became the first Governor of New York, commanded Fort Montgomery. They were in no way related to Sir Henry Clinton. They were brave men; but neither they nor General Putnam had any expectation of being attacked.

General Burgoyne was in trouble. St. Leger had failed at

Fort Schuyler; Baume and Breyman had been routed at Bennington; and he himself had been defeated at Stillwater. He had heard nothing from New York, and wondered if the army, which he expected would meet him at Albany, had started. He sent a message to Sir Henry, and the messenger, piloted by Tories, had no difficulty in getting through the American lines. Sir Henry sent him back again, with the information that he was about to move up the Hudson, and attack the forts in the Highlands. He could do it, now that General Robertson had arrived from England with two thousand fresh troops.

Sir Henry sent spies up to Peekskill to find out the situation of affairs—Tories who had enlisted in the king's service, under Governor Tryon, the former Governor of North Carolina and New York. One of the spies, Nathan Palmer, a lieutenant in a Tory regiment, was discovered at Peekskill, and arrested. A court-martial was called by General Putnam to try him. The general would not have him executed as General Howe executed Nathan Hale, without a trial. It was proved that Palmer was a lieutenant in Tryon's regiment.

Governor Tryon heard of the arrest, and sent a letter to General Putnam, claiming that Palmer was a British officer, and threatening vengeance if he was executed. The threat did not frighten Putnam, who sent back this reply:

"SIR,—Edmund Palmer, an officer in the enemy's service, was taken as a spy, lurking within our lines. He has been tried as a spy, condemned as a spy, and shall be executed as a spy; and the flag is ordered to depart immediately.

ISRAEL PUTNAM.

"P.S.—He has been accordingly executed."

The Tories kept clear of Putnam after that.

On Saturday evening, October 4th, Sir Henry Clinton and General Vaughan, with three frigates and a large fleet of schooners and boats, with five thousand men on board, left New York, and sailed up the Hudson. The wind was fair, the night dark. The Americans up in the Highlands knew nothing of the movement.

On Sunday morning, the British were at Tarrytown; and before noon, Sir Henry landed three thousand men at Verplanck's Point, eight miles below Peekskill.

Messengers rode up the river spreading the news. General Putnam sent riders in every direction alarming the people. The countrymen who were at church hastened home, seized their guns, and started to aid in driving back the invaders. They came into Putnam's camp; and by night he had two thousand men. He was sure that Sir Henry intended to march to Peekskill, and from there get in rear of Fort Independence; for the three frigates had moved up and dropped anchor within cannonshot of the fort. General Putnam sent an officer to General James and General George Clinton.

"Send me all the men you can spare," was his order.

Monday morning dawned. A heavy fog hung over the river, and under its cover Sir Henry made his next move. He had no intention of attacking Fort Independence, but was after other game.

The troops which had landed at Verplanck's went on board the boats, rowed across the river, and landed at Stony Point— all except some regiments of Tories under Colonel Bayard and Colonel Fanning, Governor Tryon's son-in-law. Governor Clinton and his brother were on the alert. They suspected that the landing at Verplanck's was only a feint. They remembered how General Clinton, leading the British army, had entered the back door at Long Island, and Major Logan, with one hundred men, was sent up to Dunderberg to keep watch. Major Logan soon sent back word that forty boats had crossed to Stony Point.

Another party of thirty men went out from Fort Clinton, over the hills behind Dunderberg, on the road leading to Haverstraw, and suddenly found themselves face to face with the British. Crack! went their rifles, and the British fired in return; but the bullets fell harmlessly around the Americans, who fled to the forts, giving the alarm.

"The British are approaching the forts," was the message which Governor Clinton sent to General Putnam, by a man named Waterbury. But the man was a traitor. He left the fort, secreted himself, and the next day joined the British.

So it came about that on Monday afternoon, while Sir Henry Clinton and General Vaughan were approaching the rear of the forts, along the steep and narrow mountain-roads, General Putnam was out on horseback reconnoitring the enemy at Verplanck's, wondering why they did not advance, and in utter ignorance of what Sir Henry was doing, till he heard the rattle of muskets from the other side of the Hudson behind Dunderberg. All the while the two generals in the forts were wondering why Putnam did not send re-enforcements—little thinking that the messenger was a traitor, and hiding in the woods.

Out on the bank of a gurgling brook, south-west of the forts, in the ravine between Bear Hill and Dunderberg, the British army divided. Lieutenant-colonel Campbell, with nine hundred men, took a narrow road leading around Bear Hill. He had the Fifty-second and Fifty-seventh regiments, a battalion of Hessians under Colonel Emerick, and a regiment of Tories. A Tory, who knew the road, piloted them. They were to attack Fort Montgomery; but had to make a march of seven miles.

Sir Henry Clinton halted with the remainder of the troops a while; for it was only three miles that he had to march to get in rear of Fort Clinton. His men rested beneath the trees till nearly three o'clock, and then moved toward the fort.

Lieutenant-colonel Campbell, with the left-hand column, winds around Bear Hill, descends into a ravine, crosses a brawling stream called by the Dutch Peploap's Kill, climbs another hill, turns east, and approaches the fort. Suddenly a cannon blazes in front of them. Governor Clinton has sent out a cannon and sixty men. The roar of the gun rolls over the mountains. The governor hears it, and sends another cannon with one hundred men.

It is an unequal contest—only one hundred and sixty against nine hundred.

While the British are forming, the Americans from behind the trees keep up a destructive fire, and the cannon roar again and again. One of the guns bursts; but they keep up the fight with the other till the British charge bayonets, and then the gunners, after driving a spike into the vent-hole, retreat to the fort.

Sir Henry Clinton is working toward Fort Montgomery along a narrow path. He marches down the valley, and comes to the shore of a pond—Sinnipink, the Dutch called it; but since the battle it has been known as Bloody Pond, for on that night blood flowed freely on its shores. Between the pond and the river the Americans have built a strong abatis; and while Sir Henry's pioneers are clearing a way through it with their axes, the Americans pour down a deadly fire. But the Americans are few and the British many, and the abatis is cleared at last; and Sir Henry with his troops is ready to attack the fort. He sends a white flag, and the officer carrying it bears the summons:

"The garrisons of both forts must surrender within five minutes, or they will be put to the sword."

To surrender is to yield their liberty without a struggle; that were unworthy of brave men. To surrender is to go to the old hulk—the prison-ship at New York—with all its horrors; that were worse than death.

"The forts will be defended to the last," is the reply which Lieutenant-colonel Livingston carries from Governor Clinton to Sir Henry Clinton.

It is four o'clock. The three frigates have slipped past Fort Independence, and make their appearance below the forts. The battle begins in earnest now. There are six hundred in the forts, when there should be fifteen hundred to make it an equal contest. Oh, if the troops under Putnam were only there! But the traitor is hiding. Putnam hears the uproar, but he is too far away to render aid.

In the British ranks is a brave officer from Poland—Count Grabowski. He leads the grenadiers in a charge upon the fort, but three bullets pierce him, and he falls mortally wounded. Up by Fort Clinton, Colonel Campbell falls. Step by step only can the British gain ground. From four o'clock till dark the battle rages.

Night comes, and under cover of the darkness the Americans

ESEK EARL IS TAKEN TO NEW YORK AND CONFINED IN THE OLD
HULK, THE "JERSEY."

231

flee, some across the river, others up the bank, and some fall into the hands of the British. One of their prisoners is the brave boy, Esek Earl, who has been in so many battles. With the other prisoners, he is taken to New York, and confined in the old hulk, the *Jersey*, at anchor between New York and Brooklyn.

Above the boom is a fleet of American vessels, but the wind is against them, and they can not escape. The crews set them on fire, push off in boats, and escape to the mountains. Magnificent the scene on that dark and cloudy night. The flames light up the mountains. From the sides of the vessels belch forth sheets of flame, as the shotted guns become heated; and then, as the magazines explode, great columns of flame shoot upward, illumining momentarily all the surrounding scene, and raining down a shower of golden light as the burning fragments fall into the river.

One hundred cannon have been lost; three hundred men have been killed, wounded, or taken prisoners. An immense amount of powder has been captured, besides other supplies. The forts are gone; the great chain is broken.

On this night of October 6th all obstructions are removed, and Sir Henry Clinton, with his army of nearly four thousand men, may move on to Albany to aid Burgoyne; but he is in no hurry. Is it because he is well satisfied with what he has accomplished? In twenty-four hours he might be in possession of Albany, and moving on to Saratoga, and the army under Gates would be scattered right and left, and the grand plan thought out by Burgoyne accomplished. Why does Sir Henry wait a week before sending General Vaughan up to Esopus and Kingston, and then only to act the part of a marauder in burning those places? Who can tell? It is one of the mysteries of history. If he were, on this Monday night, to push on, wind and tide favoring, on Wednesday he might be in Albany, and in possession of Gates's supplies. Such a movement would force Gates to leave his position in front of Burgoyne. The relief would be timely.

If to the Americans the night of the 4th at Germantown, and the night of the 6th at the base of the Dunderberg, are hours of gloom and despondency, the night of the 7th shall be one of hope upon the upper Hudson. If Sir Henry Clinton were to push on, he might even now turn the tide setting against Burgoyne. But he lingers, and the opportunity passes, never to return.

Esek is in the old prison-ship. Oh, the horrors of the place! It is crowded with men. Some are dying with fever, some with consumption. All are starving. They have little to eat, and that not fit to feed swine. The beef is tainted, their bread full of bugs and worms. They are covered with vermin. They are in rags. The air is reeking with pestilence. Their cheeks grow thin and pale. They die like sheep, and are borne out and tumbled into a trench on the Long Island shore. The officer in command is coarse and brutal. Humanity has fled from his bosom. General Clinton, as General Howe did before him, permits it all.

Esek tried to keep up a brave heart, but his strength began to fail. He loathed the food. Sometimes the bread was made of bran, or moldy meal. The meat was so foul that he could not taste it. He had no blanket, but was obliged to sleep on the bare deck. His clothes were only rags. No mother near to help him; no one to comfort him: strength going, life going, hope going day by day.

Gone at last. Out to the trench they bear him, and lay him with the others. So the brave boy gives his life to his country.

Chapter 20
SARATOGA

THE golden opportunity had passed away. The day after the battle of Hubbardton, Burgoyne, if he had pressed on with what supplies he could carry, might have reached Albany without much opposition. The few dispirited troops under Schuyler would have been swept away like chaff before the wind; but now an army larger than his own, securely intrenched, blocked his way. General Stark and the men of New Hampshire had given him his first staggering blow at Bennington; and now he had received another blow, squarely in the face, mainly from New Hampshire men through whose country he thought, when at Ticonderoga, he could march to Boston. Burgoyne received startling news from the north— that five hundred New England militia, on the night of the 25th of September, in the midst of a furious storm, had captured two hundred bateaux, an armed sloop, several gun-boats, provisions, ammunition, and two hundred and ninety-three prisoners at Ticonderoga. They had retaken Mount Defiance, and only wanted heavy artillery to force the garrison in the fort to surrender. So his communication with Canada was cut off.

On the 29th of September, General Lincoln, with two thousand fresh troops from New England, arrived at Saratoga. During all these days Dodifer and Nicholas were hard at work building forts and intrenchments, and cutting down trees. If there was a strong line on the day of battle, there was one far stronger now.

The British soldiers were hard at work. Down by the river in front of his camp, Burgoyne built a strong breastwork, and planted his cannon behind it. His camp was on a pine plain, and

The Man with the Trumpet Blew It as Loud as He Could.

he carried t h e breastwork across i t toward t h e south, then it curved and ran north-west, inclosing the field on M r. Freeman's farm. North-west of Mr. Freeman's half a mile, on a hill, the Hessians, u n d e r Colonel Breyman, threw u p f o r t s a n d breastworks.

The Indians began to leave Burgoyne. T h e y could see that the battle had gone against him, and they found that, instead of taking scalps, their own scalps were in danger.

Every night the pickets fired at each other. One night a party of farmers came into camp and wanted a frolic. One of them took a trumpet, and the others, about twenty of them, with their guns, crept close to the British lines. The man with the trumpet blew it as loud as he could, and the others set up a fearful yell.

"Surrender, or you are dead men!" they shouted; and the frightened sentinels threw down their guns and gave themselves up, thinking that the whole army was upon them, and the twenty citizens came into camp with their captives.

General Burgoyne's hopes revived, for a messenger had reached him from New York with a letter from Sir Henry Clinton. It was dated September 10th. Sir Henry said that he should go up the Hudson and attack Fort Clinton and Fort Montgomery, in the Highlands, the 20th of September.

Burgoyne expected to see Gates sending off half his army southward, but, instead of that, Gates was receiving more troops every day. It seemed as if all New England were on the march toward Saratoga. Burgoyne, not disheartened, sent several messengers by different routes southward with letters to Sir Henry, telling him to hasten to Albany; that he had provisions enough to last till the 12th of October. But on the 1st of the month the British soldiers had to get along with only half as much food as they had been receiving. Although the soldiers were on short rations, General Burgoyne and his generals sat down to good dinners; and, after dinner, drank the health of the king, the ministry, their friends, and success to the expedition. Many of the officers had their wives with them; and although the Americans were closing around them, they laughed, sung, played cards, and drank each other's health as if they were out on a grand picnic. General Reidesel had his wife and children along with him. His wife was a baroness, a good and noble woman. The nights were cool, and there were rainy days, bringing discomfort. One of the English officers had a house built for her, with a chimney and fire-place, as if the army had settled down there for the winter!

General Burgoyne wanted forage for his horses. There was a field of oats out beyond Breyman's camp toward the west, but Morgan with his riflemen were just behind it, and to get the oats a large force must be sent out.

It was the 7th of October, a beautiful morning. The Baroness Reidesel thought that she must give a dinner party to Burgoyne and his officers, and invited them to dine with her in the afternoon. They accepted the invitation. They would return from the foraging expedition in season.

Soon after breakfast, General Burgoyne, with General Fraser, General Phillips, and General Reidesel, started with about fifteen hundred men and several cannon. They took a path that led south-west to the field about three-quarters of a mile distant. They reached it, and the soldiers formed in line, and the forage men, with their sickles and scythes, began to gather the oats. Some of the officers climbed upon the top of a house and looked southward to see what they could discover. General Burgoyne wanted to know just how the American left was situated, and while the foragers were loading their carts he concluded to push on and find out. He sent the Indians and the Canadians in advance.

Nicholas was doing picket duty. He heard a noise partly behind him, and saw the Indians creeping toward him from the west. He fired at the nearest Indian, and then the guns began to rattle. The Indians came on with a whoop, and Nicholas and the other pickets had to take to their heels; but not till they had discovered that behind the Indians were the grenadiers.

The alarm had been given, and before they reached the lines Nicholas could hear the drums beating the long roll, and the shouts of the officers calling upon the men to fall in. The Indians and grenadiers came almost to the lines, but Morgan and his riflemen fell upon them and drove them back through the woods to General Burgoyne, who, instead of retreating, concluded that he would risk another battle, and ordered up the rest of the troops.

This is the way the British army was drawn up: The light-infantry, under Earl Balcarras, were farthest west; next were some British troops, under General Phillips; then the Hessians, under General Reidesel; then farther east some grenadiers, under Major Ackland; and the artillery, under Major Williams.

General Fraser, with five hundred men, was in advance of the light-infantry. General Burgoyne planned to have the Hessians and other troops in the centre begin the battle; and when the Americans came out to attack Reidesel, he intended that

Fraser should fall upon their flank, and drive them pell-mell to their breastworks. It was a very good plan, but the game of flanking was one in which Morgan decided to have a hand. He marched west, took a circuit among the hills, and got into position to fall upon Fraser's rear.

It was past two o'clock when General Poor, with the three New Hampshire regiments—the same that had begun the battle at Trenton, and also on the 19th of September—with a part of Learned's Massachusetts troops, marched out from the intrenchments. The three New Hampshire regiments were farthest east, and their line of march would bring them directly against Burgoyne's artillery. Learned's line of march would bring him against the grenadiers.

Dodifer was with General Poor, and Nicholas with Morgan. General Poor marched down the little brook called Mill Creek, muddy with the trampling of men, crossed it, and came close up to the artillery. Dodifer saw the cannon on the slope above, the artillery-men standing with lighted port-fires.

The next moment there was a roar, a crashing of the limbs of the trees above him, and a whizzing of shot over his head. The cannon had been aimed too high, and very few soldiers fell. The small-arms joined in; but the New Hampshire troops faced the fire, just as they faced the sleet and the snows of the winter storms, without flinching. They marched up the hill, almost to the muzzles of the guns, before they fired.

Dodifer and the soldiers of his company sprung upon one gun, drove the gunners, and seized the piece; but the next moment the grenadiers were upon them, and they had to give it up. They fell back, reloaded their guns, fired another volley, seized it a second time, but again were driven. The fire was rolling along the line. Learned was attacking the Hessians and grenadiers. Once more the New Hampshire boys sprung upon the artillery, but were driven back.

In the midst of this uproar, there came a volley from the west. Morgan, with fifteen hundred men, suddenly appeared; and Fraser, instead of having fallen upon the Americans, found that the Americans had fallen upon him. A part of Morgan's men fired upon Fraser's picked corps; while the balance, under Major Dearborn, wheeled, and, with a cheer, rushed down upon the light-infantry. There was fighting all along the lines. The light-infantry were facing south-east, to meet Learned; but they found Dearborn coming from the south-west; while behind them, toward the north-west, was Morgan. Attacked in front and in flank, the light-infantry began to waver; but the officers rallied them. The Hessians in front of Learned were standing firm.

It was past three o'clock when Learned's troops saw their old commander, General Arnold, ride down the lines. They received him with a cheer. He was not their commander now: there was a misunderstanding between him and Gates, and Arnold had demanded a pass to join General Washington, which Gates had granted. Gates was back in his head-quarters, and had not been upon the field. General Poor might issue orders to his own brigade, Learned to his, Morgan to his; but there was no general commander on the field.

General Arnold had heard the roar of battle. From the breastworks at Neilson's he could see the smoke, and get a glimpse of what was going on. He could remain quiet no longer, but sprung into his saddle and galloped toward the battle-field.

"Bring him back. He'll do something rash," says General Gates to Major Armstrong.

Arnold sees Major Armstrong following, and, thinking what his errand may be, dashes down the line, waving his sword. He has no right to give an order, but nevertheless gives one.

"Forward!" he shouts; and the line, with a hurra, sweep upon the Hessians.

The fight is getting fiercer. The two armies are close to-gether. Dodifer is in the thickest of the fight, his face and hands begrimed with powder. The smoke from the Hessian guns envelops him. Once more he rushes up to the muzzle of a cannon, and lays his hand upon it; and the grenadiers, under Major Ackland, rush up and fire at him. He and his comrades are once more driven back; but in the *mêlée* Major Ackland falls, with a shot through both legs. Major Williams,

HE SWINGS HIS HAT, JOINS IN THE HURRA, BUT THE NEXT MOMENT
CLASPS HIS HANDS UPON HIS BREAST AND FALLS UPON THE
GROUND.

who is commanding the artillery, is wounded, and both officers fall into the hands of the Americans.

Colonel Cilley, commanding one of the New Hampshire regiments, forms his men once more. He waves his sword, and Dodifer rushes again into the white, sulphurous cloud upon the cannon.

The artillery-men are few now. One by one the men have dropped beside the guns. Major Williams is not there to help them. The grenadiers are still ready to support them; but Major Ackland is not there to animate them. Through the cloud, up to the guns, rush Dodifer and his comrades.

"Hurra!" It is theirs. The artillery-men flee, and the grenadiers have not the courage to attempt to recover it. Colonel Cilley leaps astride the cannon, waves his sword. Dodifer helps wheel it round, lays down his gun, seizes the port-fire, still smoking beside the gun. One of the soldiers rams home a cartridge, another primes it. Dodifer runs his eye along the sight, then touches it off, and the shot goes tearing through the Hessian ranks. To take a cannon from the enemy, and turn it upon them, fills him with new life. This pays for all the toils and hardships through the wilderness to Quebec, for the defeat at Ticonderoga and Hubbardton. He swings his hat, joins in the hurra, but the next moment clasps his hands upon his breast and falls upon the ground.

A comrade bends over him. "Tell mother—that—that—I have—done—what—I—could."

Oh, brave boy! you gave all you had to give to your country —your life! The world never will know how great the gift. And the mother far away in her humble home, childless now, never again will hear the footsteps of her boy, or gaze upon his manly face; but it will be her joy to know that he did what he could for his country.

On the battle-field, Major Armstrong was trying to reach Arnold; but Arnold did not stop to give him a chance. Wherever the fight was hottest, wherever the balls were flying thickest, there was Arnold riding recklessly, giving orders without authority, and directing all the movements, while Gates was in his tent discussing the general question of the Revolution with Sir Francis Clark, who had been carried there a prisoner, mortally wounded.

On the British side is an officer, General Fraser, who sees that the fortunes of the day are turning against Burgoyne, and who is doing what he can to rally and inspirit the British. He, and not Burgoyne, is the real commander and leader. He brings order out of confusion. Now he is on horseback, now on foot in the thickest of the fight. At a critical moment he is wounded, and borne from the field to the house where the Baroness Reidesel is staying. She has invited him and Burgoyne to take dinner there. The cloth is laid, the table spread, but the dishes are quickly removed, and the brave man, with the blood oozing from his wound, laid upon the table. He was to have drunk the king's health, and taken a hand in a game of cards after dinner; but he has emptied his last goblet, played his last game. Little heeds he the roar of battle. His fighting is finished. He is thinking of his far-away home among the mountains of Scotland, bright with the heather and broom. Never more will he behold them. He laments the ambition that led him to leave a beautiful Highland home. "Fatal ambition! Poor General Burgoyne!" are the words that fall from his lips. He knows that the battle is going against Burgoyne. He knows that his own life soon will fade away.

It is stated by most historians that General Fraser was riding everywhere along the British line; that Colonel Morgan called some of his riflemen around him, pointed out Fraser, saying, "That is General Fraser; I admire and honor him; but it is necessary he should die. Take your stations in yonder bushes, and do your duty," and that soon after General Fraser fell, shot, as has been supposed, by Timothy Murphy.

There is reason to believe that there is not much truth in the story. Two of General Burgoyne's officers, after their return to England, testified that Fraser was on foot when he was shot. It is reasonable to suppose that Morgan never had seen Fraser. He had had no opportunity to make his acquaintance, never had met him except in the battle of the 19th of September.

It is quite probable that Morgan directed his men to pick off the British officers, as a great many other generals have done in battle. There was a fearful loss of officers, but it is very doubtful if Morgan specially pointed out Fraser to his men.

The British light-infantry have given way. The man who has led them on, and encouraged them by his bravery, is no longer there to lead them. Down through the woods and across the field to their intrenchments they flee. General Reidesel, General Phillips, and General Burgoyne do what they can to rally the discouraged men, but vain their efforts. The Americans follow them. General Tenbroeck, with some New York troops, comes down from the American intrenchments to take part in the contest. Arnold is in his glory. He places himself at the head of Paterson's and Glover's brigade, leads them up to the trees which Burgoyne has felled in front of his intrenchments, and fires at the British beyond them; but he can not storm the intrenchments there.

Arnold rides to Leonard's brigade and leads it against the Canadians and Tories. Nicholas is in this charge. Colonel Brooks's Massachusetts regiment storms the Canadian breastworks. With a hurra the men leap over the logs, and drive the Canadians before them. This leaves the Hessian breastwork exposed. Having carried the Canadian line, Arnold rides to Livingston's and Wesson's regiment, and, with some of Morgan's men, charges Breyman's position.

The Hessians have seen the ferocious man on a brown horse, riding everywhere upon the field, waving his sword amidst the smoke, and now he is attacking them. They fire a volley and flee, panic-stricken, toward the Hudson. But the volley brings down the fearless rider. A bullet passes through the same leg that was wounded under the walls of Quebec. Though he falls, the men whom he is leading do not falter; but rush on, over fallen trees, over the breastworks. Breyman falls, mortally wounded, and the whole of his line gives way. Some of the Hessians fall upon their knees and surrender, and others throw away their guns and flee through the woods toward their camp.

It is sunset. Arnold is lying upon the ground bandaging his leg, when Major Armstrong, who has been chasing him for two hours, rides up and delivers General Gates's orders. Arnold is ready to obey it now, for the victory is won.

The October sun goes down upon a bloody field. Hundreds have been killed, hundreds wounded. It is a gloomy night to General Burgoyne. All his bright anticipations are gone forever. He will not sit down to a Christmas dinner with Sir Henry Clinton in Albany. Nearly all his troops have been engaged, while not half of the Americans have been upon the field.

Major Armstrong Delivers General Gates's Order to Arnold.

General Burgoyne was not ready to renew the battle the next day. He was in no condition to take the aggressive. Nor did General Gates attempt it. Time would give him the victory without the shedding of blood. The militia of New England were hastening to aid him. General Fellows had three thousand men on the east bank of the Hudson, and was sending his cannon-shot into Burgoyne's camp.

General Stark, with two thousand, was on his way to Fort Edward to seize that point.

General Fraser was dead. Out from the baroness's house his brother officers bore him to his grave. It was a sad procession, and the shot from Fellows's guns covered the chaplain and the mourners with dust as they stood beside the grave. General Fellows soon saw that it was a funeral procession, and honored the brave man by firing minute-guns, so it was not hate that inspired the patriots in battle. They could honor their enemies while fighting for their liberties.

It was sunset when Burgoyne and his officers stood there, and, amidst the roar of cannon, heard the chaplain, the Rev. Mr. Brudenell, read the solemn service for the dead—"Earth to earth, and dust to dust." Darkness came on. Dark clouds rolled up from the east, and the rain began to fall. Although the tempest was raging, Burgoyne's army was on the march. At Crown Point he had said, "His army must not retreat"; but now, in the darkness and storm, it was on its way back to Fort Edward. All was confusion. The road was muddy. In the darkness men tumbled headlong to the ground. Teams broke down, or else were stalled in the mud. The Baroness Reidesel and her children, and all the wives of the officers, were out in the storm. These ladies, who had lived delicately all their lives at home, through the long and dreary night were exposed to the chilling wind and the driving rain, making hardly half a mile an hour, so crowded the road, so deep the mud, so great the confusion.

General Burgoyne halted at six o'clock in the morning. He might have gone farther, but he was on his old camp-ground, the first he had occupied after crossing the Hudson.

"Why doesn't General Burgoyne go on?" asked the Baroness Reidesel.

"He is tired, and means to halt here till night and give us a supper," said General Phillips, who was out of patience with Burgoyne.

And a grand supper General Burgoyne gave to his officers. The wife of one of the officers of the commissary department, who was no better than she should be, sat by his side at the table, and drank champagne with him, and the officers clinked their glasses, and laughed and sung songs, while the poor wounded soldiers were lying half starved under the trees and fences, and the good Madame Reidesel was making them broth.

General Burgoyne had ordered the soldiers to set fire to General Schuyler's house and mill near his encampment, and the houses of all the Whigs, thus doing by the torch what damage he could not with the sword.

General Burgoyne made an excuse for halting—because the boats in the river, containing his provisions, could not make headway against the stream as fast as the army marched. The roads were so muddy that the Americans did not begin the pursuit till four o'clock in the afternoon of the 10th. On the morning of the 11th Burgoyne found that they were upon him, and had captured some of the boats in the river. He was going to retreat along the same road down which he had come from Fort Edward, but General Fellows was in possession of it. Then he resolved to march up the west side of the Hudson, and cross the river opposite Fort Edward; but General Stark had sent Colonel Cochran to take possession of that point.

General Fellows, on the east side of the Hudson, was sending cannon-balls into Burgoyne's camp once more. There was no place of safety for the sick and wounded, or the women and children. The Baroness Reidesel and several women, with a number of wounded officers, had to take refuge in the cellar of a house, and remain there day after day, holding their breath in terror as the cannon-balls crashed through the house.

Although they were close to the river, they could get no water, except what a courageous woman brought to them. The American soldiers in the woods on the east bank of the river would not fire upon her.

On the afternoon of the 12th, Burgoyne held a council of his officers, and it was decided to make a rapid retreat to Ticonderoga—to cut their way through the Americans at Fort Edward; but scouts said it was impossible to retreat. The Americans had broken down all the bridges, and held the road.

On the morning of the 13th, Burgoyne called another council. The officers met in a large tent. Pretty soon musket-balls began to cut through the canvas. General Burgoyne was seated at a table, asking the officers what was to be done. Just then General Fellows sent an eighteen-pound cannon-shot into the tent and across the table, which set the officers thinking that something must be done very quickly.

"Shall we negotiate with General Gates?" Burgoyne asked. The cannon-ball was a powerful argument in favor of such a proposition. A drummer with a white flag went out toward the American lines, and the riflemen stopped firing. An American officer advanced to meet him, and so negotiations began for a surrender of the British army on the 17th.

But a faint gleam of hope came to Burgoyne. On the night of the 16th, a messenger from Sir Henry Clinton worked his way past General Gates's sentinel, and reached Burgoyne. He had been several days on his journey; but Tories had helped him on. He had traveled up the east side of the Hudson, and brought joyful news. Sir Henry had taken the forts on the Hudson, and had sent General Vaughan as far up as the town of Esopus. Burgoyne called his officers together once more.

"Will it be honorable," he asked, "to break off negotiations now?"

General Reidesel, General Hamilton, and several other officers, said it would not be honorable. Burgoyne thought differently. But the Americans knew what had taken place on the Hudson, and a messenger arrived from Gates with a note. The American army was drawn up in order of battle; and if the surrender was not carried out in order as agreed upon, the contest would be renewed at once. Burgoyne signed the papers, and his army marched into a field by the river, laid their arms upon the ground, and emptied their cartridge-boxes.

General Burgoyne and his officers, in their rich uniforms, rode along the bank of the river toward the American camp. General Gates came out to meet him, with the officers of his staff. Colonel Wilkinson introduced them.

"The fortune of war has made me your prisoner," said Burgoyne, raising his hat.

"I shall always be ready to bear testimony that it has not been through any fault of your excellency," Gates replied; and then the whole party rode to Gates's quarters, and had a good dinner. In the afternoon, the American army was drawn up in two lines on the interval near the river—one brigade behind another—reaching more than a mile, and several ranks deep.

Nicholas heard the fifes and drums playing "Yankee Doodle"; then he saw two officers on horseback—one carrying the Stars and Stripes; then came a company of American cavalry; and then the captive army, the British light-infantry in front. No guns in their hands now. It was a sorrowful procession. They had come to conquer, but were conquered. Five thousand seven hundred and ninety-one marched past. They had left behind forty-two cannon, and nearly five thousand muskets. Nicholas stood near General Gates's tent. He saw General Gates and General Burgoyne standing there—Burgoyne, large and stout, wearing his rich uniform covered with gold lace. Gates was small, and had on a blue frock. He saw General Burgoyne hand his sword to Gates, who took it, held it a moment, and then returned it.

So the grand army which was to divide New England from the other colonies—which, in the flush of success at Ticonderoga, Burgoyne thought could march to Boston—was on its way there to the tune of "Yankee Doodle," but not as victor.

Nicholas beheld it with joy; and then the thought came—"Oh that Dodifer were here to see it!"—he who had fought so nobly and given his life to his country. But the brave boy was at rest forever, on the hills of Saratoga—his battles ended, his victory won!

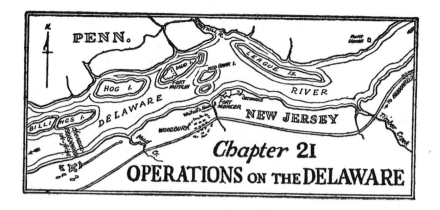

Chapter 21
OPERATIONS ON THE DELAWARE

THE shores of the Delaware River below the junction of the Schuylkill are low and marshy. The wild ducks build their nests in the reeds along the shores and upon the islands. There are Hog Island, Mud Island, and Billings Island.

The Americans had a fleet of vessels in the river; but, in addition, to keep the British fleet from getting up to the city, they placed a line of obstructions from the Pennsylvania to the New Jersey shore. On Mud Island they erected a fort, named Fort Mifflin; and on the New Jersey shore was another fortification, at Red Bank, named after General Mercer, who was killed at Princeton. On the New Jersey shore, opposite the *chevaux-de-frise* which had been placed in the river, the Americans began to throw up another fort.

General Washington hoped that General Howe, although in possession of Philadelphia, would not be able to take these forts. If they could be maintained, General Howe would find it a difficult thing to stay in Philadelphia—so far away from his ships and supplies.

The fleet, under Admiral Howe, sailed down the Chesapeake, came up the Delaware, and was ready to co-operate with the army.

General Howe sent Colonel Stirling, with two regiments, to capture the unfinished fortification (K in the plan). They marched down from Chester, and crossed the river in boats below Billings Island. There were only a few Americans in the unfinished work. When they saw the British advancing they spiked their guns, set fire to their barracks, and fled up the river to the fort at Red Bank. Colonel Stirling completed the destruction of the works, helped the fleet open a passage through the *chevaux-de-frise*, and returned.

Six small vessels sailed through the opening in the *chevaux-de-frise*. The fleet could have sailed up to Philadelphia if it had not been for the fort at Red Bank, which would be able to riddle any vessel that might attempt to pass it. That must be taken. General Howe sent Count Donop, a brave young Hessian officer, with two thousand five hundred picked Hessians, to capture it. The Hessians crossed the Delaware at Philadelphia, and marched down the New Jersey side to Haddonfield on the evening of October 21st.

The next morning Count Donop started for Fort Mercer. With his brave soldiers he would have no difficulty in capturing it, which, though it had an embankment on the river-side, was very weak landward. Colonel Christopher Greene, of Rhode Island, who had marched through the wilderness of Maine to Canada with Arnold, held the fort with four hundred Rhode Island troops. Early in the morning of the 22d, Count Donop came to Timber Creek, a little stream that empties into the Delaware above Fort Mercer, but found that the Americans had taken up the bridge, and that he must march four miles up the brook before he could ford it. It was a long and tiresome march—eight miles out of the way—and it gave Colonel Greene time to make all preparations possible. He had fourteen cannon mounted in the fort, but most of them had been placed in position to fire at the ships, and he had to change some of them to the landward side. His men worked with a will, and were ready for the Hessians.

It was afternoon when Donop reached Red Bank. He formed his men in line of battle in a piece of woods, but, before beginning the attack, sent an officer and a drummer with a white flag toward the fort. Colonel Greene sent out an officer to see what was wanted.

"The King of England orders his rebellious subjects to lay down their arms. They are warned that if they stand battle, no quarter will be given." The officer came into the fort with the message.

"Say to him that we ask no quarter, nor will we give any. We shall defend the fort or make it our tomb," was Colonel Greene's quiet but determined reply.

The Hessian officer returned to Count Donop. The British fleet in the river came up stream, and began a furious cannonade. But the shot buried themselves in the mud or flew harmlessly over the works.

Count Donop brought up his cannon, formed his men, and moved to the attack. It was nearly night, and he expected to be in possession of the fort before dark. He sent half of his men to attack on the north side, while he, with the rest, approached from the south. The fort consisted of two parts, the main fort and the outworks. The latter were unfinished; they were weak, and could not be defended. The main fort was stronger, and Colonel Greene wisely determined not to attempt to hold the outworks.

South of the fort a short distance was a brick house with "I. A. W. 1748" on one of the gables, the initials standing for James and Anna Whitall. The house had been built twenty-nine years. Mr. Whitall lived there with his wife and family. He was a Quaker, and a good Whig. Seeing that the battle was about to begin, he and his wife left the house; but his mother, an old lady, would not leave.

"God will take care of me," she said.

The Hessians, attacking on the north, after keeping up a lively cannonade for half an hour, advanced. At the same time, the British ships began to bombard the fort more furiously. From the north and the south the shot were falling into the fort.

The Hessians charged upon the outer works, but were surprised to find no one there. They set up a shout, as if they had already won the victory. There was no ditch between the main fort and the earth-works, and they imagined it would be an easy matter to rush up the bank and plant their flag upon it. They could not see any Americans. What had become of the men who had just said that they neither asked for nor gave quarter? Not one was in sight. Were they hiding, panic-stricken by the bombardment? With a shout, they rushed forward. Suddenly the fort was all ablaze. From embrasure and rampart there burst out a flame and a storm of iron hail and leaden rain that swept them down in an instant. They could not stand before it. All who could get away fled in consternation from the spot.

While this is going on, Count Donop is advancing from Mr. Whitall's house. The cannon of the fleet are sending a storm of solid shot and bombs into the fort. Suddenly the cannonade ceases, for the Hessians are about to leap over the ramparts. They rush bravely up; but now that side of the fort is all aflame. Count Donop falls, and his next in command, Colonel Mingerode. The Hessians are brave; they climb on their hands and knees up the embankment, fire into the faces of the Americans, who, in turn, the next instant blow out the brains of their assailants. The Rhode Island men have piles of grenades—hand-bombs—which they set on fire and toss over the embankment, which explode among the Hessians, who have lost their brave leader. He is lying, mortally wounded, at the bottom of the ditch. There is no one to inspirit them. They lose courage. The fire is growing hotter. More murderous the storm. A moment, and they are fleeing past Whitall's house, disorganized, panic-stricken—running in terror to Haddonfield.

It was five o'clock when the attack began, and it is not yet six, but the battle is over. The last rays of the setting sun fall upon the Stars and Stripes, still proudly floating above the ramparts; while below, heaped one upon another, are four hundred Hessians, killed or wounded. Inside the fort are eight dead and twenty-nine wounded, and nearly half of these casualties occurred through the bursting of a cannon. The Hes-

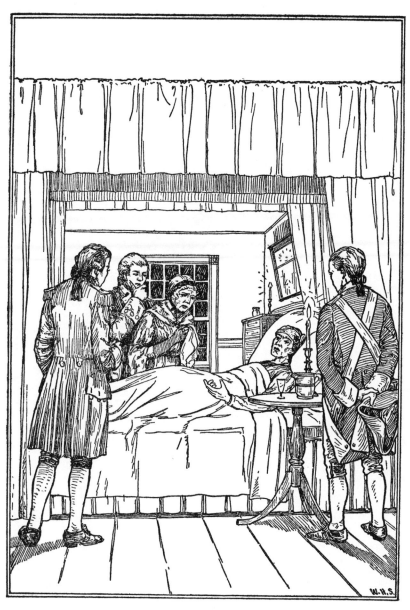

"I DIE A VICTIM TO AMBITION AND THE AVARICE OF MY
SOVEREIGN."

255

sians were so panic-stricken that they left their leader lying at the foot of the embankment.

In the evening twilight, Colonel Manduit, the French engineer, who had laid out the works, and who assisted in defending them, was out amidst the wounded. He heard a voice among the slain:

"Please take me out."

It was Count Donop. The kind-hearted Frenchman hastened to help him, conveyed him to Mr. Whitall's house, and kindly cared for him; but his wound was mortal. "I die a victim to ambition and the avarice of my sovereign," he said; and he might have added that he was slain through the incapacity of Lord North and the stubbornness of the king.

It was a terrible defeat to General Howe. Four hundred men lost, and nothing gained, and the fleet as far from Philadelphia as ever. The country rang with the praises of Colonel Greene and the brave men who had inflicted so signal a defeat upon the enemy.

Colonel Greene was greatly assisted by Commodore Hazlewood, with a fleet of small vessels in the river. He had more than twenty of all kinds—galleys, floating batteries, one brig, besides fourteen old vessels fitted up as fire-ships, with tarbarrels on board, which he could set on fire, and which would float down with the tide against the British fleet. Commodore Hazlewood had about one hundred cannon, and he kept up a hot fire upon the British fleet.

Two days later, in the morning, the British ships made an attack on Fort Mifflin. The *Augusta*, with sixty-four guns; the *Roebuck*, with forty-four; two frigates; the *Merlin*, with eighteen guns; and a galley, came up the river and opened a furious cannonade. Lieutenant-colonel Smith, of Lancaster, Pennsylvania, was in the fort, commanding the garrison. His men, from Colonel Lamb's artillery regiment, worked the guns vigorously. Commodore Hazlewood dropped down with his fleet, and the fort and fleet together made it hot for the British.

Colonel Smith sent a red-hot shot at the sixty-four-gun ship, the *Augusta*, which struck the hull, and in a very short time the ship was in flames. She was on a mud-bank, and could not get away. The fire worked its way into the seams of the ship. The sailors tried in vain to put it out. They fled to their boats, and about noon the ship blew up with a tremendous explosion. The British did not like to give up the contest, and the fight went on from one till two, from two till three in the afternoon. The *Merlin* was lying near the mouth of Mud Creek. The gunner sent a red-hot shot which struck into the side of that ship, and set it on fire, and there was another explosion. The *Roebuck*, whose commander feared that she might be served in the same way, and the other ships, dropped down the river. So in an afternoon the king had lost two fine ships.

General Howe was chagrined. There he was in Philadelphia with a great army, and yet two garrisons of less than twelve hundred men, with the fleet of Commodore Hazlewood, had prevented the ships from coming up to the city. He must take Fort Mifflin, on Mud Island, and Fort Mercer at Red Bank, or he would be compelled to abandon Philadelphia. He adopted a new plan. He saw that Fort Mifflin, on the side toward Carpenter's Island, was very weak. There were no cannon mounted to sweep that island, and he sent an expedition in the night to take possession of it. The troops met with no opposition, and in a few days he had five batteries erected, with some of the heaviest cannon of the fleet mounted. He brought up a floating-battery mounting twenty-two guns, and anchored it south-west of the fort near Hog Island, within fifteen hundred feet of the fort. Two sixty-four-gun ships and two forty-gun ships came up to take part in the bombardment. All told, the British had between two hundred and fifty and three hundred cannon, besides mortars, to rain a storm of shot and shell upon the little fort.

Every thing is ready on the part of the British. The ships advance, and the batteries on the shore open fire. All through the day the cannonade goes on, ships and batteries firing rapidly, the cannon of the fort replying slowly. Lieutenant Treat, commanding the artillery, is killed by the bursting of a bomb. The barracks are knocked to pieces. Till late into the night the fire is kept up.

At day-break the next morning the ships and batteries open once more. The shot fall thick and fast without the inclosure. Colonel Smith sits down in the barracks to write a letter to General Varnum, who is on the New Jersey shore: a shot passes through the chimney, scattering the bricks in every direction, and knocking him senseless. Lieutenant-colonel Russell, of Connecticut, takes command; and Colonel Smith, with other wounded, is taken in a boat across the river to Red Bank. Faster rain the bombs, more vigorously than ever the British sailors work the guns. From day-break till midnight, the cannonade goes on. The palisades around the fort are knocked to pieces. A cannon-shot comes through an embrasure and dismounts a gun, killing the gunner. Lieutenant-colonel Russell is worn out, and Major Thayer, of Rhode Island, assumes command. There is very little rest for the three hundred men under Major Thayer. The firing goes on till midnight, and the British only stop from weariness.

On the 12th, the ships, at day-break, open fire once more. The top of the fort is plowed through and through by solid shot. The bombs, which bury themselves in the embankment, blow out cart-loads of earth. Two more guns are disabled, the laboratory blows up, and the block-house at the north-west corner of the fort is knocked to pieces.

The hard blows are not all on one side. Major Thayer sends his shot with unerring aim into the fleet, splintering masts and spars. They crash through the sides of the vessels and make fearful havoc among the crews.

The morning dawns once more, and the Americans discover the floating-battery close to the fort. During the night, with the incoming tide, the British have come to fight at close quarters. The thirty-two pounders open. They are so near that the shot pass through the embankment. But the shot from the fort tell with greater effect upon the battery. Its thick timbered sides are smashed in, and before noon there is very little left of it—every gun is silenced.

The hard-worked men in the fort are worn out. Soldiers drop asleep beside the guns while the bombs are bursting around them. Unless relieved, they can not hold out much longer. They have boats in which, if need be, they can retreat in the night up the river to the fleet, or across to Red Bank. They will not give in, however, just yet.

A Soldier Steals from the Fort, Jumps into a Boat, Makes His Way to the Fleet, and Informs the British.

The British are nearly in despair, and are thinking of abandoning the siege. There is a traitor in the garrison. A soldier who, perhaps, has had enough fighting, steals out from the fort, jumps into a boat, makes his way to the fleet, and informs the British that Major Thayer is just ready to abandon the fort. It revives the drooping spirits of the British. Orders are sent to the ships to come to close quarters in the morning. The admiral will knock the fort level with the ground, or sink his ships in the attempt.

The sun rises, and the hard-worked soldiers in the fort see that preparations are making for a terrific assault. They behold the *Somerset*, the sixty-four-gun ship which, at day-break on the 17th of June, 1775, began a cannonade upon Bunker Hill, and the *Iris*, carrying sixty-four guns, coming up close to the fort to attack in front.

The *Vigilant*, with twenty twenty-four-pounders, and an old vessel with three guns, work their way up west of the fort, and take position where they can not be harmed by any of its guns. The ships do not get into position till ten o'clock. Then at a signal, the fire begins. From all sides, except the north, the storm is poured upon the fort. The ships are so near that the men in the rigging can pick off the gunners the moment they attempt to load a gun. The cannon, one after another, are dismounted, the carriages knocked to pieces. By noon all the cannon, except two, are disabled. There is not a safe place in the fort. Many are killed, and more wounded; but Major Thayer will not raise the white flag. All day long the storm rages. The block-houses are knocked to pieces, the palisades all leveled, the embrasures torn away, and yet the brave little band will not surrender.

Night shuts down upon the scene; but there is no diminution of the storm. The deep roar of the cannonade goes on. In the darkness Major Thayer places his wounded in the boats. Among them is Captain Talbot, with a wound in the hip, another in his wrist; but, though wounded, he has kept on cheering the men. The boats push off in the darkness, and make their way to Red Bank. Major Thayer and forty men remain till midnight. It is useless to remain longer. He will leave the spot; but he will leave in triumph. A train is laid, the match applied, and while it is burning the heroic defenders glide away in the boats, and while the rowers are pulling at the oars, the flames break out, licking up every thing that can burn about the fort. Nearly two hundred and fifty have been killed and wounded in the defense, and more than that number have fallen on board the ships.

There still remained Fort Mercer. Colonel Greene and his brave men were still there. General Howe sent Cornwallis, with two thousand men, to attack it in conjunction with the fleet. Cornwallis crossed the river from the west side below the fort, and came to the little village of Woodbury. General Washington sent General Greene across the Delaware above Philadelphia, at Burlington, with Lafayette; but Greene had a small force, and could not think it prudent to risk a battle, and on the 20th of November, seeing that he was about to be attacked, and that there was little hope of holding the fort, now that Fort Mifflin had fallen, he evacuated it, and so saved the garrison. A few of the small vessels of Commodore Hazlewood's fleet crept up past Philadelphia in the darkness, while all the others were set on fire to prevent their falling into the hands of the British.

It was a gloomy day, that 21st of November, to the little army under Washington. Philadelphia was in the possession of the British, the river was open, the forts and fleet destroyed. General Howe had a great army, and Washington was powerless to resist him.

ENERAL HOWE was quite well satisfied with what he had done. He had defeated Washington at Brandywine, repulsed him at Germantown, taken the forts on the Delaware, and was in possession of Philadelphia. Re-enforcements were on their way from England, his army was in good condition, while Washington's was growing weaker. Many of the citizens of Philadelphia had welcomed him with open arms as their deliverer, while the farmers of the surrounding country hailed him with favor, for he had British gold, which he was ready to pay for their garden-sauce, butter, cheese, eggs, cattle, and horses.

The money issued by Congress, made of paper, was poor stuff. It was only a promise to pay, and the promise was not worth much. The money was so poor that one hundred dollars would hardly buy a pair of boots. A good coat would cost five hundred dollars. Poor as the money was, Congress had not paid the soldiers in the army; and General Howe was confident, now that he was in possession of the largest two cities in America, that the rebellion would soon die out.

General Howe moved the army from Germantown down to the outskirts of Philadelphia, where the supplies could be delivered directly from the ships. He established his head-quarters on High Street, one door from the corner of Sixth Street. He was kind to the poor people in the city, allowing them to go out past the pickets to get flour at the old mill in Frankford.

General Washington was still at Whitemarsh, where he had encamped after the battle of Germantown. His army was growing weaker day by day. What to do he did not know. He could not attack Howe in Philadelphia. Where should he go, or what do? He had little to eat. His soldiers had no blankets. Some were almost naked. Many had no shoes. Winter was close at hand, and the time of many of the soldiers was expiring. Yet still he waited, hoping that Howe would make some movement.

General Howe resolved to make a movement. He saw that Washington was growing weaker; he would strike one more blow, and finish the war. He would make a night march, fall upon Washington like a thunder-bolt, and scatter the Americans to the winds, or perhaps capture the entire army. None but his most trustworthy officers should know of the movement.

General Howe's adjutant-general was quartered at Mr. Darrah's house, on South Second Street. It was a long brick building, with a balcony over the lower story. Mr. Darrah was a Quaker, but he was a Whig, and had a noble wife—Lydia.

"Lydia," said the British adjutant-general, one day, "I expect some friends here to-night, and I want the upper back-room made ready. And, one thing more, Lydia, be sure to have all the folks in the house early to bed."

"It shall be as thee dost desire," said Lydia.

In the evening, General Howe and several of his officers came to the house. The servants were all in bed. Lydia admitted the gentlemen.

"You can go to bed now, Lydia, and lie till I call," said the adjutant-general.

Lydia went to her room, lay down without undressing, but not to sleep. What were the officers there for? Why so much secrecy? An irresistible impulse seizes her to know what is going on. In her stockings, she glides noiselessly to the door of the chamber, bends her ear to the keyhole, and hears the adjutant-general read an order which General Howe has written:

IN HER STOCKINGS SHE GLIDES NOISELESSLY TO THE DOOR OF THE
CHAMBER.

"To-morrow night the army will make a secret march to surprise and capture the American army."

Back to her room she glides. An hour passes. The officers are ready to leave, and the adjutant-general knocks on her door. She is not asleep, but all her senses are awake as never before. She makes no answer. Another rap—still no answer. A thumping now—she is sleeping soundly, the adjutant-general thinks. She awakes. She will be out in a moment. She arises, waits a little while, then appears in the hall, to open the street-door for General Howe and his officers. She goes back to bed; but all night long she is thinking, and praying that God will aid her in what she is about to do.

Lydia wanted some flour. She rode on horseback in the morning to General Howe's head-quarters, and obtained a pass to go to the old mill in Frankford. It was five miles to the mill; but while the grist was grinding, she had time to ride beyond it toward Whitemarsh. She rode till stopped by an American sentinel. Major Craig was in command of the pickets. Lydia called him aside, whispered a few words in his ear, and rode back, took her grist, and returned to Philadelphia.

Night comes. The British army is astir, marching secretly, but rapidly northward. Just before day-break, the American pickets, who have been charged to be on the watch, discover the British approaching. Word runs down the line, but General Washington is ready. The army is under arms and in line of battle.

General Howe forms his line, but is surprised to find Washington prepared for him, with his army so advantageously posted that he does not dare to attack. He must change his plan. He marches, counter-marches; there is some skirmishing; but Howe does not think it prudent to bring on a battle. Back to the city march the British. The adjutant-general rides to his quarters.

"Lydia, I would like to see you in my room," he says to the true-hearted woman. "Lydia, were any of your family up on the night that I received some company?"

"Nay, they were all in bed at eight o'clock."

"Strange, very strange. You, I know, were asleep, Lydia; for I knocked three times at your door before I could wake you; yet it is certain we were betrayed. I am at a loss to think who could have given information to Washington of our intended movement. We found him drawn up in line of battle, and, like a pack of fools, we had to march back again."

Foiled in his effort to surprise Washington, General Howe settled down in Philadelphia for the winter, while Washington, with his army dwindling every day, looked around to find winter-quarters. Pitiable the condition of the troops—shoeless, and almost naked.

"I will give ten dollars to the man who will get up the best shoe out of a raw hide," was the offer of Washington. He could not get shoes, and the soldiers took the hides of the cattle killed for beef and made moccasins of them.

Valley Forge was the place selected for winter-quarters, and thither the army marched. What an uneasy march it was through the snow by the barefooted, ragged men! All the way there were blood-stains. They had to ford the river on that wintry day; and when they reached the place selected for the encampment, they had to sleep on the frozen ground till they could build huts. They had few axes, but in a very short time each brigade had its cluster of houses. Each brigade was a village by itself, laid out in streets, each house sheltering sixteen men. They built fireplaces and bunks and ovens. Besides their houses, they had to build intrenchments and forts, guarding against a surprise from the British.

The camp was on the west bank of the Schuylkill. It was a strong position—so strong that General Howe did not care to make an attack upon it. General Knox had his cannon planted to sweep all the approaches. The snow was deep. Very little provision could be had, and less clothing. Congress had no supplies, the soldiers no money; Congress failed to pay them; starvation stared them in the face. Oh, the dreary days of that terrible winter!

"For some days past there has been little less than a famine in the camp," wrote Washington on the 16th of February. "Some of the men have not had any meat for a week."

Sickness broke out, and the men began to die. They could get no hay for the artillery horses. The people in the vicinity were Tories, who carried every thing they had to sell to P h i l a d e l- phia, where they could obtain gold. There were men in Congress, and officers in the coun- try, who were do- ing what t h e y could to degrade Washington from t h e command. Gloomy the days! But amidst the gloom the great man commanding the army n e v e r faltered, nor did General Greene, nor Sullivan, nor Wayne; not one among the officers, nor among the sol- diers. They were starving, but they would be free.

Baron Steuben Instructs the Troops at Valley Forge.

A brave man came into the camp, an officer from Prussia, Baron Steuben. He had come across the ocean to aid the Americans, and Con- gress made him inspector-general. The troops were undisci- plined, and so were the officers. They knew nothing of mili- tary drill, but under the instruction of this noble man they quickly learned how to handle their guns, how to wheel, and march, and change front. He was sharp and strict, but was as kind-hearted as a child, and the soldiers loved him. Starving, almost naked, yet learning how to fight. So the winter passed away, General Howe never once molesting them.

The people of England were dissatisfied with the way things were going on in America. General Howe was commander-in-chief, and his brother, Admiral Richard Howe, was in command of the fleet. The winter had passed, and General Howe had been spending his time in Philadelphia, with a great army quartered there. He had made no effort to molest Washington, with his handful of starving and almost naked troops at Valley Forge, only twenty miles away. In the autumn he had turned away from helping Burgoyne—had won a victory at Brandywine, but had been all but defeated at Germantown. He had declined a battle at Goshen, had marched out to White-marsh to surprise Washington, but had returned, not daring to make an attack. He had spent the winter in dissipation at Philadelphia, the army doing nothing.

There was so much dissatisfaction with General Howe in England that he resigned, and Sir Henry Clinton was appointed commander-in-chief. General Howe was to sail on the 19th of May, and his officers got up a grand entertainment in his honor.

Weeks were spent in making preparations. It was held on the 18th of May. First there was a procession of boats on the river. All of the boats belonging to the fleet were gayly decorated with flags, and filled with the officers of the navy and army and ladies. Bands of music played, and salutes were fired as the procession moved down the river from Mr. Knight's wharf to Mr. Wharton's house, where upon the lawn in front of it triumphal arches and spacious pavilions had been erected.

The officers landed, the grenadiers and light-infantry were drawn up to receive them, and they marched beneath the triumphal arches to the lawn, where a tournament was to be held. Two small pavilions had been erected for the tournament. On the front seats of each were seven young ladies, dressed in Turkish costume, wearing turbans, and exhibiting the favors which they intended to bestow upon the gallant knights who were to enter the lists in their behalf.

Now was heard the blowing of trumpets, and a company of knights dressed in the costume of the days of chivalry, in white and red, mounted on horses gayly caparisoned, accompanied by their squires, came down the avenue. In advance of them came a herald, with two roses on the lapel of his tunic, with the motto, *"We droop when separated."*

Then came Lord Cathcart upon a powerful horse. He was chief of the knights. Two negro slaves wearing white breeches and blue sashes, with large silver clasps around their necks, held his stirrups. On his right hand walked his two esquires, one bearing his lance and the other his shield, with a device of Cupid riding a lion, and upon it the motto, *Surmounted by Love.* The "Knights of the Blended

Then Came Lord Cathcart upon a Powerful Horse.

Rose," and the "Knights of the Burning Mountain," with their esquires, all in gorgeous costume, made their appearance, riding in front of the pavilions, wheeling, curveting, throwing down their gloves, riding at each other full tilt, firing their pistols, flourishing their swords, and doing a great deal of foolery.

When the tournament was over, they dismounted, and escorted the ladies into the great pavilions, and had lunch, tea, and liquors; and the knights kneeled before the ladies, and received their favors. From the pavilions they went into the great dancing-hall, which had been erected, and gayly painted and decorated, for the occasion.

The officers had been through the city, and called upon the citizens to lend their mirrors to add to the display, and had obtained eighty-five, which were placed around the room in a way to reflect and re-reflect its bewildering scenery. Leading from the hall were side rooms where the dancers could obtain refreshments. The bands came in and took their places, and the dancing began, and was kept up till ten o'clock, when there was a magnificent display of fire-works in front of the house, and all Philadelphia was there to witness it. At midnight supper was announced.

Suddenly one side of the ball-room opened, and the amazed dancers perceived that what they had supposed to be a blank wall was a series of folding-doors, which had been concealed. They saw before them a magnificent saloon, two hundred and ten feet long, forty wide, and twenty-two high, with alcoves for sideboards. The ceiling was carved, and painted a light stone-color, with vine-leaves and festoons of flowers. Fifty-six pier-glasses reflected the scene, all superbly decorated with flowers. There were eighteen chandeliers, with twenty-four lights each, suspended from the ceiling, and one hundred branches, or side lights, with three candles in each. There were four hundred and thirty plates laid. Twenty-four black slaves, in Oriental costume, with silver collars on their necks, bent low, almost touching their heads to the floor, as General Howe and the other officers entered. Toward the end of supper the herald of the Blended Rose, with his trumpeters, came into the hall and proclaimed the toasts—the king's health, the queen's, the royal family, the army, the navy, the knights, and the ladies—the bands playing, and the company draining their wine-glasses at each toast.

After supper, those who cared to dance went back to the ball-room, while those who preferred to play cards retired to the pavilions, and played till morning, betting high, and some of them getting so drunk that their servants had to carry them to bed. The next day General Howe sailed for England, leaving Sir Henry Clinton in command.

Chapter 23~STONY POINT

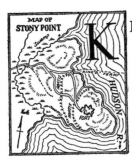

KING'S FERRY was the place where troops and provisions were taken across the Hudson, a line of communication of great value to General Washington. General Clinton thought that he could strike a damaging blow by securing it. The ferry was from Verplanck's Point, a rocky headland on the east side, to Stony Point on the west side. At Verplanck's stood Fort Lafayette, guarded by seventy men. Stony Point, another small fortification, was guarded by twenty men.

On the night of May 31st, 1779, Sir Henry Clinton sailed up the Hudson with several ships of war and a large force. He sent General Vaughan with troops to the east shore. Both started at midnight, Clinton to take Stony Point, Vaughan to take Fort Lafayette. The twenty men at Stony Point discovered Clinton's approach, and fled. Sir Henry took possession of the fort, turned its guns upon Lafayette, and the seventy men had to surrender, for General Vaughan had cut off their retreat.

Having captured the forts, Clinton set his soldiers to work to make Stony Point a formidable fortress, which was not a difficult matter, for the Point was a rocky hill projecting into the river, with a marsh behind, over which the tide flowed, and which was crossed by a causeway and bridge. Two lines of abatis were built between the fort and the marsh, which was nearly half a mile from the fort, while the fort itself was a strong work, large enough to require a garrison of seven hundred men, with cannon mounted to defend it on all sides.

274

All communication between New England and the other colonies now was at West Point or above, which was a great inconvenience to Washington, who wished, if possible, to gain possession of King's Ferry once more. But he had no troops to spare to make a regular attack. If captured at all, it must be by a surprise. There was one general in the army who was well fitted to attempt the capture of Stony Point by such a movement—the general who, when a school-boy, was always building forts, and marshaling his playmates, neglecting his studies until his good old uncle, who was educating him, gave up in despair of his ever being a scholar. This was General Wayne—"Mad Anthony," the soldiers called him, because he was terribly in earnest about what he undertook.

General Washington met General Wayne at Sandy Beach, fourteen miles from Stony Point, to talk over the matter. Wayne was ready to undertake such an enterprise.

"I'll storm hell, general, if you will only plan it," said Wayne.

"Hadn't we better try Stony Point first?" Washington replied.

This was the plan: To make a night march; the men, with their muskets unloaded, to cross the marsh at low tide; a party in advance with axes to clear away the abatis; the soldiers to wear white cockades, to distinguish each other in the darkness, and rush, with fixed bayonets, into the fort.

General Wayne and Colonel Febiger reconnoitred the fort. A deserter informed General Wayne in regard to its construction, and how the cannon were placed. General Wayne selected his troops, and thought out his plan of attack, but kept his plan to himself, and sent out small parties to guard all the roads, and prevent any one from giving information to the British of any movement he might make.

The fort was a series of redoubts on the summit of Stony Point and an abatis, which extended across the Point a little distance from the marsh. There was a second abatis, extending nearly across the Point, strengthened by three redoubts, in which there were brass twelve-pounders.

At twelve o'clock on the 15th of July, a hot summer day, General Wayne starts with his troops, three regiments of Continental light-infantry—one under Colonel Butler, one under Colonel Febiger, and one under Colonel Meigs—also a battalion of Massachusetts troops, under Major Hull, and two companies of North Carolina troops, under Major Murfey; also some artillerymen, to work the cannon in the fort, if he succeeds in taking it. He moves along narrow roads—so narrow and rocky and uneven that the men march some of the way in single file. The sun goes down, and the twilight comes on. At eight o'clock, the head of the column is at Mr. Springsteel's, a mile and a half from the fort. No

He Orders Each Soldier to Pin a Piece of White Paper to His Hat.

man is allowed to speak. In silence the men march, in silence they come into line, throw themselves upon the ground, and eat their supper of bread and cold meat.

General Wayne forms his men into two columns. The right column contains Febiger's and Meigs's regiment and Major Hull's battalion. Colonel Butler's and Major Murfey's troops compose the other. General Wayne will command the right, and Colonel Butler the left. He places one hundred and fifty men in advance of his column, under Lieutenant-colonel Fleury; and in advance of them twenty pioneers, under Lieutenant Knox; and in front of the other, one hundred men, under Major Stewart; and twenty pioneers, under Lieutenant Gibbon. The men do not know what they are to do. Up to this time, Wayne has kept the plan to himself and his chief officers. He orders each soldier to pin a piece of white paper to his hat. They will be able by that to distinguish friend from foe.

"We are going to attack the fort," he said; "and the first man inside of it shall have five hundred dollars, and immediate promotion; the second, four hundred; the third, three hundred; the fourth, two hundred; the fifth, one hundred. If any of you are so lost to the sense of honor as to attempt to retreat or skulk, any officer is authorized to put you to death. I shall share the dangers with you. This is the watch-word, '*The fort is our own.*'"

Till half-past eleven the men rest; and the brave general, having matured all his plans, writes a letter to a friend in Philadelphia, asking him to take care of his young children if he falls in the assault. This done, the columns, in silence, move toward the fort. They come to the marsh. General Wayne moves to the right, and Butler to the left. The tide has not wholly ebbed, and the water is two feet deep on the marsh.

A picket stands at the top of the hill south of the bridge. Two men approach him stealthily, and before he can give an alarm he is a prisoner. The columns divide—Wayne going down the hill toward the marsh near the river, and Butler toward the bridge. The men enter the water. A picket on the side toward the fort hears them, fires his gun, and gives the alarm. The sentinels in the fort hear it, and the drums beat; the British officers and soldiers leap from their barracks and seize their arms.

A moment later, and the cannon are flashing. On through the water, across the miry marsh, to the hill, the troops move with unloaded muskets. The bayonet alone is to win the victory. Up to the abatis rush the pioneers with their axes. Some fall, never more to rise; but the others work on, cutting away the timbers.

They make an opening, and the column, like water pouring through a mill-race, rushes through. A moment, and they are at the second abatis. A few minutes of hard work there, with the bullets falling like hail around them, and the men are streaming through the second opening, and forming to rush upon the batteries. A shot strikes the brave leader—a musket-ball, tearing his scalp and glancing from the skull. He falls, with the warm blood streaming over his face. "Forward! forward! Carry me into the fort; let me die there!" he shouts. On, over rocks and fallen trees, led by Fleury and Febiger, rush the men, to avenge the fall of their leader.

"*The fort is our own!*" Febiger shouts it. "*The fort is our own!*" It goes up from five hundred voices. On over the breastworks, plunging the bayonet into all who resist, like a tornado they sweep, bearing down all before them. Cannon blaze in their faces, but there are no answering guns. Nothing can resist the furious assault. Over on the left, at the same moment, Butler is sweeping over the breastworks. "*The fort is our own!*" is the answering cry, ringing out over the hills.

The British see only an array of dusky forms in the darkness, an army of black shadows pouring into the fort, encircling them on all sides. They fire at the shadows, and the next moment the shadows are trampling them to the earth, and the bayonet is doing its bloody work. "Mercy! mercy! Don't kill us! We surrender! Mercy! mercy!"

Just such a cry went up in the woods of Long Island from American lips, but British ears were deaf to the cry. It was fun to pin the rebels to the earth with the bayonet, to cut and mangle them while they cried for mercy. Shall not the victors have their revenge? Shall they not have the satisfaction of driving home the bayonet and avenging their comrades? No. There is no revenge so sweet and satisfying as mercy. It is the

"CARRY ME INTO THE FORT; LET ME DIE THERE!" HE SHOUTS.

glory of this hour of triumph that the cry is not made in vain. The moment that resistance ceases, the slaughter stops. Let it be remembered forever that there, in the darkness at Stony Point, in the hour of triumph, with the memory of past wrongs rankling in their hearts, the men who are fighting for their liberty heed the cry for mercy. No blood shed in revenge stains their victory.

Fifteen minutes ago the Americans were wading through the water on the marsh; but the fort is their own; and their brave leader, stunned, not killed, is receiving Colonel Johnson's surrender. In these fifteen minutes, fifteen Americans have been killed and eighty wounded; of the British, nineteen have been killed, seventy-two wounded, and four hundred and sixty-seven captured.

At two o'clock in the morning, General Wayne writes this letter to Washington:

"Stony Point, 16th July, 1779. 2 o'clock A.M.
"DEAR GENERAL,—The fort and garrison, with Colonel Johnson, are ours. Our officers and men behaved like men who are determined to be free. Yours most sincerely,   ANT^Y WAYNE.
"GENERAL WASHINGTON."

Morning came, and the artillery-men turned the cannon upon the British vessels, compelling them to slip their cables and drift down stream. Great was the rejoicing over the exploit of "Mad Anthony" and his men.

Chapter 24
MONMOUTH

THE ship which brought Sir Henry Clinton's commission as commander-in-chief also brought an order for him to evacuate Philadelphia, and concentrate his troops at New York. War had been declared between England and France, and it would not be an easy matter to supply the army at Philadelphia, so far inland, with all the French navy afloat upon the sea, and American privateers swarming along the coast, on the watch for supply-ships.

Sir Henry Clinton was a more energetic officer than General Howe, and he began at once to prepare to evacuate Philadelphia; but he had such an amount of baggage, so many shiploads of supplies, that a month passed before he was able to begin his march. The vessels finally were loaded. The officers bade farewell to the ladies with whom they had danced, and were ready for their departure.

General Clinton had about ten thousand men. He gathered up all the horses and wagons he could find, sent out parties to scour the country and bring in all they could lay their hands upon, taking them without offering any pay in return. He collected all the boats of the fleet, and had them moored along the shore below the city. He let it be understood that the army was going by water, thinking thus to deceive Washington, who was still at Valley Forge keeping a keen lookout.

On the 17th of June, General Clinton started. The soldiers

left their barracks, marched down to the river bank, stepped into the boats, and were ferried across to the New Jersey shore —not all, for the Hessians from Anspach had been so long in America that they began to like the country; and Sir Henry was afraid that, if he undertook to march them across New Jersey, they would desert in a body. It was about nine o'clock when the army began to cross; the boats were going from shore to shore all through the night. By nine o'clock on the morning of the 18th, General Clinton was at Haddonfield—five miles from the river. The baggage was there, and General Knyphausen's division was appointed to guard it. The Rangers and Yagers, under General Leslie, were mounted on good horses —the best in the army—and started in advance to scour the country, robbing and plundering the inhabitants. General Clinton started for the Raritan River, where he would embark the troops. He had so many wagons and horses loaded with packs that, with his troops, the column was twelve miles long.

If General Clinton supposed that Washington was all in the dark as to his movements, he was mistaken, for, on the 30th of May, Washington had made all preparations to march to the Hudson the moment General Clinton started. His orders were all written out; the baggage was kept in condition to be packed in a moment.

The army consisted of five divisions. The first was commanded by General Lee, and consisted of Poor's New Hampshire brigade, Varnum's Rhode Islanders, and the Connecticut brigade. The second division was commanded by General Mifflin, and consisted of three brigades, mostly from Pennsylvania. The third was commanded by General Lafayette, and consisted of North Carolina and New York troops. The fourth was commanded by Baron De Kalb, and consisted of Glover's, Paterson's, and Learned's brigades of Massachusetts troops. The fifth was commanded by Lord Stirling, and consisted of Virginia and Maryland troops. There were sixteen brigades, besides the artillery and the cavalry—in all, about ten thousand.

Besides these, there were the troops under General Maxwell, and the New Jersey militia under General Dickinson—about two thousand more. General Washington directed General Maxwell and General Dickinson to break down the bridges on all the streams in advance of Clinton; and these troops were scattered here and there to do what they could to impede his march.

General Washington sent a trusty man—Captain M'Lane—into Philadelphia to ascertain what was going on. He crossed the river with the troops, went through the ranks at Haddonfield, saw the order in which they were to march, then made his way back to the city, and before ten o'clock on the morning of the 18th, while Sir Henry was at Haddonfield, Captain M'Lane was riding into Washington's camp at Valley Forge with the news. Before night the whole army was in motion, leaving the place forever consecrated to liberty by its terrible suffering and patient endurance.

General Greene was quartermaster-general. He had made admirable arrangements to supply the army with food. General Lee had been exchanged for General Prescott, who had been captured in Rhode Island, and was once more in command of his division. General Washington wanted to attack the British at the first favorable opportunity; but General Lee and a majority of the generals thought it better to hover on Clinton's flanks and rear, and cut off his men piecemeal. The army crossed the Delaware, the second and fourth divisions at Coryell's Ferry, above Trenton, and the other divisions at Sherard's Ferry.

General Clinton did not wish to fight a battle except on ground of his own choosing. He found it slow marching along the sandy roads. He soon saw that General Washington would give him trouble if he undertook to march to the Raritan River; for Washington, although he had farther to march, was moving swiftly.

On the 25th of June, Clinton concluded to make a rapid march to Sandy Hook, and turned east for that purpose.

On Saturday, June 27th, Captain Elijah Favor, engineer and aid to General Washington, was riding from division to division, exploring all the roads. General Washington was at Englishtown, six miles west of Monmouth, with Mifflin's, De Kalb's, and Stirling's divisions. Elijah started with an order to General Lee, who was commanding in advance, "to attack the enemy unless there should be powerful reasons to the contrary." He found General Lee halfway between Englishtown and Monmouth Courthouse, encamped near Freehold meeting-house, a wooden building, with a weathercock on the steeple, and old moss-covered gravestones around.

Not far beyond the meeting-house was the parsonage-house, a small, one-storied building, with a steep roof, a chimney at each end, a wellsweep and a barn near by. Beyond

Captain Elijah Favor Was Riding from Division to Division, Exploring All the Roads.

the parsonage was an orchard, and beyond that a swamp. He crossed the swamp on a corduroy road, and came to a hill east of it, where Mr. Wikoff lived. Near Mr. Wikoff's was a hedge-fence. Elijah was accustomed to observe the natural features of the country, and he saw in an instant that a body of men sheltered by such a hedge might make a stout resistance to an enemy in front. South-east from Mr. Wikoff's was Mr. Carr's house, about half a mile distant.

"The British are at the court-house," said Mr. Wikoff.

Elijah rode toward Mr. Carr's house, where he found General Lee's pickets. From Mr. Carr's he could see the Queen's Rangers and some infantry encamped in a field just north of the court-house. He could see that there was a road leading north from the court-house to Amboy, and another leading east toward Middletown and Sandy Hook.

"General Clinton has sent his baggage in advance to Middletown," said Mr. Carr, "and these are only the rear-guard. There are more troops up in that direction," he added, pointing north-east.

Elijah turned north, for he was almost up to the British pickets, and rode through the fields till he came to a road leading from the meeting-house to the Amboy road, rode up that to the Amboy road, where he could see the British grenadiers encamped on the east side of another swamp in a field. Having seen this, he hastened back to the meeting-house, saw Generals Lee and Lafayette, and reported what he had seen.

A little after midnight, Elijah rode from General Washington's headquarters to General Lee's with an order. General Washington wished General Lee to send six or eight hundred men south of the court-house to make an attack upon the British the moment they were ready to move on.

It was Sunday morning. General Lee read the order, looked at his watch, and saw that it was nearly one o'clock. It would be light by three, and the British would begin to move before sunrise.

"I will send Colonel Morgan," said General Lee.

Captain Edwards, Lee's aid, wrote an order to Morgan, directing him to march at once and join General Dickinson, who was south-east of the court-house, and to make an attack as soon as the British started. A few minutes later, Colonel Morgan was on the march.

"The British are getting ready to move," was the word which General Dickinson sent in.

General Lee ordered his troops to leave their packs by the meeting-house, and those who were lame and worn out to guard them. The troops were soon ready to move, but there was no one to guide them. None of the officers knew the ground. Elijah offered to act as guide. With six cavalry-men to act as scouts, the column started up the road leading from the meeting-house to the Amboy road.

Colonel Grayson's Virginia regiment led the column, followed by Colonel Jackson's Massachusetts regiment. Then came Scott's, Varnum's, Wayne's, and Maxwell's brigade, and Colonel Oswald's artillery. Altogether, General Lee had about four thousand men.

The sun had risen. The air was sultry. Not a breath stirred the leaves of the maples. The farmers, knowing that a battle was imminent, had flocked in from the surrounding country to see it, and walked along with the soldiers. There was no beating of drums, for General Lee did not want to let the British know that he was on the march.

Colonel Grayson came to the Amboy road, marched across it, turned north-east, crossed a little brook winding through a swampy piece of ground. They were on the left flank of the British encamped on the plain. Colonel Jackson, General Scott, and General Maxwell followed. General Wayne marched straight across the road to a piece of woods, and was in front of the British.

The pickets were firing at each other down by the court-house. He rode down in that direction. North-east of the court-house he could see the Queen's Rangers, five or six hundred, and as many grenadiers, getting ready to make a charge. He found General Lee talking with General Dickinson. "The whole British army is close by," said General Dickinson, "and I think they will send a column to flank us on the right."

It was nine o'clock, and the sun was intensely hot. The soldiers wiped the perspiration from their foreheads, drank at the brook, and filled their canteens. The British cavalry came trotting over the plain to make a charge, but Jackson's men fired a volley, and they fled in great confusion.

Captain Oswald wheeled up two of his cannon across the swamp. He had only one ammunition-wagon, and it was so heavy that he could not get it across, and the soldiers carried the cartridges in their arms. He sent his shot whirring across the plain, plump into the ranks of the British. The British artillery opened—one twelve-pounder and five six-pounders. Oswald's gunners fell, one by one, till at last there were not men enough to work one of the guns.

General Wayne was under Lafayette, and his brigade moved down near the court-house. Lafayette thought it a good time to make a charge and capture the British cannon.

"Be ready to charge," was Wayne's order to his troops. His soldiers believed in him. He was so fearless on the battle-field that they called him "Mad Anthony."

"Retreat!" was the order that came to Wayne from Lee. Wayne could not understand it, but, instead of attacking, he began to retreat by the court-house. General Lee had discovered that Sir Henry Clinton, who had started for Middletown, had faced about with his divisions, and was rapidly advancing. The information he received in regard to the British was contradictory. He did not wish to bring on a general engagement, but to cut off the rear-guard. The ground upon which he was located was not favorable, and he ordered the troops under Lafayette to fall back.

Contradictory orders reached Scott, Grayson, Maxwell, and Jackson. Some of the regiments were advancing, others standing still, others retreating. Soon all was confusion. The British cavalry made a charge, and added to the confusion. Back through the woods and fields, and across the swamps, the troops marched—some of them going upon the run—panting in the heat, back past Mr. Carr's house, through grain-fields and over fences.

General Washington had reached the meeting-house, where Lee's men had left their knapsacks. He was glad to know that, after all the months of waiting, he was at last up with the enemy. He gave the command of the right wing to General Greene, and the left to General Stirling, urging them to hasten on. He did not know what was going on in front, but just beyond the meeting-house he met a fifer who was running, and who was very much frightened.

"What are you running away for?" asked Washington.

"The army is retreating," said the fifer.

"The army retreating! I'll have you whipped, sir, for telling such a story!" said Washington, who turned to a cavalry-man and said, "Here, keep this fellow under guard."

Washington rides on. He meets another man.

"Do you belong to the army?"

"Yes, sir."

"Where do you come from, and what are you retreating for?"

"The whole army is retreating."

"I can not believe it."

"What Are You Running Away For?" Asked Washington.

"I will go forward, your Excellency, and see what this means," says one of Washington's aids, Colonel Harrison, who rides away upon the gallop.

"What are you retreating for?" he asks of Captain Jones, in Colonel Grayson's regiment.

"All of the troops are retreating."

"What are you retreating for?" he asks of Captain William Smith.

"That is more than I can tell."

Colonel Harrison meets Colonel Ogden, and asks the same questions.

Colonel Ogden is red in the face. He is hot and panting and angry, not at the question, but because the army is retreating. He swears a big oath.

"We are flying from a shadow, sir;" and then there are more oaths.

Colonel Harrison meets Colonel Mercer.

"You will find out presently what we are retreating for. You will see several columns of infantry and horsemen in a few minutes," says Captain Mercer.

"There are no more British now than when they marched from Philadelphia, and we came here to meet foot and horse," is the reply of the plucky colonel.

He meets Lieutenant-colonel Rhea, of New Jersey.

"What are you retreating for?" is the question.

"There is no need of our retreating, and we are not ordered to retreat to any particular place."

General Washington rides across the swamp near the parsonage, ascends the hill upon the other side of it, and meets General Lee.

"What is all this?" Washington asks, with a flushed face.

"Sir? sir?"

It is all that General Lee can utter at the moment. Perhaps he does not quite understand the question, and he sees that Washington is very angry.

"Whence this retreat, and what the meaning of this confusion?" Washington asks.

"My orders have not been obeyed," Lee replies.

"It is only the rear-guard and a covering party that you are retreating from."

"Perhaps so; but the enemy is stronger than I am, and I did not want to risk being cut off."

"You ought not to have solicited the command, unless you intended to fight."

"It is not for the interest of the army to have a general action, and, under the circumstances, I did not feel warranted in bringing on one."

General Washington makes no reply, but rides forward.

The troops commanded by Lafayette and Wayne are coming from the court-house, marching past Mr. Carr's house. Colonel Oswald orders Captain Cook to place two of his guns in the orchard near Mr. Carr's. Cook unlimbers them, and opens fire once more upon the British.

Maxwell, Scott, Grayson, and Jackson are retreating through the woods on the left. Varnum's brigade is coming back by the hedge-fence. The British cavalry are pressing hard upon the rear of those retreating from the court-house. They are close upon the two cannon which Oswald has had in position on the plain.

Elijah sees, and so does every body else, that, unless a stand be made on the hill between Mr. Carr's house and the swamp, the guns will be lost. He remembers the hedge-fence, and points out the spot to General Wayne.

"Take position there!" shouts Wayne to Lieutenant-colonel Olney, leading Varnum's brigade. The panting men, just ready to drop fainting to the earth, overcome by the heat, file around the fence, and take position behind it. Past them go the retreating troops. Cook has got his two cannon into position. Oswald is there with Cook. On come the British. The cannon thunder, and Varnum's men pour in a deadly fire, and the British cavalry-men tumble from their horses, and the grenadiers reel to the earth.

Up to this moment there has been no battle, only a little skirmishing and cannonading. A golden opportunity has been lost through a misunderstanding of orders, through indecision, through contradictory information, through disinclination of Lee to bring on a general engagement. Far different would have been the aspect of affairs, if Scott, Jackson, Grayson, Maxwell, and Wayne had been directed to fall with all their force upon the British early in the morning. But now they are all in retreat. The militia, under Dickinson, are scattered everywhere, while Morgan, who has been making a long march to be ready to fall upon the British flank, is chafing like a lion under the change that has taken place in Lee's arrangements. It will not do for him to attack now. Lee and Washington meet once more by the hedge-fence. It is no time for the commander-in-chief to be angry now. He needs Lee's services.

"Will you take command here, sir?" Washington asked.

"Yes, sir; and your orders shall be obeyed."

Washington rides across the causeway to the parsonage. The main army has arrived. In a moment Greene is arranging his division on the right, and Stirling on the left.

"Form in rear!" is Washington's order to the retreating troops; and Grayson, Maxwell, Scott, Jackson, Wayne, all form behind the new line.

General Knox has been riding over the field. He sees where he can plant his cannon to good advantage. The British, under Cornwallis, have been coming round upon the left, and now Clinton advances from the court-house. Varnum retreats across the swamp. Captain Cook brings back his guns, and the British artillery and infantry take possession of the hedge-fence, and the battle begins in earnest.

It is past noon. The sun hangs like a brazen ball in the sky. There is not a breath of air to cool the fevered brows of the soldiers in either army. Men drop fainting to the earth, stricken down by the sun. Some of the skirmishers are in an orchard, and fight beneath the shade of the apple-trees. Some gain the covert of the woods, secure themselves behind the trees, and pour a galling fire upon the red-coats. Some find shelter in the parsonage barn. Spectators have climbed upon the roof of the meeting-house to watch the strife. Some are standing in the church-yard. A cannon-ball comes bounding over the ground, and mortally wounds a man who is sitting upon a grave-stone.

Oswald's men work their guns with great vigor, sending solid shot and grape-shot across the swamp into the ranks of the British. One of the gunners, an Irishman, falls. He is married,

THE ARMY CHEERS HER AS SHE RAMS HOME CARTRIDGE AFTER
CARTRIDGE.

293

and his wife Molly has been with him through all the campaign. She is bringing water from a spring for the gunners to wet the sponges when they swab the cannon. She puts down her bucket, seizes the rammer, and takes his place at the gun. The army cheers her as she rams home cartridge after cartridge.

All through the afternoon the fight goes on. No more retreating now. The drill which the soldiers have had under Baron Steuben, at Valley Forge, is telling in this battle. Since that terrible day for the British at Bunker Hill, Sir Henry Clinton has seen no such obstinate fighting. Cornwallis makes an attempt to turn Stirling's left, but is driven. Clinton pounds

away at Wayne in the centre, but without avail. He tries to turn Greene's right, but Knox brings up his spare guns, and sends a storm of shot and shell into the advancing ranks.

The sun goes down with the roar of the conflict still rolling far away. The troops of both armies are exhausted; but Washington, having restored order out of confusion, having held his ground against every attempt of Clinton and Cornwallis, is determined to renew the attack in the morning. He sends General Poor, with the New Hampshire troops from Stirling's position, round upon the left, to be ready to begin the attack at daylight.

The troops eat their supper without leaving their ranks, and lie upon their arms. Washington issues his final orders, wraps himself in his cloak, and lies down with them.

Midnight. The British are astir. They, too, have been lying

upon their arms. Silently they rise and move away, regiment by regiment, battery after battery, the pickets going last: all so quietly and secretly, that General Poor's pickets hear nothing of the departure.

Day breaks, and General Poor is ready to begin the attack; but there is no one to be attacked—none but the wounded and the dead; for Clinton has fled, and is on his march to Middletown, leaving all his wounded behind him. He is too far away to be overtaken. He has lost nearly one thousand in killed, wounded, and prisoners, while Washington has lost less than three hundred. So Washington brought victory out of defeat.

Chapter 25
AFFAIRS IN RHODE ISLAND

THE British were in possession of the town of Newport, in Rhode Island. General Prescott, who had succeeded Earl Percy, was in command in the summer of 1777. He was proud, haughty, and a tyrant. He arrested many of the citizens, threw them into prison, and kept them there month after month, preferring no charges against them.

When walking the streets, if he saw two or three citizens talking together, he would shout, "Disperse, you damned rebels!"

Every man was expected to take off his hat to him. One evening as he was riding out to his quarters, he overtook a Quaker, who walked along minding his own business, taking no notice of the ruffian general, who rode his horse against the inoffensive man, pinned him against the wall, knocked off his hat, and told his guard to arrest him.

He gave splendid parties, and lived like a nabob, plundering the poor, defenseless people, and cultivating the friendship of the rich Tories.

There was a brave, cool-headed man in Providence, Colonel William Barton, who resolved to capture the tyrant. Colonel Barton received information that Prescott had taken Mr. Overing's house for his head-quarters. Mr. Overing lived about midway the island, five miles from Newport, the house overlooking the blue waters of Narragansett Bay. It was a large, old-fashioned, two-storied house, with a gambreled roof, and trees around it, nearly a mile from the water.

Colonel Barton and John Hunt, a soldier in Colonel Elliot's company of artillery, talked over the expedition. John was born near Mr. Overing's house, and knew every room in it, and the grounds around, and where would be the best place to make a landing.

Colonel Barton selected Captain Eleazer Adams, Lieutenant Andrew Stanton, Lieutenant John Wilcox, and Lieutenant Samuel Potter, men as cool and courageous as himself, to be his officers. He selected Joshua Babcock and Samuel Phillips as sergeants, and thirty-four men, every one accustomed to rowing, all brave men, and ready to follow their leader anywhere without asking any questions.

It was past nine o'clock, on the night of July 10th, 1777, when Colonel Barton started from Warwick Point, on the west shore of Narranganset Bay, with six boats. Their oars were muffled. The men rowed in silence. It was a long pull down past Prudence Island and over to the other shore; but the strong-armed rowers sent the boats swiftly through the water. There were three British frigates at anchor which they must pass, and the frigates had guard-boats here and there, which must be avoided. They heard the ships' bells strike the hour of midnight as they glided past the frigates.

John Hunt knew the best place for a landing—a little cove sheltered by trees. Silently the boats came to the shore, and silently the men laid down their oars and stepped upon the beach. They were divided into parties, one to keep the boats, the others to approach the house from different directions. Each man knows what he is to do. Up a sheltered ravine they move. South of them, not a hundred rods distant, are the head-quarters of the cavalry, and north of them, not more than eighty rods, are the head-quarters of the guard; and these brave men are slipping in between, to seize a general and carry him away! It is a bold undertaking. Half of the party moves toward the house under cover of a piece of woods; the other crosses a barley-field into the road, and approaches the front of the house, where a sentinel is pacing his beat. John Hunt and Colonel

"YOU ARE MY PRISONER, SIR. COME IN SILENCE, AS YOU VALUE YOUR LIFE."

Barton are in advance, and right behind are the true men, ready to act their part.

"Who comes there?"

No answer.

"Who comes there? Advance, and give the countersign."

"We have no countersign. Have you seen any deserters?"

The answer quiets the sentinel's fears, and in an instant he is a prisoner, disarmed, and a pistol at his face.

"Make the least noise, and you are a dead man."

Quickly the door is opened. Major Barrington, Prescott's aid, hears men tramping through the hall and ascending the stairs. He springs to a window, and leaps to the ground, but only to find himself a prisoner.

General Prescott hears the disturbance, sits up in bed, wondering what is going on. The door of his room opens, and Colonel Barton and his men rush in. The candle-light falls upon the frightened Briton.

"You are my prisoner, sir. Come in silence, as you value your life."

"Will you not let me dress?"

"No time for that. Put on your cloak."

General Prescott's cloak is thrown over his shoulders, one of the party gathers up his breeches and stockings, and they descend the stairs. Two men lock arms with him, and at a quick-step the prisoners are borne to the boats. Silently the boats move away past the frigates and guard-boats. The rowers could hear a commotion on shore—drums beating, guns firing, rockets shooting upward; but their arms were strong, the night was dark, and before daylight the boats were at the Warwick landing.

"You have made a bold push," says Prescott, now that he was permitted to speak.

"And have been fortunate," is Barton's quiet reply.

Morning dawned, and there was a commotion. A coach drove into town, in which were seated Colonel Elliot (who owned it), Colonel Barton, and the hated British general and his major, guarded by Colonel Barton's soldiers. Every body rushed into the street to see the crest-fallen prisoners, rejoicing at the capture of the hated tyrant.

Prescott was sent to General Washington, then on the Hudson. He passed through Lebanon, Connecticut, and the party guarding him stopped at Captain Alden's tavern for dinner. Among other dishes on the table was one of succotash—boiled beans and corn. Prescott never had seen any such food, and did not know how delicious it was; for corn in England is only fed to hogs, and beans to sheep. He threw the dish upon the floor.

"Do you give me pigs' feed?" he said, in a rage.

That roused Captain Alden, who got his horse-whip, and gave the haughty fellow a terrible whipping, and taught him a lesson which he remembered, for he was very careful not to throw any more dishes upon the floor.

In May, 1778, General Pigot, who was in command of the British in Newport, sent Lieutenant-colonel Campbell, with six hundred men, to burn some boats which the Americans were building at Warren. They sailed on a frigate and in boats. At daylight the people in Warren were astonished to find an army marching into town with drums beating and colors flying. The British burned the boats and the meeting-house, entered the houses, captured the citizens, and marched on to Bristol, burned twenty houses there, snatched rings from the fingers of the women, stole their silver shoe-buckles, pillaged the houses, and started back.

Word was sent to Providence of what was going on. Colonel Barton started, with twenty men, on horseback. The farmers in the surrounding towns joined him. They came upon the British at Bristol Ferry, and boldly attacked them. Colonel Barton and four of his men were wounded, but several of the British fell before they reached their boats.

On the retreat through Warren, a drummer with a big bass-drum fell behind. Some women, seeing that there were no troops near, seized whatever they could lay their hands on for weapons—brooms, shovels, and tongs—ran out, and surrounded him.

"You are our prisoner," they shouted.

"I am not sorry to be captured, for I am very tired," said the drummer, giving himself up.

In July, 1778, a large number of vessels arrived from England with troops. It was supposed that the British intended to attack Providence a n d march to Boston. General Pigot had s e v e n thousand men; while General Sullivan, who was at Providence, had only sixteen hundred.

But the 29th of June was a joyful day to the Americans, for twelve French line-of-battle ships and four frigates sailed into Narragansett Bay. It was the fleet of Count D'Estaing —the first French fleet to arrive on the coast to aid the Americans.

Some Women Seized Brooms, Shovels, and Tongs, Ran Out and Surrounded Him.

There was great consternation among the British at Newport. Three British vessels over in the East Bay were at once blown up, and four frigates and a corvette were run ashore and burned in Newport Harbor—the *Cerberus*, twenty-eight guns; *Falcon*, sixteen; *Lark*, thirty-two; *Orpheus*, thirty-two; *Juno*, thirty-two; *Grand Duke*, forty; *Flora*, thirty-two—in all, the vessels carried two hundred and twelve guns. This was a sad loss to the British, but it was better to destroy them than to have them fall into the hands of the French.

General Sullivan was in command at Providence. The militia flocked in from Massachusetts and New Hampshire, as well as from Rhode Island. Generals Greene and Lafayette came with some of the Continental troops. Elijah Favor came: he was a major now.

On the 9th of August, General Sullivan crossed the narrow strait at the north end of Rhode Island with about eight thousand men. At the same time, D'Estaing landed twenty-five hundred troops on the island of Canonicut, in the harbor. But that very afternoon another fleet appeared in sight—thirteen line-of-battle ships and twenty-three others—Lord Howe's fleet from New York. The French troops were re-embarked, and D'Estaing sailed down the bay to meet Howe in the open ocean.

The wind was east, thick clouds rolling in from the sea, the wind blowing a gale, and the rocky shores white with surf; but the fleets engaged. The French captured the *Senegal,* frigate, and a bomb-vessel; but D'Estaing's own vessel, the *Languedoc,* had its masts and spars badly splintered. A storm came on, and the admirals, instead of sending each other to the bottom, had quite enough to attend to in managing the vessels.

For two days and nights the storm raged. The troops suffered severely. They had no shelter except the fences and walls. They were wet through, their provisions were spoiled, their powder damaged. Fair weather came, but the French fleet, instead of returning to Newport, sailed for Boston.

A grand opportunity was lost. Had the French fleet remained in the harbor, and the French troops co-operated with the Americans, with the fleet to help, the British lines could have been carried, and the army captured; but now the Americans must retreat.

On the night of the 28th of August the army fell back twelve miles to Butts's Hill, at the north end of the island. Elijah Favor rode here and there to see where the troops could be advantageously placed, and fortifications erected to cover the retreat. He saw that there were two roads—one over on the east side, and one near the west side of the island. He was quite sure that the British would advance up both roads in pursuit, and they did.

At daylight there was a commotion in the British camp. Lieutenant-colonel Campbell and the Twenty-second regiment marched in haste up the east road about five miles, and came to a cross-road which ran up the hill toward the west past Mr. Gibbs's house. A part of the regiment went up the cross-road, little thinking that there was a regiment of Americans lying in wait for them behind Mr. Gibbs's stone wall, and that Colonel Laurens, Colonel Fleury, and Major Talbot, with the rear-guard of the Americans, were holding the roads; but suddenly there was a flashing of guns, and nearly half of the Twenty-second regiment went down before the murderous fire. Two Hessian regiments came to the support of Lieutenant-colonel Campbell, but before they arrived the rear-guard was retreating to the main army, near Butts's Hill.

The British followed, and by noon the whole army was drawn up in line of battle on Quaker Hill and Anthony's Hill, about a mile from Butts's, while the fleet sailed up the bay to throw shot and shells into the American camp.

General Greene was in command of the right wing of the Americans. He had Glover's, Varnum's, Cornell's, and Colonel Christopher Greene's brigade. It was the same Colonel Greene who commanded at Red Bank, and defeated Count Donop. General Greene posted his men in the woods between Anthony's and Butts's Hill, and waited for the British.

It is nearly two o'clock in the afternoon when the Hessians descend the slope of Anthony's Hill and approach Greene's line. They are confident of driving the Yankees; but suddenly the woods blaze with musketry, and the advancing line is thrown into confusion. The Hessians fire a few volleys, but are driven.

The day is very warm, and the Hessians in the open field suffer from the heat and the terrible fire poured upon them, while the Americans in the shade suffer very little. Though the ships are sending broadsides into the woods, few are killed or wounded.

The British are ready at last for a grand attack. General Pigot sends a large force to drive Greene from his position, and the battle begins in earnest. The troops approach the woods and open fire. The British artillery on the hill are throwing shot and shell upon Butts's Hill, and the American cannon there are replying. The ships fire broadsides; but General Sullivan has sent some heavy guns down to the water's edge, and the Americans train these guns so correctly that the shot take effect upon the vessels, which very soon cut their cables, and sail away from the destructive fire.

General Sullivan sees that Pigot is massing nearly all of his troops in front of Greene, and sends out a party to attack Pigot's right wing; and the militia attack with such vigor that Pigot does not dare to weaken his right wing to strengthen his left.

Pigot resolves to make a grand charge upon Greene. His men advance, but are cut down almost as rapidly as the British were at Bunker Hill. Colonel Christopher Greene's regiment is composed of negroes, many of whom have been slaves; but they fight for their liberty now with desperation. The British and Hessians approach the woods to drive the Americans out with the bayonet, but are unable. The lines waver and break, and the Americans rush out, capture a cannon, and return in triumph to their lines.

The sun goes down. Two hundred and eleven Americans have been killed, wounded, or captured, while the British have lost, including prisoners, one thousand and twenty-three.

Thus closed one of the best-managed battles of the war. But General Sullivan, though he had repulsed the British, saw that he must retreat to the main-land, for Sir Henry Clinton had arrived with four thousand men, and the ships could come up on both sides and cut off his retreat. Silently the troops marched away in the darkness, and before morning the whole army was on the main-land.

AVANNAH was in the hands of the British, and so was the whole State of Georgia. The Tories outnumbered the patriots. Sir Henry Clinton thought that South Carolina could be made loyal by a vigorous campaign, and that North Carolina and Virginia would soon wheel into line as loyal provinces. The loyal cause was far more hopeful in the South than in the North. To bring back those revolted provinces, he sailed from New York with five thousand men, and a large fleet, under Admiral Arbuthnot, to subdue Charleston, and anchored at Edisto Inlet, south of Charleston, on the 10th of February, 1780. The times were hard in South Carolina. The paper money was of so little value that it took seven hundred dollars to buy a pair of shoes. The people were nearly discouraged, and the patriotism which had flamed so gloriously in '76 was dying out. Many of the people were ready to swear allegiance to the king.

General Lincoln was in command at Charleston. When the British landed, he had only fourteen hundred men, and more than half of these were from North Carolina, and their term of enlistment was nearly ended. Lincoln did not think that he could hold the city; but Clinton stayed a month at Edisto before beginning operations, and Lincoln changed his mind and began to throw up intrenchments west of the town, for he saw that Clinton would be likely to attack from that direction. The town is situated on a tongue of land between the Cooper and Ashley rivers. Re-enforcements were on their way—seven hundred Virginians, under General Woodford, who came to take the place of the Carolina troops. Governor Rutledge, the State Executive, called upon the militia to turn out; but few came, however, and General Lincoln could muster only about two thousand men.

On the 20th of March, Admiral Arbuthnot got his fleet over the bar. He did not attempt to attack Fort Moultrie; but though the guns of the fort fired at the fleet, he sailed past it, and anchored within cannon-shot of the town. General Clinton had already marched up the shore, and seized Fort Johnson, on the south side of the harbor. From there he marched up the south bank of the Ashley. The boats from the fleet went up past the town, ferried the troops across the river, and on the 1st of April the siege began. On the 2d of April, Lord Cornwallis arrived from New York with three thousand troops, and the British took possession of the country east of Cooper River. No fresh provisions could be carried into Charleston now. All communication with the outside world was cut off. Lincoln thought that he could force his way out through Sir Henry's lines between the Cooper and the Ashley, but the people implored him not to abandon the city. The American general and the inhabitants agreed upon terms of capitulation—to give up the city, if the troops could be allowed to retire; but Sir Henry, having got the American fort in his grasp, would not accept the terms, and the siege went on. Day and night bombs were bursting and cannon-shot crashing through the town. The Tories in the city were doing what they could to help the British. A flag was sent out to know what Sir Henry would consent to, and word came back that troops, ships, supplies, every thing, must be surrendered without any conditions. Private property would not be molested, and the prisoners might be paroled. General Lincoln would not surrender on such terms, and the firing began. All through the day and night of May 10th shells were bursting in the town. Women and children were killed, and there was no place of safety. The fleet came up, and were ready to bombard the town. To hold out any longer was useless; more than that, it would be inhuman; and on the 12th of May the Americans marched out and gave up their arms. Four hundred cannon fell into the hands of the British, and two thousand prisoners. Two hundred and ten of the influential citizens signed an address of congratulation to Clinton. The Tories cheered, swung their hats, and many of them enlisted in the royal service. People from the country came in and swore allegiance to the king. Sir Henry was greatly gratified. In a very short time Carolina, as well as Georgia, would be wholly loyal. He divided his army— sending Cornwallis, with about three thousand men, toward North Carolina, and Lieutenant-colonel Conger, with nearly two thousand, one hundred and fifty miles west to a place called "Ninety-six." He sent another detachment from Savannah to Augusta. These would overawe the patriots, and the loyalists would be in power once more.

There was only one body of American troops in the State. Colonel Abraham Buford had raised four hundred men, and was on his way to Charleston with two pieces of artillery when the city capitulated. He was one hundred and forty miles from Charleston in the north-west, retreating to North Carolina. Sir Henry Clinton had one energetic cavalry officer, Colonel Tarleton, a young lawyer from Liverpool, twenty-six years old, a thick-set, swarthy man, with black eyes, and sullen, revengeful temper. Sir Henry directed him to disperse this last remnant of patriot soldiers in the South. Tarleton had seven hundred men on horseback—a part of them cavalry, and the rest mounted infantry. He went like the wind, one hundred and five miles in fifty-five hours; and before Buford mistrusted that the British were near him, he found himself surrounded.

Tarleton sent a summons to surrender. "Sir," the summons began, "resistance being vain, to prevent the effusion of human blood I make offers which can never be repeated. You are now almost encompassed by a corps of seven hundred troops on horseback: half of that number are infantry, with cannon; the rest, cavalry. Earl Cornwallis is likewise within a short march, with nine British battalions."

This was a lie. Cornwallis was far away, and Tarleton had

only about four hundred men—the other three hundred having been tired out. Colonel Buford considered them humiliating, and would not accept them.

While the flag of truce was raised, while Buford was conferring with Tarleton's officers, Tarleton was arranging his men. It was a violation of all the rules of war—an expedient which an honorable-minded man would have scorned to use. But Tarleton was not an honorable man. Buford's men stood at ease, not expecting an attack. The flag of truce went back to Tarleton's lines, and a moment later the British cavalry, with drawn swords, were rushing from all directions upon the Americans. In a moment the lines were broken. A few fired their guns, but most of the soldiers threw them down and gave themselves up as prisoners. Then began the butchery. One hundred and thirteen men killed outright; one hundred and fifty wounded. Only fifty-three were spared.

Tarleton made no effort to restrain his men. He saw the defenseless men cut down by his savage soldiers, and murdered in cold blood. Buford and a few others escaped. The British loss was only five killed, and fifteen wounded.

Tarleton left the wounded lying upon the field of slaughter, and, with his prisoners and the two captured cannon and wagons, marched back to General Cornwallis, who wrote an account of the achievement to Sir Henry Clinton. "I can only add," he said, "the highest encomiums on the conduct of Lieutenant-colonel Tarleton. It will give me the most sensible satisfaction to hear that your excellency has been able to obtain for him some distinguished mark of his majesty's favor." The favor of the king for butchering three hundred men who had thrown down their arms!

General Clinton, Lord Cornwallis, and Colonel Tarleton perhaps thought that such a massacre would intimidate the people, and make them loving subjects of the king; but it had just the opposite effect. The patriots on their farms among the Carolina hills were more determined than ever to resist the British.

Not far from the place of the massacre was a school, kept by Mr. Humphries. One of the boys attending school and studying Latin was named Andrew Jackson, thirteen years old. His older brother had been killed at Stono Inlet, near Charleston, by the British. Andrew was not at all awed by the slaughter of Buford's men, nor were the settlers, who formed themselves into a company as soon as Tarleton departed, and Andrew was one of the number. A few weeks later a party of British came back to Waxhaw, where Andrew lived, to plunder the inhabitants. The company assembled at the meeting-house, and the British attacked them. Andrew and another brother escaped; but the next day the Tories told the British where they were secreted, and they were captured.

Andrew was placed under guard. One of the British officers came up to him.

Out Came the Ruffian's Sword.

"Here, sir, clean my boots!" he said, imperiously, to the boy.

"I am a prisoner of war, sir, and I look for such treatment as I am entitled to," said Andrew.

Out came the ruffian's sword. A blow was aimed at Andrew's head. The boy threw up his left arm to ward it off, and the bright blade came down upon the arm, cleaving the flesh to the bone. His brother also was wounded in the head, because he would not do the bidding of the brutal fellows. Not satisfied with this, they were thrust into jail. No surgeon came to dress their wounds. The older brother, Robert, soon sickened and died, and Andrew was left alone in the world. He was exchanged a few days later. He paid the British off in 1815, at New Orleans, when commander of the American army. From the little old tumble-down house in which he was born at Waxhaw, he marched on through life to be President of the United States.

When General Washington discovered, in May, that Sir Henry Clinton had sailed southward, he sent Baron De Kalb, with General Smallwood and fourteen hundred troops from Delaware, Maryland, and Virginia, south. They started from Morristown, New York, on the 14th of April. A long and weary march was before the troops.

It was the 6th of July when they reached Hillsborough, in North Carolina. The news of the fall of Charleston and the massacre at Waxhaw reached General Washington, and he saw that De Kalb, though a brave officer, was not the man to organize an army in the South, and General Gates was appointed commander of the Southern department.

It was a hard task that Gates had before him. A majority of the people in South Carolina were Tories. The patriots were crushed out. There was no public spirit. It was the hot season of the year. Loyalists swarmed, ready to give information to Cornwallis and withhold it from Gates, to send him on a false scent, or betray him at every opportunity. He had no money and few supplies. But there were patriots in North Carolina who had turned out under General Caswell. The patriots in South Carolina were not all dead. Colonel Sumter had raised a few hundred men, and was harassing the British wherever he could get a chance, cutting off their supplies, capturing a few prisoners here and a few more there. Cornwallis learned that Gates was approaching, and hastened from Charleston to Camden, one hundred miles north-west. General Gates sent a part of his little force to Colonel Sumter, who was farther south, and marched with the rest toward Camden, where twenty-five hundred British and Tories had concentrated under Cornwallis. General Stevens, with seven hundred Virginia militia, joined General Gates.

The American army was at Rugeley's Mills, thirteen miles north of Camden. Gates intended to make a night march and surprise Cornwallis. Colonel Armand, with some cavalry, led the column, followed by the Maryland and Delaware brigades, under Colonel Smallwood and General Gist. This division was under De Kalb. Then came the North Carolina militia, under General Caswell, and the Virginians, under General Stevens. It was ten o'clock when the column started. There were about four thousand in all.

One day a strange cavalcade came into Gates's camp—twenty or thirty men on horseback, in a great variety of costumes, some in uniform, some in citizen's dress, some in deer-skins—white men and negroes—but all had rifles. Their leader was Francis Marion, a brave, keen-eyed, active man, who, with his few men, was a constant thorn to Cornwallis, cutting off his supplies, pouncing upon his scouting parties, here one day, somewhere else to-morrow, hiding in swamps, eluding the British, riding a hundred miles, and striking a blow and disappearing before Cornwallis could overtake him. People called him the "Swamp Fox."

Marion was a partisan leader, but Gates did not have a high opinion of partisans, and took no pains to cultivate Marion's friendship, and so deprived himself of a valuable ally.

Cornwallis, in Camden, has conceived the idea of making a night march and surprising General Gates. His officers know the country; they say that Gates is in a weak position at Rugeley's Bridge. The Tories will guide and aid him.

At the same time that Gates begins to move, Cornwallis is also on the march. Silently, through the darkness, the two armies approach each other along the road parallel to the Wateree River, and about two miles east of it.

It is two o'clock in the morning. The American cavalry cross

Graney Quarter Creek, a little stream running into the Wateree. They ascend the hill south of it, and march past a clearing. The road is sandy. The column is winding through the woods. The road passes between two swamps, and just south of the swamps is another little stream, Sander's Creek. The British column has crossed Sander's Creek, and is between the swamps.

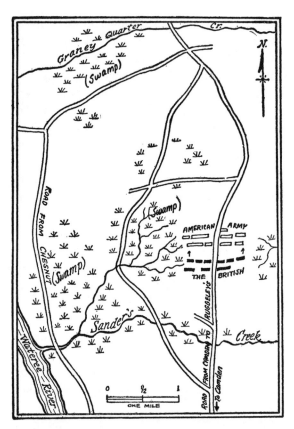

Plan of the Battle Fought Near Camden, S. C., August 16, 1780.

The two armies are face to face. Both are surprised. There is a quick flashing of muskets. Some of Armand's troops are killed at the first fire, and the others fall back, throwing the column into confusion. Colonel Porterfield, brave officer, who has commanded one of the flanking parties in the march, falls mortally wounded. Colonel Armstrong, commanding the right flank, rallies his men, pours a volley into the British lines, and both armies come to a standstill.

General Gates is surprised, so is Cornwallis; but Cornwallis sees that he has an advantageous position. There is a swamp east of him, a swamp west of him. Gates can not flank him on either side. He can form his men in a line between the swamps and win a victory.

Gates does not know the ground. It is dark. The men see nothing of the enemy. He calls a council of his officers. "Gentlemen, you know the ground better than I do. What are your opinions?" he asked.

The officers did not know the ground.

"It is too late to retreat," says General Stevens.

"Then nothing more is to be said. Gentlemen will please take their posts," Gates replies.

It is a simple matter for Cornwallis to form his men. He has only to parade them across the road, and out in the woods on either side. General Webster commands on the east side, and Lord Rawdon on the west.

General Gates places the Second Maryland brigade and the Delaware troops west of the road, under General Gist. The North Carolina militia, under General Caswell, are posted in the centre. The Virginians, under General Stevens, are sent east of the road, and the First Maryland brigade, under Smallwood, is placed in the rear, on the east side of the road.

The artillery of both armies is placed in the centre. All of this is done in the darkness. Day dawns. The American artillery opens. General Stevens's men never have been under fire. They do not know what a battle is. They advance boldly to attack the British regulars, who have been in many engagements. They will drive the British with their bayonets. But suddenly the British, under Webster, are in motion toward the Virginians, who fire one volley, then turn and flee, panic-stricken, from the field, many throwing away their guns.

A moment later, all the North Carolina militia, under Caswell, except Dixon's regiment, do the same. The whole of Gates's left wing has given way: only the Continental troops and Dixon's right are left to oppose Cornwallis. The two armies are about equal in number now; but Cornwallis has all the advantage of position.

Lord Rawdon advances upon the Americans, who receive his fire and return it. The American artillery (four pieces) pours grape and canister into the British ranks, and makes fearful havoc. The Marylanders charge upon the British and throw them into confusion. Some of the British flee. Oh, if the militia had only stood their ground, they would have driven the British pell-mell down the road, and across Sander's Creek to Camden. Smallwood advances with his brigade to take the place of the fugitives. He is too late. His troops are too few, and General Webster, with the whole right wing of the British, closes in upon him, and gains his flank. The battle rages from swamp to swamp. In the centre, on both sides, the artillery is flaming.

No order comes from Gates to De Kalb. But an opportunity has come. Things are favorable for a charge.

"Forward! forward!" The order runs along the line. The troops under Gist advance, pour in a volley, and make terrible havoc in the British ranks. The British are driven, and fifty prisoners taken. Cornwallis rallies his men, and hurls his whole force upon the Marylanders. The line that has stood so firmly, the men who have fought so nobly, are cut down in an instant. The day is lost. The artillery-horses are shot, the gunners bayoneted. The Americans flee—some across the swamp, others down the road, others through the woods. The British cavalry, under the blood-thirsty and implacable Tarleton, ride over the fugitives, trampling them down, slashing their heads open, showing no mercy. Once more it is a massacre. The brave De Kalb falls, pierced by eleven bayonet-wounds. The Delaware regiment is annihilated; more than a third of the Americans are slaughtered, after giving themselves up as prisoners. Seven hundred are killed, wounded, or captured. The British loss was nearly five hundred. All the baggage, two hundred wagons, and eight cannon fell into Cornwallis's hands. The Tories, seeing that the patriots are defeated, inhumanly murder the fugitives who ask for food at their doors.

Tarleton went in pursuit of Sumter, who was on the west side of the Wateree, surprised him, massacred nearly two hundred men, took a large number of prisoners, and scattered the whole of Sumter's force.

Just before the battle at Camden, General Gates was so sure

THE BRITISH OFFICER CLIMBED UP A CHIMNEY, BUT WAS QUICKLY
PULLED OUT.

of victory that he sent General Marion with his followers to destroy all the boats on the rivers between Camden and Charleston, in order to prevent Cornwallis's retreat. Marion was at work destroying the boats, when a negro brought him word that Gates was defeated, De Kalb killed, and the whole army routed, and that a party of British were coming to capture him, and near at hand. In a moment Marion and his men were dashing through the woods to a swamp not far from Nelson's Ferry, where he concealed his men. They were but thirty.

Marion's scouts were on the lookout. One came riding in, saying that a party of British, with the prisoners captured at Camden, had started for Charleston.

"How many prisoners are there?" Marion asked.

"About two hundred."

"How large is the guard?"

"We counted ninety."

"Ninety! These we must have," said Marion.

Through the day Marion remains in the swamp. His men rest beneath the leafy shade of the oaks. Long trails of moss hang pendent from the trees, waving in the summer breeze. So deep the shade, that at midday there is only twilight where the brave men lie concealed. At night, no one could find them there.

The sun goes down. Their horses are fresh. The thirty will follow their beloved commander wherever he may lead. Out from the gloomy depths of the swamp they ride to the open ground, and, like the wind, they dash away, and reach the Wateree River, where the ferry-man informs him that he has just set the prisoners on the other side of the stream. The ferry-man is a Tory, and does not know that it is Marion whom he is paddling across.

The British, with the prisoners, have halted for the night at the Blue Tavern. No pickets are out. The British officer in command of the party has no thought of a surprise, for the Americans have been utterly routed at Camden. Like a thunderbolt, the thirty fall upon the guard. In a moment, they are captured, all the guns of the British stacked in the yard before the tavern seized, and the prisoners released. The British officer in charge climbed up a chimney, thinking thus to hide; but he was quickly pulled out, well covered with soot. Thus, without losing a man, the "Swamp Fox," whom Gates had looked down upon, released all the prisoners, and captured ninety British.

Chapter 27
WEST POINT

AFTER the capture of Forts Montgomery and Clinton, on the Hudson, in September, 1777, when Burgoyne was at Saratoga, General Washington and Congress saw the necessity of having a strong fort erected farther up the river at West Point, to protect the ferrying of troops and supplies between New England and the other colonies. Nature had made it so strong a place that it was not difficult to build a fortress which the whole British army could not capture.

The young officer from Poland who had planned the intrenchments at Stillwater—Thaddeus Kosciuszko—was employed to plan the intrenchments, and Captain Elijah Favor was directed to aid him. They began work on the 20th of March, 1778, staking out the lines, and setting a large number of soldiers at work. The walls were of earth and logs, fourteen feet high, and twenty-one wide at the base. It was eighteen hundred feet around the main work. There were bastions and ditches, and it had many angles. It could be approached from one side only —that toward the river; and for a defense there, they erected a strong oak palisade—driving the logs into the earth, and bolting them together at the top. One hundred guns of all kinds were placed in the main fort and the surrounding works.

To make it impossible for the British ships to get past it at night, it was decided to have a great iron chain stretched across the river just above the fort. The links were large, and the whole chain weighed one hundred and eighty tons. The soldiers floated great pine-logs down the river, and laid them side by side, to buoy the chain; fastened it to the logs with iron staples, and bolted each end to the ledges on the shores. The fort was so strong, and was so conveniently situated, that General Washington had his supplies of powder stored there.

While the fort was building, Elijah had his head-quarters at a house owned by Mr. Beverly Robinson, on the east side of the river, and two miles down stream. It was a delightful place, close by the river, with a piazza on the south side, and surrounded by apple, plum, and cherry trees. Mr. Robinson was a Tory, and had fled to New York, and had been commissioned a colonel in the British service. Mr. Robinson's sister was Mary Phillipse, the young lady to whom, in 1756, General Washington paid his addresses, but who had married General Washington's old companion in arms, Major Morris.

After the British evacuated Philadelphia, General Arnold was sent by General Washington to take possession of that city. He lived in fine style, gave good dinners, and spent more money than he received. He was forty years old, and a bachelor; but he saw a girl who charmed him—Margaret Shippen, youngest daughter of Judge Shippen, who was only eighteen. His love was reciprocated, and she became Mrs. Arnold.

General Arnold was in debt, and men who are hard pressed for money not unfrequently do that which is not lawful. He was in command, and a military commander in time of war has great power. He oppressed the citizens, used the army teams for his own use, engaged in speculations, but lived in great style, and instead of diminishing his debts, become more deeply involved. The people of Philadelphia were offended at his exactions, and the President and Council of the State preferred charges against him to Congress, and a court-martial was ordered to investigate them.

General Arnold had spent money in Canada, and he sent a bill to Congress, claiming that a large amount was due him. Congress did not think that he was entitled to what he claimed, and Arnold resigned his commission. He was angry that a court should be called to investigate the charges against him.

General Arnold's young wife held in kindly remembrance one of the young British officers, who, by his wit, his genial nature, his poetical talents, his ability to paint pictures and make off-hand sketches, had made the winter so agreeable—Major John André—and who was now with Sir Henry Clinton in New York —his quarters at Mr. Kip's house, on the shore of the East River. Friendly letters passed between them. One day, among other letters received by Sir Henry Clinton by flag of truce from the American lines, was one from Philadelphia. The writer did not give his full name, but signed himself *Gustavus*. He stated that he was a person of importance in the American service, but he was dissatisfied with what Congress was doing. He did not like the alliance with France, and he was ready to leave the Americans and become loyal, if he could be assured of the safety of his person, and be indemnified for the loss of his property. Sir Henry Clinton was quite willing to find out who this person of some consequence might be.

"You will please answer that under a disguised hand and an assumed name," were his instructions to his adjutant-general, Major John André; and the major wrote a reply, inviting further correspondence, and signed the letter John Anderson— *John André's own;* and so it came about that, during the winter of 1779–'80, there was a correspondence between Mr. Gustavus, of Philadelphia, and John Anderson, merchant, of New York.

Sir Henry Clinton had a suspicion that Mr. Gustavus was General Arnold, for the court which had investigated the charges against Arnold had condemned him to be reprimanded for oppressing the people of Philadelphia, and other irregularities. Arnold expected to be triumphantly vindicated, and it was terribly galling to his proud spirit to be conducted into the presence of General Washington and receive a reprimand. He bore it with becoming acquiescence, however, and renewed his professions of loyalty to the patriot cause. He would still serve his country. Little does General Washington know of the thoughts that are coursing through the brain of General Arnold as he stands before the commander-in-chief and the officers of the court.

"One may smile, and smile, and be a villain."

What he is thinking of we shall perhaps see by-and-by.

Months pass. Summer comes. General Arnold is a patriot. He has not allowed the rejection of his claim by Congress, nor the finding of the court-martial, to dampen his ardor for his country. The time has come for active operations; but his wound received at Saratoga will not permit him to ride horseback. He would like to be reinstated in command as major-general. He could command at West Point. General Washington would like to have him command the right wing of the army, but General Arnold declines the honor on account of his wound, and so is appointed to command the impregnable and all-important fortress at West Point, where all the powder is stored—the stronghold protecting the Hudson, and which the whole British army can not capture.

Sir Henry Clinton was still receiving letters from Mr. Gustavus, who was no longer in Philadelphia, but somewhere up the Hudson. Mr. Gustavus was in the mercantile line. He had something to sell, and wrote about tobacco and dry goods. His letters were addressed to "Mr. John Anderson, Merchant, to the care of James Osberne, to be left at the Reverened Mr. Odell's, New York."

Mr. Gustavus was a man of consequence now. He had something besides his influence to sell. He could turn over a fortress, with one hundred cannon, powder, balls, provisions; and, with the fortress, he could sell an army, a nation.

On the 31st of August, a boat sailed down the Hudson, with a white flag fluttering in the breeze. There was a gentleman on board the boat by the name of Heron, a member of the Connecticut Legislature. He carried a package of letters, and among them one for John Anderson, merchant. Mr. Heron did not know who wrote it, nor what was in it; but Mr. Heron had a talk with Sir Henry Clinton, and informed him that he, though a member of the Connecticut Legislature, was dissatisfied with Congress, and that the rebellion would soon come to an end through its weakness.

On that same day, in the afternoon, a ship sailed down the Narrows for England, with Colonel Dalrymple on board, and other officers of the English army. They carried information too important to be put on paper, which they would whisper in private to Lord North, and be taken by him into the royal closet, where they would whisper it to the king, that a British fleet would go up the Hudson with troops, and capture West Point. A plan was being arranged under which it would immediately fall into the hands of the British. Before Washington was aware of it, the rebellion would be crushed, and Washington's army scattered to the winds, or else captured, and the French also.

The ship arrived in England, and a day or two later it was known in London that the rebellion was soon to receive its finishing blow.

Mr. Gustavus, up the Hudson, was ready to do some trading with Mr. John Anderson, merchant, of New York. Thus far they had carried on the negotiations about tobacco and dry goods by correspondence, but it was desirable to have a private interview. Mr. Gustavus was living with a young and beautiful wife and their young babe, in Colonel Beverly Robinson's house, nestled on the east bank of the Hudson, just below West Point. Colonel Beverly Robinson was a loyal subject of the king, holding a commission, and knew Mr. Gustavus personally, and was selected to arrange a meeting.

Colonel Sheldon, commanding the cavalry in Westchester County, received a letter from New York written by John Anderson:

> "New York, September 7th, 1780.
> "Sir,—I am told my name is made known to you, and that I may hope your indulgence in permitting me to go out with a flag, which will be sent to Dobbs's Ferry, Sunday next, the 11th, at 12 o'clock, when I shall be happy to meet Mr. G——.   "John Anderson."

Colonel Sheldon never had heard of John Anderson, and did not quite know what to make of it. He sent the letter to General Arnold.

"If a man by the name of John Anderson comes to the lines, send me word by express, and bring him to head-quarters," were Arnold's instructions.

Sunday came. There was to be a meeting on this day on the east shore of the Hudson, near Dobbs's Ferry. No church bell would ring, there would be no crowd of worshipers, no preaching or praying, no minister; but Mr. Gustavus would meet Mr. John Anderson and talk over a little trade they had in hand.

On Saturday night General Arnold went down the river from Robinson's house, and spent the night at the house of Mr. Joshua Smith, at Long Clove, two miles above Haverstraw. He intended to cross to the east side of the river in the morning, to the neutral ground, between the outposts of his own lines and those of Sir Henry Clinton. Possibly he would meet somebody from New York there. He had heard that Mr. John Anderson, merchant, of New York, was to be there on Sunday morning. Mr. Anderson and Colonel Robinson went up the river on Saturday afternoon, but, by some mistake, instead of going to the spot where they were to meet Mr. Gustavus, they went on board the *Vulture* frigate.

Sunday morning the sailors on the *Vulture* see a boat coming down the Hudson. An American major-general is seated at the stern. The boat carries no white flag. It is within cannon-shot, and the sailors ram home a shot and let it fly at the boat, which quickly turns about to get beyond reach, and so there is no meeting on this Sunday morning between Mr. Gustavus and Mr. Anderson on the east bank of the Hudson. General Arnold goes up the river to the Robinson house, and Major André returns to Sir Henry Clinton, at Kip's house, each wondering how there happened to be no meeting.

Count Rochambeau had arrived at Newport, in Rhode Island, with a French army, and General Washington was to go eastward to Hartford, to meet him there and arrange a campaign.

Sir Henry Clinton was getting impatient. The importance of obtaining West Point grew upon him, and he sent Colonel Robinson up the river to see what could be done about it. Colonel Robinson went on board the *Vulture,* and the ship, with a white flag flying, sailed up the river to Teller's Point, and came to anchor. Colonel Robinson delivered a letter to Colonel Livingston, in command of the Americans there, addressed to General Arnold. The letter was forwarded to Robinson's house. General Arnold was at dinner with a company of officers when the servant put the letter into his hands.

"The enemy have sent Colonel Robinson up the river asking for an interview with me," he remarked.

The second in command at West Point was Colonel Lamb, the man who had his jaw shot away by the side of Montgomery, on that fearful night at Quebec, on the last day of December, 1776. Mr. Lamb was related to Colonel Robinson; but he was a true patriot, and Robinson a Tory.

"To grant such a request would be exceedingly impolitic. It would give the public ground for suspecting improper connections," was Colonel Lamb's outspoken remark.

General Arnold showed the letter to General Washington.

It is considered highly improper for the commander of a post to grant such an interview. A trustworthy officer may be sent, but it is better to have nothing to do with business that pertains to the civil authorities.

General Washingon and General Arnold ride side by side to Peekskill, and pass the night. On the following morning General Washington bids Arnold good-bye. They never will meet again. The one goes east to Hartford; the other returns to the fine old mansion on the banks of the Hudson.

It would be discourteous not to take notice of the letter sent by Colonel Robinson; for, in war, commanders of armies should pay particular regard to any courteous request of an enemy. The messenger who goes down to Teller's Point carries this reply:

"I will send a person in whom you can confide, by water, to meet you at Dobbs's Ferry, at the landing east side, on Wednesday the 20th, who will conduct you to a place of safety, where I will meet you."

The letter is not intended for Colonel Beverly Robinson, but for John Anderson.

In the Kip house, on the 20th of September, Sir Henry Clinton is giving his last instructions to his youthful and beloved adjutant-general, who is going up the Hudson to transact some important business—the purchasing of the strongest fortress in America. The last words are spoken, and the light-hearted officer leaves Sir Henry's apartment. Upon the veranda he meets Polly Kip, the merry daughter of the host. Major André has been so long an inmate of the house that he may address her familiarly. He stands before her, with his boyish face and pleasant smile, in his handsome uniform. Perhaps, as he gazes upon her, his thoughts fly far away over the sea to an English home, and he thinks of the days when he so stood before Honora Sneyd, his true-love, whose portrait, painted by himself, is this moment inclosed in a locket upon his neck. Alas! she is the wife of another, and never again will he clasp her to his heart. He beholds the fair, fresh countenance of the light-hearted Dutch girl.

"Come, Polly, I am going up the river. We are old friends; kiss me good-bye."

"Oh, you be hanged!"

Polly will not give such a favor—not even to Sir Henry Clinton's young and brilliant and good adjutant-general. Little does Polly Kip, little does Major André, think the words spoken in jest may be prophetic of impending doom.

John Anderson is sailing up the Hudson with wind and tide in his favor. He does not land at Teller's Point, but goes on board the *Vulture,* and spends the night.

Autumn has come. The apples are ripening, and an old farmer on the east side of the Hudson, near Teller's Point, is making cider. A party of American militia are drinking and carousing around the press, and the farmer, to get rid of them, informs them that the *Vulture* has come up the river, and is at anchor just off the point.

"You had better go down and bother the British, than to stay here and bother me," he says.

It is a good suggestion. The young men think that they will take a look at the *Vulture*. They are ready for a lark. How

"YOU HAD BETTER GO DOWN AND BOTHER THE BRITISH, THAN TO
STAY HERE AND BOTHER ME."

would it do to hang out a white flag and toll a boat out from the *Vulture*, get it within gun-shot, and then give a volley? The bumpkins know little of the rules of war, and care less. It will be a capital joke, and so they hang out a white cloth.

Mr. John Anderson and Colonel Beverly Robinson see it. That is the place where they are to meet a messenger from General Arnold. Captain Sutherland, commander of the *Vulture*, sends a boat to see about the white flag; but as the boat nears the shore suddenly there is a cracking of rifles, and the bullets splash the water or splinter the boat. It is treachery unheard of, a violation of all the rules of warfare, and the officer in the boat goes back to the *Vulture* boiling over with wrath; and the captain of the ship, hot with anger, sends a letter to General Arnold, wanting to know the meaning of such treachery, and John Anderson begins to suspect that he has been made a fool of. Twice he has failed of meeting Mr. Gustavus.

The trustworthy man whom General Arnold had selected to meet Mr. John Anderson and conduct him to a place of safety was Mr. Joshua Smith, owner of the house at Long Clove, on the west side of the Hudson, just above Haverstraw. Mr. Smith was a Whig—at least he claimed to be one. He was an intelligent man, and owned a large farm. His brother was a Tory, and was in New York with General Clinton; and some of Mr. Smith's Whig neighbors were quite confident that Mr. Smith at Long Clove kept Judge Smith informed of all that was going on up river, and that what Judge Smith knew Sir Henry Clinton knew. General Arnold came to the conclusion that Mr. Smith was just the man to meet Mr. John Anderson, and bring him to a place where he could confer with him on important public matters.

Would Mr. Smith be willing to send his family away for a few days? The matter was of a nature which General Arnold wished to keep from the public, and Mr. Smith was ever ready to do what he could for his country, and was ready to oblige General Arnold, and so carried his wife and children up the river to Fishkill on a visit, and the house was at the service of General Arnold.

General Arnold came down the river to Mr. Smith's house. Would Mr. Smith be kind enough to go down the river in the night to the *Vulture,* and bring a Mr. John Anderson, merchant, of New York, to a point on the shore below Haverstraw? General Arnold would supply him with passes. He might go in the day-time, by flag of truce, but it was better to do it in the

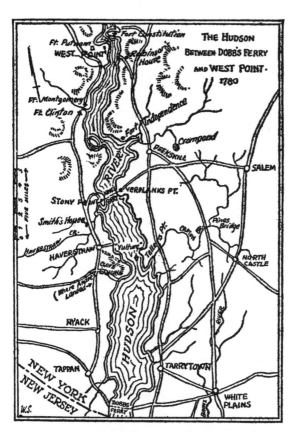

night. Mr. Smith had some hesitation about going in the night, but it was at the request of a major-general of the American army, who had fought gallantly in Canada and at Saratoga; it was a matter of great public importance, and he could not refuse. He obtained two boatmen, Samuel and Joseph Colquhoun, two of his tenants, and in the darkness they leave Long Clove, and go down past Haverstraw to the *Vulture.* The sentinel on board the *Vulture* hails them. They are friends, with passes from General Arnold. Mr. John Anderson steps on board, and they pull to the shore. In the darkness, the boatmen and Mr. Smith can only see that he is a young man, wrapped in a blue cloak.

The boat reaches the land. Mr. Smith climbs the bank, and

finds General Arnold standing beneath the dark and gloomy fir-trees at the foot of the palisades. Mr. John Anderson—for such is the gentleman's name, as Mr. Smith understands—steps upon the land and meets General Arnold, and the two move away a little distance.

No lisp of their conversation is heard by Smith or the boatmen. Hour after hour passes. The morning dawns. The bargain is not completed, but it is quite time that Mr. John Anderson should be on his way back to the ship. He is ready, but the boatmen are not. They have had a long pull; their arms ache. Besides, Samuel and Joseph Colquhoun are Whigs. They are simple-hearted men. They did not wish to go to the *Vulture* at the outset, and they will not make a second trip. The sentinel challenged them roughly; the officer on the deck of the *Vulture* was rude to them; the sailors chaffed them. They do not care to be chaffed a second time. Possibly their neighbors will ask them what they went for. Possibly they have a little distrust of this midnight meeting, although General Arnold, commander at West Point, is one of the parties.

Mr. John Anderson is anxious to be off. General Arnold wishes them to go; Mr. Smith importunes them.

"No, our arms ache. Besides, Colonel Livingston, who is in command over on the east side at Teller's Point, is going to cannonade the *Vulture* in the morning," say the boatmen to Mr. Smith, who reports their answer to Mr. John Anderson.

"Oh, they can reach the ship, and get out of the way before the cannonade begins; and the flag that carried them to the ship will protect them on their return," says Mr. Anderson.

But the boatmen will not go. Day is breaking. Up in the woods Mr. Smith's negro servant is waiting. He followed General Arnold from Smith's house, and is holding General Arnold's horse, and the horse which he himself rode. The business which Mr. Anderson has in hand is not quite completed, and it will be best for him to mount the negro's horse and ride with General Arnold up to Mr. Smith's, beyond Haverstraw. They mount the steeds and ride away, and the boatmen and Mr. Smith and the negro glide along the western shore of the river, reaching Mr. Smith's house almost as quickly as the riders.

The roar of a cannon breaks upon the morning air. Colonel Livingston has begun, and the balls go plump into the sides of the *Vulture,* at anchor near the mouth of the Croton River. John Anderson hears the uproar, looks out of the window, and sees the *Vulture* spreading her white wings to the morning breeze and sailing away. He feels a sinking of heart. What would he not give at that moment to be on board!

After Breakfast They Go into a Chamber, and General Arnold Shows Him a Paper.

General Arnold and the merchant breakfast together. Arnold is very careful to address him as Mr. Anderson. After breakfast they go into a chamber, and General Arnold shows him a paper—a plan of West Point. They talk about money, about troops being placed in particular localities on a particular night in squads, where they might run a chance of being captured, if a British force were suddenly to appear. General Arnold says that a link has been taken out of the great iron chain, and that, if a British fleet should happen to get past the fort, the sailors could quickly separate the boom, and the two ends would swing round against the shores. If a British army should happen to be marching some night up toward West Point, it would be an easy matter for some of the officers, dressed in American uniform, to gallop into the fort and see how the troops were situated. They could do it very easily if they had the countersign; and as General Arnold knows what the countersign is to be, he will just whisper it to Mr. Anderson.

This is the 22d of September, and on the 26th, at midnight, a British army will be marching to surprise the garrison at West Point.

It was ten o'clock in the forenoon when General Arnold got through his business with Mr. John Anderson. He left some papers with Mr. Anderson, bade him good-bye, stepped into his barge, and the rowers pulled up stream to the Robinson house. Mr. Anderson looks at the papers, pulls off his boots, and puts the papers inside of his stockings. He hardly knows why, only General Arnold suggested it. He might carry all there is on the papers in his head; but perhaps they will be of value to Sir Henry Clinton. It would be better for him if he were to burn the papers. The ashes would tell no tale. It would have been better if he had held a white flag in his hand when he came on shore last night, even if no one saw it in the darkness.

Through the day Mr. Anderson remains at Mr. Smith's house. He looks out of the window and views the landscape. Evening comes. Just as twilight is fading away, Mr. Smith and a stranger ride down to King's Ferry. The ferry-man is well acquainted with Mr. Smith.

"We are on our way up river," Mr. Smith remarks to the ferry-man. The stranger with Mr. Smith is a nice-looking young man, dressed in a beaver hat a little the worse for wear, a plum-colored coat trimmed with tarnished gold lace, nankeen small-clothes, and white-topped boots. Good boots they are. Over all is a blue cloak with a heavy cape. They cross the river. Mr. Smith and Mr. Anderson mount their horses, with a negro servant following, for Mr. Smith is a man of consequence.

They gallop up the road leading toward West Point, away from New York, away from the *Vulture*. They come to a road turning off to the right hand. A guide-board, standing at the junction, with an arrow pointing down the road over which they have ridden, has this direction:

> *"Dish his di Rode*
> *tu de Kishnigs Farry."*

Mr. Smith wishes to ride toward New York, but he has informed the ferry-man that he is going "up along," and it will not do to turn to the right here; they ride on two miles farther, and then turn south-east. A sentinel halts them, but they have passes. Captain Boyd, in command of the sentinels, examines the passes:

"Head-quarters, Robinson House, September 22d, 1780.
"Joshua Smith has permission to pass the guards to White Plains and to return, he being on public business by my direction.
"B. ARNOLD, *Major-general."*

"Head-quarters, Robinson House, September 22d, 1780.
"Permit Mr. John Anderson to pass to the White Plains, or below, if he chooses, he being on public business by my direction.
"B. ARNOLD, *Major-general."*

"The passes are all right. The best road is by North Castle. The Tarrytown road is infested by Cow-boys, and you had better not attempt to get on to-night," says Captain Boyd.

Mr. Smith thought it prudent advice, and halted at a farm-house till morning.

John Anderson and Mr. Smith were up by day-break on the morning of the 23d of September. Mr. Anderson had not been asleep. He had a haggard look, and had grown old. Mr. Smith and Mr. Anderson would not stop for breakfast, but before sunrise were galloping southward on important public business; and Mr. Smith was ignorant as to what that business might be. He may have had a suspicion that something not quite right was going on; but General Arnold had not enlightened him in regard to it.

Twelve miles, and they halted for breakfast. It was at a small house. The Cow-boys had been there during the night and robbed the lone female occupant of almost every thing. She could only give them some hasty-pudding, which the Dutch called *soupann*. Curious that this same John Anderson should have written, a few weeks before, a poem called "The Cow Chase," in which he had ridiculed the men who, while fighting for their liberty, could get nothing but water and hasty-pudding. These were his lines:

> "For many heroes bold and brave,
>   From New Bridge and Tapaan,
> And those that drink Passaick's wave,
>   And those that eat soupaan."

"I must bid you good-bye here," Mr. Smith said, while eating his pudding.

They were close to the Croton River. Mr. Anderson would find no sentinel beyond that. He would be on neutral ground. If he were to fall in with either the Cow-boys or the Skinners, Mr. Smith would be of no service to him. The Cow-boys were a set of rascals who shouted "God save the king!" but who plundered every body. The Skinners were another set of ruffians who shouted "Hurra for Congress!" but who plundered all they met. Sometimes the Cow-boys and Skinners joined their forces, and made raids among the farmers, drove off their cattle, and robbed them of their provisions. Besides these, there were bands of militia, composed of the farmers, who joined together to protect themselves from the Cow-boys, the Skinners, and the British. If Mr. Anderson were to fall in with either party he would get along just as well alone as with Mr. Smith. They bade each other good-bye. Mr. Smith and his negro servant rode to the Robinson house, where Mr. Smith sat down to General Arnold's table to dinner, and informed General Arnold that Mr. Anderson was well on his way to the British lines. The general was well satisfied with what Mr. Smith had done.

Mr. Anderson pursues his solitary way. He comes to two

roads, one leading to Tarrytown, the other farther east; but both leading toward New York. Which shall he take?

Is it that the right-hand road will take him down through Sleepy Hollow, where a little brook winds down from the hills, and where the little old Dutch church is standing? There have been delightful legends since then about Sleepy Hollow? It was there that Ichabod Crane, the tall, lean, and awkward school-master, fell in love with Katrina Van Tassel, sung with her in the old church, sat in her father's kitchen during the long evenings, looking into her eyes, and thinking how delightful it would be to have Katrina forever by his side in a kitchen of their own. Going by the way of Sleepy Hollow, John Anderson would cross the bridge by the old mill, where the ghostly horseman, enveloped in a cloak, on a fiery steed, carrying his head on the pommel of the saddle instead of on his shoulders, chased the school-master and threw his head at him, and so frightened Ichabod that he fled from Sleepy Hollow, and left Katrina to be married to his rival, Brom Bones.

John Anderson, as he rode along the solitary road over the hills and through the valleys, with no one to keep him company, was thinking how soon he might come across a British sentinel. Is there any reason why he should take the right-hand road rather than the left? No, for the distance by one is no greater than the other, and both are equally safe.

He turns to the right. Oh, if he had but taken the left! He goes to his destiny, and with him goes the destiny of a nation.

Mr. Anderson is thirsty, and asks for a drink of water at Mr. Hammond's farm-house, and the little Hammond boy, who holds his bay horse by the rein, notices that it is a good horse, but that there are burrs in its mane and tail, that the rider wears a plum-colored, silver-laced coat, and nice boots.

"How far is it to Tarrytown, my lad?"

"Four miles."

"Four miles! I did not think it so far."

His is a pleasant voice. The traveler rides on, and meets some Quaker farmers.

"Friends, are there any troops out below?"

The men wearing broad-brimmed hats have seen none.

Mr. Anderson meets a man on horseback, an American officer. His hair stands on end; his heart leaps into his mouth. It is an officer whom he knows, and who knows him—Colonel Samuel P. Webb. They stare at each other, and pass on. He has now reached the Hudson. A little farther, and he will meet British sentinels. He is light-hearted once more.

The traveler has reached Sleepy Hollow. The air is still on this sweet September day. He hears the water falling over the dam by the mill; he can see the little old church, and before him is the bridge where the ghostly horseman threw his head at Ichabod Crane.

Beyond it, on the south side of the stream, is a

"Friends, Are There Any Troops Out Below?"

wood of oak, and chestnuts, and alders, and matted grape-vines. Three young men are seated in the bushes beneath the vines. They have been there but a little while, but having been out all night, have sat down to rest, and are playing cards. There are four other men on a hill at a little distance, looking toward Tarrytown to see if the British down below are making any movements. They do not belong to the army, but call themselves militia. The officer up at Salem has given them liberty to come down toward Tarrytown to see what they can discover, and to punish the Cow-boys, if they can get an opportunity.

One of the men under the grape-vines is John Paulding. He is only twenty-one years old; he is six feet high. Twice has he been arrested and taken to New York a prisoner. He obtained the uniform which he is now wearing from a German Yager, and made his escape; and here he is with his rifle, on the lookout for somebody on whom he can make reprisals.

David Williams, another of the three, marched to Canada under General Montgomery. He has nothing to do now, and is working for his board for whomsoever will employ him, and his food consists principally of johnny-cake.

Isaac Van Wart lives up by Pine Ridge. But here are the three. They hear the sound of a horse's hoofs. One is engaged in shuffling the cards.

"There comes a trader, going to New York," says Van Wart.

"He is a gentlemanly-looking man, is well dressed, and has topboots on. Hadn't you better stop him?" says Williams to Paulding, the captain.

All three spring to their feet, and seize their rifles.

"Halt!"

It is the command of the man who has been twice a prisoner. The traveler reins in his horse.

"Where are you going?"

"My lads, I hope you belong to our party."

"Which party is that?"

What shall the traveler say? He is close to Tarrytown. He is going south. Of course, these are Cow-boys, or else British soldiers in disguise. One wears a Yager uniform. It will not do to hesitate.

"The lower party."

"So do we."

The youthful heart beneath that plum-colored coat bounds with exultation.

"Thank God, I am once more among friends!"

How strange and wonderful that in these words lie the destiny of a nation and the future history of a continent!

"I am glad to see you. I am a British officer, out of the country on particular business, and I hope you won't detain me a moment."

He pulls his gold watch from his pocket. Better have left it in the fob.

"You are our prisoner," says Paulding.

"Ha! ha! Here is General Arnold's pass!" The traveler pulls the pass written by Arnold from his pocket. "My God! I must do any thing to get along," he says in a low voice to himself.

The man in the Yager uniform reads it.

"Had you shown this first, I would have let you go, but now I must examine you. Dismount!"

It is a peremptory order, and John Anderson, so near the British lines and yet at this moment farther from them than ever, is led to the roadside, to the shelter of a gigantic tree.

"You will bring down the displeasure of General Arnold by doubting me."

"We must search you."

"I have no papers. You will bring yourselves into trouble."

"Take off your cloak!"

His cloak is laid aside, and the plum-colored coat. There is a British uniform beneath it.

"Let us see your boots!"

They find nothing in his boots. How about his stockings?

"Here is something!" Paulding's hand is upon the fatal paper.

Ah! Why did he take that paper in Benedict Arnold's handwriting? What good could it do him! He could have remembered it all. Fatal mistake! Three half-sheets.

"West Point" is written on the outer sheet. Paulding uses wicked words at times.

"By God, he is a spy! Where did you obtain these papers?"

No answer.

"What will you give us to let you go?" Van Wart asks.

"All that I have, and a hundred guineas, and any quantity of goods."

"I won't release him for ten thousand guineas," says Paulding, with an oath.

"Will you escape if we give you an opportunity?"

"Of course I will."

"Then we will not let you."

"Take me to the nearest American camp," says John Anderson. He will talk no more.

It was twelve miles to the nearest American outpost, at North Castle, where John Anderson was delivered by his captors to Colonel Jameson, who examined the papers found in Anderson's stockings.

"Will you please inform General Arnold that John Anderson, with a pass signed by him, has been arrested?" said the prisoner.

It was Colonel Jameson's duty to report the arrest to General Arnold, and he concluded that he might as well send John Anderson at once to head-quarters, and transmit the papers to General Washington. Lieutenant Allen, with four soldiers of the Continental militia, was ready to start with John Anderson for West Point.

A company of cavalry on dapple-gray horses, under Major Tallmadge, came galloping up. Major Tallmadge was appointed by Washington to guard this section from the depredations of the Cow-boys and Skinners, and to carry on a secret correspondence with spies in New York. His troops wear glittering helmets with horse-tail plumes, and have bear-skin holsters manufactured in France. They have been out on a scout.

Tallmadge was a young man only twenty-six years old, but his was an old head on young shoulders.

"A man was arrested," said Colonel Jameson, "down near Tarrytown this morning. He had a pass from General Arnold, and was going toward New York. He had some papers in his stockings stating the number of guns at West Point, the number of soldiers, and where they are posted. His name is John Anderson, and I have just sent him to West Point to General Arnold, and dispatched the papers to Washington."

"BY GOD, HE IS A SPY! WHERE DID YOU OBTAIN THESE PAPERS?"

343

Major Tallmadge listened intently. He remembered that a few weeks before Colonel Sheldon had received a letter written in New York by John Anderson, who was to be taken to Arnold's head-quarters. And now John Anderson had been arrested going toward New York with important papers on his person. What was the meaning of it? General Arnold was in correspondence with the enemy. The papers found on John Anderson were in Arnold's handwriting. Major Tallmadge turned the matter over in his mind. "General Arnold is a traitor!" he exclaimed. That was the conclusion he arrived at.

"That can not be," said Colonel Jameson, astonished at the suggestion.

"You ought not to let Arnold know of it."

"It is my duty. He is my superior, in command of the department."

"I will take all the blame if you will send a man to bring Anderson back."

Colonel Jameson could not believe that Arnold was a traitor, but concluded to have Anderson brought back.

Early in the morning Anderson is sent to Colonel Sheldon's head-quarters at South Salem. Lieutenant King has charge of him, and walks with him in the yard in front of the house. He is an affable gentleman, and soon wins the confidence of John Anderson.

"I must make a confidant of somebody. John Anderson is not my name. I am Major John André, Adjutant-general of the British army."

The prisoner breathes more freely now.

"The papers found on you have been sent to General Washington, and he, and not General Arnold, will decide what shall be done with you," is the information imparted to Major André.

Paper and ink are supplied him, and he writes a full and frank letter to General Washington, claiming that he is not a spy. Against his intention he was conducted inside of the American lines. He came in his British uniform. He signed the letter

John André, Adjutant-general, and an officer started with it in search of General Washington.

Washington is at Fishkill, on his way west from Hartford. He meets the French envoy, M. De Luzerne, who has just come from General Arnold's head-quarters, and is on his way east. They stop at Fishkill for dinner, and one of the guests at the table is Mr. Joshua Smith, who, after escorting Mr. John Anderson to the Croton River, has ridden up there to get his family; General Arnold having no further use for his house, his important public business having all been transacted.

General Washington having returned from Hartford by the *upper* road, and Colonel Jameson's messenger having gone to Hartford by the *lower* road, the former has heard nothing in regard to the arrest of one John Anderson; and for the same reason Major André's letter has not come into the American commander's hands.

Mr. Smith sits at the table, ignorant that Mr. John Anderson has been arrested, ignorant that John André and John Anderson are one and the same person.

The sweet, sad season of the year has come. The changing foliage is bright with autumnal hues. General Arnold and his young wife are at the Robinson House. A sentinel, on the morning of the 25th of September, is pacing his beat before the door. From West Point comes the roll of the morning drum. Only once more will the drummer beat it there beneath the Stars and Stripes. To-morrow night the cross of St. George will float above the ramparts, and the Stars and Stripes will soon be seen no more on the Western continent. The flag will be heard of no more, except in history, as the flag of the rebels, who were subdued by the valour of the British troops, and by the defection of one of the most trusted and popular American officers. Such may have been the thoughts that flashed through the brain of Major-general Arnold, as he listened to that morning's reveille.

Early in the morning, a light traveling-wagon drives into the door yard. It is General Washington's baggage van, and the officer in charge has the pleasure of presenting the compliments of General Washington and the Marquis de Lafayette, who, with their suites, will do themselves the honor of breakfasting at the Robinson house. A little later the marquis rides up to the door with his suite and other officers.

General Washington has turned aside to examine the fortifications by the river, and begs that Mrs. Arnold will not delay breakfast on his account.

The breakfast-table is spread in the large room. It is a low apartment with wainscoted walls and great beams overhead. The beautiful young wife presides with charming grace at the table.

A horseman rides into the yard and halts beneath the cherry-trees—Lieutenant Allen. He comes from Colonel Jameson, and has a letter for General Arnold. Colonel Jameson has deemed it his duty to report to his superior the capture of a man by the name of John Anderson, and to state that the papers upon him have been forwarded to General Washington. General Arnold breaks the seal, and reads the letter at the table. He is a little embarrassed; but the conversation goes on, and General Arnold takes part in it for a few minutes.

"Excuse me, gentlemen; I have some business that will require my attention a few moments. Please make yourselves at home meanwhile."

He leaves the room and calls one of his aids: "Have the barge ready instantly. I must cross to West Point without delay. Order the coxswain and crew at once."

He calls Lieutenant Allen aside: "You must not mention to any one that you have brought a letter from Colonel Jameson."

He spoke to the hostler: "Bring a horse, quick. Any horse —a wagon horse, even!"

His orders are peremptory, and the men move quickly to obey.

The guests are eating alone, for the young wife, accustomed to all her husband's moods, sees that something unusual has occurred. She excuses herself, rises from the table, and passes into her chamber.

One of his aids' horses is at the door. The coxswain of the

barge, Mr. Larvey, is mustering the crew. General Arnold meets his young wife in her chamber. He kisses their babe.

"We must part at once, and perhaps forever."

The loving arms that clasp his neck unclose, and with a wild outcry she swoons upon the floor.

"Take care of her," he says to the chamber-maid, that moment entering. He descends to the breakfast-room.

"I beg your indulgence, gentlemen; but Mrs. Arnold has been seized with sudden illness," he says to the Marquis de Lafayette and the other officers, still sitting at the table. He seizes his holster, with pistol and powder-flask, leaps into the saddle, and dashes down the hill to the water.

"Take your places!" He shouts it to the oarsmen standing on the shore, leaps from the horse, springs into the barge.

"Push off!"

The barge glides from the shore.

"I am going to the *Vulture* with a flag of truce, and must get there as quick as I can, and back again to meet Washington. You shall have two gallons of rum, my boys, when you get back."

It is eighteen miles to the *Vulture*—a long pull; but swiftly the boat glides down the stream, and while on their way Major-general Arnold examines his pistols, re-primes them, cocks and uncocks them, and conducts himself as the barge-men never have seen him before.

Colonel Livingston is still at Teller's Point. He sees the barge of General Arnold moving swiftly down stream, General Arnold himself holding the white flag—his pocket-handkerchief tied to a cane. What is the meaning of it? A major-general never goes with a flag of truce. Colonel Livingston will go out and see the meaning of such a procedure; but before he can summon his rowers, the barge is alongside the *Vulture*, still lying at anchor in the river, but beyond the reach of Livingston's cannon.

General Arnold unties the handkerchief, and with it wipes away the great beads of sweat upon his brow. He climbs the side of the ship. Colonel Beverly Robinson is on board: he is there waiting for Mr. John Anderson, merchant; but the merchant's foot nevermore will press the deck of the *Vulture*. In the cabin, to Robinson and Captain Sutherland, the traitor narrates the story. The plan has failed—André is a prisoner; but Arnold has escaped, to enter the king's service. He goes upon the deck, and calls the coxswain, Larvey, and the crew on board.

"You must enter the king's service, or I shall detain you as prisoners," he says.

The malignity and hate so long smothered has taken fire, and this is its first outburst.

"If General Arnold likes the King of England, let him serve him. *We love our country, and intend to live or die in support of her cause,*" are the words of the coxswain. Glorious Larvey! Words that shall never die. A century has passed since they were uttered, but how thrilling to read them! Six of the boat's crew swear their allegiance to America.

Captain Sutherland turns with contempt from Arnold. He will not interfere, however, with Arnold's orders, and the heroes are prisoners for the time being. They are taken to New York, but are at once released on parole by Sir Henry Clinton.

General Washington and the officers of the army had not forgotten how the brave man from Connecticut, Nathan Hale, was executed, without trial, as a spy; but not so should Major André suffer. He was tried by court-martial, found guilty, and condemned to die.

The American army was at Tappan, in New York, and there, in the presence of all the soldiers, he was hanged. He was so kind and genial and gifted, that all who knew him loved him. Every kindness was shown him, and many of the soldiers shed tears when they saw him die. In England his fate was sorely lamented, and the king caused a monument to be erected in Westminster Abbey to his memory; and yet he suffered justly for he was a spy.

Chapter 28
KING'S MOUNTAIN
AND THE COWPENS

AUGUST 16th, 1780, at Camden, was a sad day for the patriots of the South. There was no army to oppose the British; but, though Gates was defeated, the Whigs living up in the mountains had no intention of yielding. They would still be patriots. The Tories, on the other hand, joined Cornwallis in large numbers; and Cornwallis concluded to raise a Tory army, and also to send a force into the mountains to crush out the Whigs. He dispatched Major Ferguson, of the Seventy-first regiment, with one hundred and ten regulars and as many more Tories, to march up to the mountains, and compel the Whigs to take the oath of loyalty, or else harry them out of the country.

Ferguson started and marched north-west. The Tories flocked to his standard, and in a few days he had a force of eleven hundred men, who plundered the people, burned their houses, drove off their cattle, and in some instances committed brutal murder.

Men who live among the mountains are always lovers of liberty; and the more the Tories plundered and burned, the more the Whigs resolved that they would not be subdued. Messengers rode here and there, summoning the patriots to arms. They answered the summons, and from all the mountain glens hastened to the rendezvous. It was harvest-time. They could find potatoes and pumpkins and corn ripening in the fields, and so needed no commissariat, no long train of wagons. Each man had his powder-horn and bullet-pouch filled with ammunition. They could make quick marches. At night they could lie down and sleep sweetly beneath the evergreen pines. In the woods were deer; and they were all true marksmen, and could bring down a buck upon the run. They knew that Ferguson was on the march— that in a few days the Tories would be burning their houses.

Colonel Campbell gathered four hundred men from Washington County; in Virginia, Colonel Isaac Shelby rallied two hundred and forty; and Colonel John Sevier came with two hundred and forty North Carolinians. Colonel M'Dowell came with one hundred and sixty who had fled from before Ferguson. Colonel Cleaveland came with three hundred and fifty from the counties of Wilkes and Surrey; and Colonel James Williams came with four hundred from South Carolina. They met at the Cowpens, near the North Carolina line. Ferguson was about thirty miles away, at King's Mountain, on the line between North and South Carolina, fifteen miles east of Broad River. Colonel Campbell was chosen commander. They had come out to fight, and determined to strike a blow, and not wait to receive one. It was resolved that nine hundred of their best men should make a forced march, and strike Ferguson unawares, and the rest were to follow as rapidly as possible.

It is after dark, on the 6th of October, when they start. They leave the Cowpens, move eastward, cross the Broad River, and push on for King's Mountain. They know the roads. The column winds through the forests. In the morning, they halt, rest their horses a while, and resume the march.

Ferguson is resting securely on the mountain. He knows that the Whigs are gathering in the West; but he is in a strong position, and does not expect to be attacked.

The mountaineers halt within a mile of Ferguson's position. Colonel Campbell forms his little army, less in number by two hundred than the foe he is seeking. Colonel Campbell's own regiment, with part of Colonel Cleaveland's and Colonel Shelby's, takes the right; Colonel Sevier, the left; Colonel Williams and the rest of Cleaveland's form the centre. It is three o'clock in the afternoon. In this order they move so silently that they are within a quarter of a mile of Ferguson before they are discovered. Colonel Campbell has sent his wings around, as Stark sent his at Bennington, to close in upon the enemy, and make the attack from every quarter.

There is a sudden commotion in Ferguson's ranks, a quick springing to arms. A moment later, Shelby's and Campbell's regiment are pouring their fire into the ranks of the confused Tories. It is in the forest. A little brook winds beneath the trees. There are hillocks here and there, and sheltered places, from which each party may fire upon the other.

The Mountaineers Are On All Sides, and Have the Advantage.

The other regiments hear the rattling of the guns, and hasten on. Five minutes later, they, too, are engaged. The Tories are astonished at the suddenness and fierceness of the attack. They had joined Ferguson, expecting to have fine opportunities to plunder their neighbors, and now they are in battle, and the bullets are pouring in upon them from every quarter. Ferguson orders his regulars to charge, and for a moment the mountaineers are driven; but they rally and drive the regulars in turn. The Tories fight with desperation from behind rocks and trees, and the mountaineers attack with equal courage. If a Tory exposes himself, if he steps from behind a tree, bullets come from several directions. The mountaineers are on all sides, and have the advantage. Colonel Ferguson falls, and the command devolves upon Captain Depeyster. He is unaccustomed to such a mode of warfare. He can charge an enemy; but to meet an enemy behind rocks and trees is not the way they fight in England. He forms a few of his men, to charge and break the line of the Whigs. They rush down the mountain side, but from front and flank the bullets come; his men drop, the others turn and flee. But whither shall they flee? They run north, but find themselves confronted by Colonel Cleaveland. They are hemmed in, and there is no escape. Depeyster raises a white flag. A shout of triumph goes up from the victors. Now is the time for revenge. Down at Waxhaw, Tarleton murdered Buford's men in cold blood. No plea for mercy stayed the sword. But no such slaughter shall tarnish this victory of the mountaineers, and the firing ceases.

Yet among the prisoners are twelve Tories, who have been implacable in their hate; who have plundered the people, burned their houses, and hanged all who opposed them; whose hands are red with blood; they shall suffer. Ropes are thrown over the branches of a tulip-tree, and twelve are hanged—the meting out of a just retribution to those who have shown no mercy.

The rivers in North and South Carolina rise in the Alleghanies, and run south-east to the sea. In North Carolina is the Dan, which passes into Virginia, and becomes the Roanoke. South of the Dan are two small streams, one called Reedy Fork, and the other Troublesome Creek, rising amidst the hills. Below the junction the stream is called the Haw for forty miles or more. At the south-east corner of Chatham County, nearly in the centre of the State, another stream comes in from the west, called Deep River, and from this point to the sea the stream is called Cape Fear River.

South of these is the Yadkin, which rises away up in the northwest section of the State, runs across the State into South Carolina; but in that State it is called the Great Pedee. Beyond these is the Catawba, which in South Carolina, for one hundred miles or more, is called the Wateree, and for a short distance the Congaree, and lastly the Santee. It empties into the Atlantic about forty miles north of Charleston.

In the fall of the year, up near the mountains, there are sudden freshets, and at such times for a day or two the rivers can not be forded.

On the 2d of December, 1780, General Greene took command of the Southern Department, at Charlotte, North Carolina, a village of thirty or forty houses, about ten miles east of the Catawba, and twenty from the South Carolina line. He had in all about two thousand men; but only eight hundred were fit for duty, for many of the soldiers were nearly naked, and they had no blankets.

"The troops may be said to be literally naked," General Greene wrote to Thomas Jefferson, Governor of Virginia. On the day he took command there were not three days' provisions in camp. He had not a dollar of hard money. He had Continental paper money, but one hundred dollars of Continental money were worth only one silver dollar. The people would not touch it. General Gates had decided to have the army spend the winter at Charlotte, and had begun to build huts there; but General Greene resolved at once upon a winter campaign, and on the 16th marched south-east into South Carolina, and encamped on the east side of the Great Pedee, on Cheraw Hill. He wanted shirts for his soldiers, but had no money.

"Pay in salt," he said to his quartermaster, and so obtained the shirts, although he had little salt to spare.

The soldiers belonging to North Carolina were in the habit of going home when they pleased. "That must be stopped; no more going home without leave. I will hang the first offender," said Greene.

A man went home, was arrested, and executed, and there was no more going home after that. Troops joined him from Virginia—four hundred infantry and three hundred cavalry. General Morgan was with him—the man who had marched with Arnold to Canada, who commanded the infantry at Stillwater and Saratoga. He was nearly as poor as the soldiers, had but one shirt now, and whenever he wanted it washed he had to wrap himself in his cloak.

General Otho H. Williams, who had marched from Maryland to Boston, in 1775, as lieutenant in a rifle company, and acted as adjutant-general, and who had been in the battle of Camden, was there; and now young Henry Lee, of Virginia, came with Colonel William Washington.

He Had No Cannon to Batter the Buildings Down, but He Mounted a Pine Log on a Pair of Cartwheels.

Colonel Washington had just captured, on the 4th, a party of Tories at Rugeley's Mills, twelve miles from Camden, the place from which Gates had started to attack Cornwallis. There were one hundred and twelve Tories under Rugeley, who owned the mill. Colonel Washington came upon them suddenly and surrounded them. The Tories ran into Rugeley's log-house and barn. Williams had no cannon to batter the buildings down, but he mounted a pine log on a pair of cart-wheels, aimed it at the house, and sent a summons to Rugeley to surrender before he opened fire upon the buildings, and Rugeley and the whole one hundred and ten gave themselves up. There was hearty laughing among the Americans when the crest-fallen Tories discovered the deception.

Cornwallis was at Winnsborough; and General Greene divided his army by sending Morgan to harass Cornwallis's foraging and scouting parties. General Morgan was more than one hundred miles west of General Greene, close to the North Carolina line, at a place where the farmers who pastured their cattle on the hills brought them up at night for milking, and it was therefore called the Cowpens. Morgan has about one thousand men—all infantry except one hundred and twenty men under Colonel Washington.

General Cornwallis sees that Greene has divided his army, and is too far away to aid Morgan, and resolves to send Tarleton, with eleven hundred of his best troops, to crush him at a single blow. At the same time, he intends to move with his troops from Winnsborough north, midway between the Catawba and Broad rivers, and will cut off Morgan's retreat into North Carolina, and then move on to invade that State, march northeast, get in the rear of Greene, and cut him off from Virginia.

General Morgan keeps his eyes open. He does not intend to be surprised. His spies inform him that Tarleton, with eleven hundred men, is coming like the wind to crush him. About half of his men are militia. He knows that they will be likely to run at the first fire, as they did at Camden; and in the battle which he intends to fight he will fix things so that they can not flee with any hope of escaping. He selects his position not far from the bank of the river, where there is no ford and where the water is deep. Tarleton will attack him from the front to drive him toward the river. It is in the woods, where there is no underbrush. There are no swamps near to which his militia can flee. He posts his first line on a ridge of land, and behind it about two hundred feet is another higher ridge, on which he establishes his second line.

There are Tories in Tarleton's ranks, and the hate is bitter between Whig and Tory. Morgan has no cannon. He knows that early in the morning Tarleton will make his appearance after a long night's march. He considers that Tarleton's men will be weary, while his own will be fresh.

Morning comes, and Morgan is up early. The scouts bring information that Tarleton is not far away. Morgan gives his men a hearty breakfast, and while they are eating it he passes through the lines and looks at their guns.

"This is the way to use a bayonet," he says, as he shows a raw soldier how to stand a charge. "This is the way to swing the sword," he says to a dragoon. "Hold up your heads, boys. Stand your ground till you have fired three times, and the day is yours." He believes that

"This Is the Way to Use a Bayonet," He Says

by that time the militia will not be frightened at the whistling of bullets, and will get over the idea of running away.

Morgan puts his best troops—Howard's Marylanders, who have been in battle—on the highest ridge in the centre, and his two companies of Virginians on the left. The Virginians are old soldiers; some of them fought at Monmouth, Brandywine, and Germantown. On the left he places his riflemen. Lieutenant-colonel Howard has command of the line. Out in front of their line he places the Georgia and North Carolina militia, and in advance of them one hundred and twenty picked men, with rifles, who can bring down a squirrel any time from the highest trees. Behind the second hill he places Colonel Washington with his cavalry—out of sight, ready to move in an instant.

The Tories in Tarleton's ranks know the ground. "The woods are open, and free from swamps. Morgan is about six miles from Broad River, close by a creek," they say to Tarleton. Tarleton is delighted. Long before the fugitives can reach the creek he will cut them to pieces.

"Lay aside your knapsacks, and every thing except your guns and ammunition," are Tarleton's orders. He will have his men go into the fight so that they can be as light of foot as the Americans, to trample them down the moment he gets them upon the run. He does not stop to take breakfast. He will finish the little job he has in hand, and eat breakfast afterward.

"File right, and attack the left flank," are Tarleton's orders to the light-infantry. He sends a three-pounder to open fire. The light-infantry file into position. The Seventh regiment forms in front of Morgan's centre with the other three-pounder. He sends fifty dragoons to the right flank and fifty to the left. A battalion and two hundred cavalry are placed in a second line.

While Tarleton is forming, Morgan goes along the line. "Be firm—keep cool—take good aim. Give two volleys at killing distance, and the victory is yours. You of the main line, here on the hill, must not lose heart when you see the skirmishers and the militia out in front of you fall back. That is a part of the plan. They will draw the fire of the British, and then fall back."

He says this, knowing that the militia will run. He came to the Carolinians and Georgians. "Let me see—which is most entitled to credit, the Georgians or Carolinians? I'll let you decide that question here." So he encourages them—each to do

their best.   He takes his position on the hill where he can overlook all.

The fifty British dragoons on the right and the fifty on the
left are advancing.   They are going to make a charge upon each
flank, and double up Morgan's line in a twinkling.   The rifles
crack.   One saddle emptied—another—another—another.   But
still the British dragoons come on—the militia begin to fall back.
Another empty saddle—another.   The British cannon begin to
thunder.   Another saddle emptied—more—fifteen in all, and
the horses are running wild.

The militia are falling back, but they are not frightened, and
the men in line on the hill keep steady ranks, as the militia fall
behind them.   There comes a hurra from the British, who have
driven the riflemen and skirmishers, and will make quick work of
it now.   They advance upon the run.

The hill is a sheet of flame, and the British come to a walk.
They were going to charge bayonet, but conclude to pour in a
volley first.   Three volleys have been fired on each side.   The
Americans are getting used to the whistling of bullets, and they
have no thought of running.   Tarleton is surprised.   He did not
expect such resistance.   "Forward the second line," is his order.
He will hurl his whole force upon the rebels, and smite them
down with a single sledge-hammer stroke.

"Now is the time."   It is Morgan's order to the cavalry behind the hill.   Out from the shelter of the sand-hill move the
troopers.   Through the woods they ride, and fall suddenly upon
the British dragoons, and put them to flight.

Tarleton's second line is moving upon Howard—swinging out
upon his right to outflank him.

"Right company, change front!" is Howard's order; but the
men think he has ordered a retreat, and begin to fall back.
Howard sees the mistake.   He will not countermand the order,
for the men are not frightened.   He will take a new position.

Morgan sees the movement, and hastens to the spot. "What
are you retreating for?" he shouts.

"Simply a change of position, to protect my right flank."

"Are you beaten?"

"Do those men march as if they were beaten?"

"Right! I will ride back and select the best position, and when you reach it face about and let them have it."

Off to the new spot rides Morgan.

"Hurra! Hurra!" It is the shout of the British coming upon the run. Now they will sweep all before them.

Colonel Washington is by Morgan's side.

"They are coming like a mob. Turn and let them have it, and I will charge them," he shouts to Howard.

"Right about face!"

The retreating men face suddenly about. There is a flash and rattle. The British come to a sudden halt. Down from the hill ride the dragoons with Washington leading them.

"Give them the bayonet!" It is Howard's shout. Back over the ground across which they have just retreated move the Marylanders. Like a thunder-bolt Washington's cavalry sweep on. The British line goes down. Some of the soldiers throw away their guns and flee, some are cut down by the sword, others hold up their hands and beg for mercy.

The victory is won! It is not a half-hour since Tarleton began the battle and now his army is a panic-stricken mob. Eighty killed, one hundred and fifty wounded, six hundred prisoners, two cannon, eight hundred muskets, thirty-five wagons, one hundred cavalry horses—lost in fifteen minutes.

Morgan has lost twelve killed and sixty-one wounded.

"Give them Tarleton's quarter—kill them!" It is the cry of the Whigs against the Tories.

But Morgan will not permit a man to be put to death. Such a victory shall not be marred by the slaughter of men after they have surrendered.

ON the day of the battle of the Cowpens, Cornwallis was thirty miles east of that place, between the Broad and Catawba rivers. It was astounding intelligence which a dragoon brought to him on the evening of the 17th of January. Tarleton defeated! routed! Eight hundred men lost! Impossible! But the fugitives were coming in. There was no doubt about it. Instead of crushing Morgan, Tarleton, with superior numbers, had suffered an ignominious defeat. It was intolerable. Cornwallis would quickly punish the rebel general. By marching rapidly due north, he could cut off Morgan before that officer, with his prisoners and plunder, could reach the Catawba. General Leslie was close at hand, advancing from Camden with about one thousand men, and upon his arrival he would push ahead.

But over at the Cowpens on that same night General Morgan was thinking of what Cornwallis would be doing. That he would determine to rescue the prisoners, was certain. That he could do it, unless Morgan stirred himself, was equally clear.

At midnight Morgan left the battle-field with his exultant army. He had two cannon now, and wagons and provisions. The roads were miry; it was raining; and he could make only ten miles in twenty-four hours. He crossed the Broad River and pushed for the Little Catawba, reached it, and crossed with his provisions and baggage. Cornwallis had lost his prey. Two days later he reached the ford, chagrined to find that Morgan was in advance of him.

Bitter the disappointment. He would have Morgan yet. "Burn all the surplus baggage," is his order, and, to set an example, burns his own. He will keep only four wagons, for the sick, for hospital stores, and ammunition. He will live on the country and march day and night, to rescue the prisoners and punish the rebel commander.

Morgan is down with rheumatism. His troops need rest; but his scouts inform him that Cornwallis is burning his baggage. Morgan comprehends the meaning of it, and it is high time for him to move. His army is smaller than it was. The Georgia and South Carolina militia have returned to their homes, and the Virginia militia have stayed out their time.

On Cheraw Hill, one hundred miles east of the Cowpens, is Greene's camp. Great the rejoicing there at the news of the victory at the Cowpens.

"Be ready to march," is Greene's order on the 25th of January. A messenger hastens northward. He is to ride clear across North Carolina to the Virginia lines with this order: "Have boats in readiness, so that the army can cross the Dan." Boats in readiness! What can General Greene, who is down at Cheraw, want of boats away up there in Virginia, two hundred miles away? But General Greene has looked over the chessboard, and sees the kind of move that Cornwallis may make, and it is well to be prepared. Another messenger hastens north-west to the Yadkin on a similar errand. "Send recruits," is his letter to Governor Thomas Jefferson, of Virginia; also to Governor Thomas Nash, of North Carolina. "Hang on Cornwallis's rear; cut off his detachments," is the word sent south to the Swamp Fox, Francis Marion, who is one day in one place, and hiding in a swamp the next, moving so rapidly that the British know not where to put their fingers on him. "March north-west to Salisbury," is the word to General Huger, whom he places in command of his little force at Cheraw; then mounting his horse, with twenty dragoons to accompany him, he strikes across the country to join Morgan.

Morgan is marching north-east, aiming for Salisbury; while Cornwallis, being east of him at the outset, is marching nearly north, to intercept him before he reaches the Catawba. Rapid the retreat, but swifter the pursuit. Morgan reaches the river, sends his baggage and prisoners across, and then his little army. Just as the sun goes down, the British, under O'Hara, reach the river; but O'Hara does not dare to attempt to cross till reenforcements arrive, and when they come it is evening. Cornwallis decides to let his troops rest till morning, and then he will cross and seize his prey. But all night long the rain falls in torrents, and in the morning the river is a wild and turbulent stream—too deep to be forded.

While the rain is pouring, General Greene rides into Morgan's camp. He is covered with mud, and weary, but receives a hearty welcome from Morgan.

"What is your line of retreat?" he asks.

Morgan points it out—still north-east.

"That will not do; Cornwallis will overtake you;" and he selects another road. He sends a messenger to Huger, who is moving toward Salisbury, to change his route and to make rapid marches.

The flood goes down almost as rapidly as it rose. The water is still deep, but Cornwallis is determined to secure his prey. He is near Beattie's Ford. Six miles below Beattie's Ford is Cowan's Ford. Cornwallis decides to send Lieutenant-colonel Webster to Beattie's Ford, to make a feint of crossing, while he steals off at midnight with the main army, to cross at Cowan's, and get in rear of Morgan. Needless strategy, for Morgan has left the river and is on the march; but Colonel Davidson, with seven hundred North Carolina farmers, is at Cowan's, guarding the ford. The river is wide, but the British wade across it. The farmers fire a volley or two, but the British greatly outnumber them. Colonel Davidson falls, and they flee —most of them to their homes. About three hundred retreat to Tarrant's tavern, toward Salisbury. They halt at noon.

Tarleton—more savage and blood-thirsty than ever after his defeat—thinks to surprise them; but they are on the alert, and Tarleton has the mortification of seeing twelve of his men killed and fifteen wounded. There are some old men and boys around Tarrant's unarmed, but they are Whigs, and, in revenge, his soldiers slaughter them indiscriminately.

Greene is only seven miles away; a messenger reaches him: "Davidson is dead. The militia are dispersed. Cornwallis is over the Catawba."

With a heavy heart, the commander turns toward Salisbury. He rides up to the door of Mr. Steele's tavern. Dr. Read is there awaiting his arrival.

"What! alive, general?"

"Yes; tired, hungry, alone, and penniless."

The hostess is a true-hearted woman. A few minutes later a breakfast is ready; and while he is eating it she places a bag filled with bright silver dollars in his hands, saying, "You need them, and I can do without them."

Over the mantel hangs a portrait of King George. General Greene, with a heart too full for utterance at the devotion of the noble woman, turns the portrait to the wall, and writes with his pencil upon the back, "Hide thy face, King George, and blush."

It is fifteen miles to the Yadkin. Greene rides on. The river is high, but no matter for that: the messenger whom he sent up this way on the 25th of January was faithful to his trust, and boats are plying from shore to shore. Before night the army is upon the other side of the stream. So, then, that forethought about boats was not idle thinking.

Morning dawns. Cornwallis has been marching all night. He comes to the Yadkin. There is the dark rolling river between him and his prey. The bird is just beyond his reach. He can only gnash his teeth and cannonade the American camp. His cannoneers can see the top of a log-cabin sheltered by a ledge of rocks. Somehow they understand that General Greene has taken it for his head-quarters. The general is writing dispatches. A cannon-ball passes through the roof, tears up the shingles, rattles the splinters upon the table; the general looks up a moment, and goes on with his writing. "It will be impossible for Greene to get across the Dan," say the spies to Cornwallis; and

IN REVENGE, TARLETON'S SOLDIERS SLAUGHTER THEM
INDISCRIMINATELY.

the British commander resolves to make one more effort to secure his prey. As soon as the river falls he will have him. Northward moves Greene's little army toward Guilford, fifty miles distant. "Join me there," is the word to Huger, who is forty miles east of Salisbury.

The roads are frozen at night, and knee-deep with mud at midday. The streams are swollen, the bridges gone. The men are shoeless, coat-less, and without blankets. He reaches Guilford, where the troops from Cheraw join him on the 9th of February. All together, Greene has only two thousand and thirty-six men, and Cornwallis is by the Yadkin with three thousand of his picked troops. He is chafing like a baffled hound. He must get at Greene. He marches up the west bank of the Yadkin, thirty miles to Huntsville; the river is

MAP OF
GEN. GREENE'S
OPERATIONS IN
THE SOUTH

SCALE OF MILES
0 20 40 60 80 100

shallow there, and he can ford it. He is only twenty-five miles from Guilford, due east, and he is nearer than Greene to the shallow fords of the Dan. He thinks that Greene has no boats on the Dan, and is sure of his prey.

"It is not prudent to fight if we can avoid it," is what Greene's officers in council think, and it is in accordance with Greene's opinion. Then there will be a race for the Dan.

Greene has already sent off his heavy baggage, but he must have a rear-guard that can move rapidly. Morgan is sick with the rheumatism; and Colonel Williams, the brave-hearted Marylander, is appointed to command it. He has all the cavalry under Colonel Humphreys, Howard's infantry, and the riflemen—seven hundred, in all, of the best men of the little army, as true as steel every one of them.

It is seventy miles from Guilford Court-house to the Dan. Cornwallis is twenty-five miles west, pushing north-east, and Greene is also marching north-east. Greene takes the main road. Colonel Williams swings out between the two armies on another road.

General O'Hara is in advance, with the British cavalry and a body of light-infantry, and the van-guard of the British and the rear-guard of the Americans are constantly exchanging shots.

At three o'clock every morning Williams is on the march, not halting till the middle of the forenoon for breakfast. A rest of an hour, or till the British appear, and then the soldiers are on the road again, marching thirty miles a day through the mud, making their way with bleeding feet. There are snow-squalls; but through the rain and sleet and snow, across the swollen streams, the little army pushes on. The militia have deserted. "All but eighty have left me," is Greene's letter to Governor Nash, of North Carolina.

February 13th was the third day of the race. Williams was eating breakfast when a Whig citizen rode up. "The British van-guard are close upon you!" he shouted.

"Reconnoitre them," said Williams to Captain Armstrong.

Williams's force moves on, all except Colonel Lee, with a squad of the cavalry, who secrete themselves in the thick woods. There is a clatter of horses' feet, and Armstrong and a little bugler, on a jaded pony, come riding in, with a squadron of British cavalry at their heels. The little bugler, a boy of thirteen, gives himself up; but the next moment a broadsword cleaves his head open, and he falls dead.

"Charge!" The secreted Americans wheel into the road, and eighteen of the British are pitched from their saddles, while two Americans only fall in the encounter. The leader of the British is Captain Miller, who is taken prisoner.

"You butchered that poor little bugler, you ruffian, and now you shall hang for it!" are the quick, hot words of Williams.

"I did not do it. It was a drunken soldier."

"You could have prevented it."

The soldiers fix a noose, but the British army is close at hand, and there is no time to execute the sentence; they hurry away, keeping fast hold of the prisoners.

All through the day the race goes on. At every little stream the Americans, under Williams, wait and give their pursuers a volley.

Night comes—cold, dark, rainy. Williams sees a fire in the forest. Is it possible that Greene has halted to try the wager of battle? Williams's heart sinks within him. It must be that Cornwallis, by forced marches, has got between Greene and the Dan, and a battle, with the odds against the Americans, is inevitable. But two days ago Greene was there, and halted a few hours, and the fires have been blazing the while. Three hours' rest, and Williams is moving. He halts once more for breakfast. A horseman rides in from the north.

"The greater part of our wagons are over the Dan, and the troops are crossing," is the word from Greene.

Hurra! hurra! hurra! So loud the shout that it reaches the ears of the British close at hand, and they wonder what it may mean.

"*Irwin's Ferry, 5½ o'clock.*—All our troops are over, and the stage clear. The infantry will cross here. Major Hardman has posted his party in readiness on this side, and the infantry and artillery are posted on the other, and I am ready to remain and give you a hearty welcome," is the second note from Greene.

Up to the river march the wearied troops. Into the boats they leap, and reach the other shore.

Safe the army, safe the prisoners, safe the baggage. It has been a chase of two hundred miles. Ah! that was wise forethought, the sending of that messenger from Cheraw to the Dan, to secure all the boats on the river.

Cornwallis is chagrined. He has burned his baggage, marched two hundred miles, his troops are worn out, and he has been defeated and baffled at every move. There will be a pretty story afloat over in England in regard to his being checkmated by a Yankee blacksmith from Rhode Island who knows nothing of military science.

Chapter 30
GUILFORD COURTHOUSE

CORNWALLIS was at Hillsborough, forty miles south of the Dan. It was an important town—a place where the Legislature met every other year. A majority of the people in that section of the country were Tories. Cornwallis raised the royal standard, and called upon all good, loyal subjects to rally around it. The Tories were delighted. General Greene had been driven out of the State, the loyal cause was in the ascendant. Now that a royal army was there, they would rally and subdue the Whigs. Men came to Cornwallis offering to raise companies. He had seven offers in a day. His lordship was delighted. Greene had escaped him, but there was not a regiment of American troops in the State. He could write home a glowing letter to the king. He was far from his supplies, which were at Wilmington, fully one hundred miles away; but the loyal people would feed him, and he would soon be able to push north into Virginia.

On the 17th of February, he sent Tarleton north-west, with about four hundred men, to bring in the loyalists in that direction who were gathering under Colonel Pyle. On the very next day Greene sent Colonel Lee and Colonel Pickens across the Dan, and made preparations for the whole of his little army to follow. He had no intention of sitting down and allowing the Tories to come to Cornwallis. If he could only keep them in awe, his lordship in a very short time would move somewhere else. Greene went with Lee and Pickens a day's march, giving them instructions, and returned in the night to his army.

Lee and Pickens heard that Tarleton had passed north-west, and they followed on his track. They captured two of Tarleton's officers, and found out where Tarleton was. Tarleton does not know that Lee and Pickens are on his track, and Lee and Pickens inform the country people that they are Tories on their way to join Tarleton: by so doing, perhaps they will be able to get within striking distance before Tarleton discovers who they are.

The column is winding along the forest roads. Tarleton is not more than three or four miles away, resting in perfect security, thinking that Lee and all of Greene's army are forty miles distant on the other side of the Dan. Two Tories ride into Lee's lines, thinking the troops are Tarleton's.

"We come from Colonel Pyle, who is close at hand, coming on a crossroad with four hundred loyalists," they say.

"Ah, indeed!"

"He will soon be here," they repeat.

Colonel Lee sends word to Pickens to place his riflemen in the woods out of sight. The riflemen wear green twigs in their hats.

"Will one of you please ride back to Colonel Pyle with Colonel Tarleton's compliments, and ask him if he will be so good as to draw out by the roadside, that my troops may pass on to their encampment."

Lee makes the request. He has determined to capture the whole force of four hundred mounted Tories. He will get his whole line in front of them, halt it, and inform Colonel Pyle that the whole force are prisoners. Pyle's men have their muskets slung upon their shoulders, and will not be able to make resistance. The lines move along. Lee meets Colonel Pyle, and shakes hands with him. Suddenly there is firing down the lines. The trick has been discovered, and the Tories begin to fire. Terrible their mistake. They are at a disadvantage. Lee would fain capture them without shedding a drop of blood, but the *mêlée* has begun. It lasts scarcely five minutes; but when it is over ninety Tories are stretched upon the ground. Pyle escapes to a little pond close by, and conceals himself by its reedy shores. The whole body is captured or dispersed. Tarleton was only two miles distant. He heard the firing, and prepared for battle. Lee concluded to wait till morning before attacking, and in the night was joined by three hundred mountaineers who had heard of Greene's retreat, and had voluntarily left their homes and hastened to his aid.

Morning came, but Tarleton was not to be seen: he was on his way east to Hillsborough, too far to be overtaken. The Tories, who were intending to flock to Cornwallis's aid, concluded to wait a little while. They were amazed to find the Americans on the move, and astonished at the fate of the four hundred under Colonel Pyle.

On the 23d, Greene, with his whole army, was south of the Dan. The Tories were more downcast than ever, and the Whigs, so lately discouraged, plucked up heart again. The militia hastened to join Greene.

Cornwallis was astounded when he found Greene south of the Dan and on the head-waters of the Haw River, which becomes the Cape Fear River farther down. He suddenly found his foraging parties cut off, and his troops constantly harassed by Marion, Williams, Pickens, Sumter, and Lee, who would be in one place to-day and somewhere else to-morrow, and who kept the Tories in such awe that very few came to join the royal standard. Cornwallis moved out from Hillsborough to the Haw to strike a crushing blow; but he could not get at General Greene.

The 10th of March came. The trees were clothed in green, wild flowers bloomed by the wayside, the air was filled with their fragrance; but on this day the soldiers of the two armies had little time to admire the beautiful in nature.

Greene had four thousand two hundred and forty-three infantry, and one hundred and sixty-one cavalry. Only one thousand four hundred and ninety were Continental troops, the rest militia, who had come out for a few weeks' campaign. In a short time they would all be on their way home. General Greene wanted to fight, and he determined to take a good position and offer battle to Cornwallis. He might not win a victory; but a battle, even if not a victory, might be a blow which would cripple Cornwallis. Greene would take care that a defeat should not be a rout. His cavalry were superior to Cornwallis's, and could cover a retreat. The ground around Guilford Courthouse would be a favorable position. The main road runs north and south; another road runs off west, at right angles, and leads to the Reedy Fork of the Haw River.

The court-house stands at the junction of the roads, with a field north of the Reedy Fork road, and another old field south of it, extending one hundred rods or more. There is a piece of woods, and south of the woods corn-fields on both sides of the road, where the farmers have just planted their corn; and beyond the fields there is a ravine, with a little brook winding through it. The ground slopes all the way from the courthouse to the brook, a distance of more than half a mile.

Cornwallis is south-west of Guilford, near New Garden meeting-house. He is surprised to hear that Greene has advanced nearly twenty miles from the Reedy Fork and is ready to offer him battle. For two weeks he has been trying to get at him, and now Greene is waiting for him. He can not decline such an offer. He has twenty-five hundred disciplined British troops and several cannon, and he will crush the man whom he has been endeavoring, not only for the last two weeks, but all winter, to catch,

On the southern border of the forest behind the log fence, along the northern edge of the corn-field, Greene posts the North Carolina militia and some riflemen, under Colonels Butler and Eaton. They have a splendid position, protected by the fence, and will have a good chance at the British as they come across the corn-field. Behind them, about nine hundred feet, he places the second line, the Virginia militia, in command of General Lawson, east of the road, and General Stevens west of it. Back by the court-house, along the road leading to Reedy Fork on the top of the hill, he places the Continental infantry. They are twelve hundred feet in the rear of the Virginians. General Huger commands on the west, and Colonel Williams on the east side of the Salisbury road. Greene, with the remainder of his troops, is near the court-house. Colonel Washington, with his cavalry and some infantry, is placed to support Huger on the west; while Colonel Lee, with his cavalry, is stationed on the east to support Williams. Greene has four pieces of artillery. Captain Singleton, with two six-pounders, takes position in the road between the corn-fields, and the other two pieces are on the hill south-west of the court-house.

General Cornwallis is forming his men. The North Carolinians see the British coming from the woods. The Seventy-first regiment, Highlanders, swings out east of the road. A Hessian regiment, under Colonel Bose, follows. General Leslie commands the wing. The Twenty-third and Thirty-third regiments, under Colonel Webster, file to the left, west of the road. The artillery is in the centre, with the light-infantry and the Yagers behind. A battalion of the Guards, under Lieutenant-colonel Norton, file east to support Leslie and General O'Hara, with the Grenadiers and second battalion of the Guards, file west to support Webster.

The two six-pounders, under Singleton, open fire, and the British guns reply. Slowly the British advance across the corn-field. The North Carolinians open fire too soon. They do not wait, as Stark's men waited at Bunker Hill. The bullets, for the most part, go wide of the mark; only here and there a man drops. On the British move. They are within good distance, and they halt and fire a volley.

"Charge!" Leslie shouts it. With a hurra the line sweeps across the corn-field, and the North Carolinians drop their guns, throw away knapsacks and canteens, and flee like a flock of sheep through the woods.

"Stand! stand! Come back! come back!" shout the officers; but in vain. In a moment they are gone. Foolish men! If they had but reserved their fire till the British were within ten rods, if they had stood their ground behind the fence, far different would have been the result of the battle. Back through the woods, through the second line they streamed, all except a handful, under Colonel Campbell, who bravely maintain their ground a while.

But the British are brought to a stand, for the flanking troops of Colonel Washington and Colonel Lee are galling them. Cornwallis half-wheels the Hessian regiment to face the east, and attacks Lee; and the Thirty-third regiment, with the light-infantry, makes a similar movement west to attack Washington. He fills the gap in the line by advancing two battalions of the Guards. It is a well-executed movement, like that which a checker-player makes when he keeps the way to a king-row well guarded.

On toward the Virginians moves the compact line of British. The Virginians pour in a deadly fire, and there is confusion in the British ranks; but the men are old soldiers, and discipline holds them. The Virginians retreat, not panic-stricken, but in excellent order. Cornwallis is confident of an easy victory. The British, under Webster, come out into the field in front of the Marylanders, under Colonel Gunby. The Marylanders have been in many a battle. Their muskets blaze, and then they rush forward down the hill, charging bayonet. It is discipline against discipline. Webster's line wavers, gives way, and the men flee in confusion toward the woods. Oh, for another regiment like that from Maryland! Vain the wish; they are the only veterans on the field. Greene has no troops to throw in behind them, to press on and follow up the work. Stevens is wounded, the Virginians in retreat; and Leslie and O'Hara, on the British side, are just ready to fall upon the Second regiment of Marylanders, under Colonel Greene. Gunby goes down beneath his horse, but Howard takes command. The cavalry under Washington charge the British.

Cornwallis's horse is shot beneath him, and he has the mortification of seeing his best troops fleeing from the field. The fight must be stayed, the pursuers driven, or the day is lost.

"Open with the artillery!" he shouts.

"It will kill our own men," O'Hara replies.

"I know it, but it must be done."

Crash go the British cannon, and British and Americans fall before the murderous storm. In a moment the British soldiers drift past the artillery, and the Americans are stopped. It is the crisis of the battle—the end of it.

On the east side of the road the British are advancing. The American militia are retreating. Greene surveys the scene. He sees what has been gained, and what may be lost. He has inflicted a terrible blow upon Cornwallis. He can retreat now, and save his army. To remain and attempt to win the victory will end in failure, and he issues the order for retreat. The horses are shot, and he must leave his artillery behind him.

"You will cover the retreat," is his order to the Second Marylanders. The regiment takes its stand, and the army files away in good order, ready, if pressed, to turn at any moment and smite the pursuers. Lee and Washington, with the cavalry, remain with the Marylanders. Tarleton would like to rush upon them, but Cornwallis has narrowly escaped an utter rout, and calls him back. About four hundred Americans have been killed and wounded, while Cornwallis has lost six hundred and thirty-three.

This battle, in its results, was one of the most important of the war. In December, when Greene took the command of the Southern Department, the British and Tories were masters of the Southern States. They held a line of posts from the Atlantic to the mountains. Cornwallis had fully four thousand men in the field; but now he was forced to abandon the interior and make a hasty retreat to the sea-coast, at Wilmington. The Tories were disheartened, and the Whigs triumphant; and the cause of liberty, which had been so gloomy, was bright once more.

General Marion was north of Charleston, not far from the Santee River, when a British officer came with a flag of truce to see him about exchanging prisoners, and was taken into the camp blindfolded. The officer had heard much about Marion; and instead of finding, as he had expected, a man of noble presence in an elegant uniform, he saw a small, thin man, in home-spun clothes. Around were Marion's soldiers, some of them almost naked, some in British uniforms, which they had captured—a motley set, with all kinds of weapons, large muskets, rifles, shot-guns, swords made by country blacksmiths from mill-saws. The business upon which the officer had come was soon settled.

"Shall I have the honor of your company to dinner?" said Marion.

The officer saw no preparation for dinner. A fire was burning, but there were no camp-kettles, no Dutch ovens, no cooking utensils.

"Give us our dinner, Tom!" said Marion to one of his men.

Tom was the cook. He dug open the fire with a stick, and poked out a fine mess of sweet-potatoes. He pricked the large ones to see if they were done, blew the ashes from them, wiped them on his shirt-sleeve, placed the best ones on a piece of bark, and laid them on the log between Marion and the officer.

"I fear our dinner will not prove so palatable to you as I could wish, but it is the best we have," said Marion.

The British officer was a gentleman, and ate of the potatoes, but soon began to laugh. "I was thinking," he said, "what some of my brother-officers would say if our Government were to give such a bill of fare as this. I suppose this is only an accidental dinner."

"Not so, for often we don't get even this."

"Though stinted in provisions, you, of course, draw double pay."

"Not a cent, sir. We don't have any pay. We are fighting for our liberty."

The officer was astonished. They had a long and friendly talk, and the officer, bidding Marion good-bye, went back to Georgetown.

Colonel Watson was in command of the British there. "What makes you look so serious?" Colonel Watson asked.

"I have cause to look serious," the officer replied.

"Has Marion refused to treat?"

"No, sir; but I have seen an American general and his officers, without pay, almost without clothes, living on roots and drinking water, and all for liberty! What chance have we against such men?"

"WE DON'T HAVE ANY PAY. WE ARE FIGHTING FOR OUR LIBERTY."

The officer was so impressed by what he had seen, that he could fight no more, but disposed of his commission and returned to England.

General Greene sent Marion and Lee south to get between the British and Charleston, and cut off their supplies. They marched to Fort Watson, a strong fortification on the east bank of the Santee River, about fifty miles north of Charleston. It was built of logs, stood on a hill, and was garrisoned by one hundred and twenty men, commanded by Lieutenant M'Kay. They sent him a summons to surrender; but he was a brave officer, and informed them that he intended to defend the fort. He knew that Lord Rawdon would soon be there to aid him with several hundred men. Marion and Lee knew that Lord Rawdon was on the march, and they resolved to capture the fort before he arrived.

They saw that there was no well in the fort, and that the garrison had to come out and creep down to the river to obtain water. The riflemen soon stopped that. Then M'Kay set his men at work digging a well, and carried it down to the level of the lake, and had a good supply of water.

Lee and Marion knew that there was a large amount of supplies in the fort, for, besides what was inside, there were boxes and barrels outside. Some of the militia tried to creep up and get a barrel; but the garrison killed one and wounded another. A brave negro, named Billy, with Marion, looked at the supplies, saw that one of the hogsheads was only a few feet from the edge of the bluff, and resolved to try what he could do. He crept up very near without being seen, then, before the British could fire upon him, he was crouched behind the hogshead. The ground was a declivity, and soon the British soldiers saw that the hogshead was in motion. They fired at it, but they could only see some black fingers clasping the chimbs, and in a few minutes the hogshead disappeared down the hill.

Billy obtained an axe, broke open the hogshead, and found that he had captured one hundred and fifty shirts, one hundred knapsacks, fifty blankets, and six cloaks. He distributed them to the soldiers, many of whom had no shirts. Marion named the negro "Captain Billy," and every one treated the brave fellow with great respect.

Rawdon was close at hand. Marion and Lee could see the light of his camp-fires on the hills in the west. Whatever was

In the Morning They Saw a Tower Higher than the Fort.

done must be done quickly. But what could they do? They had no cannon; and even if they had, they could not batter down the fort; but a bright thought came to Colonel Mahan—to build a tower which would overlook the fortification. As soon as night came, all the axes in the camp were in use. The British could hear the choppers, and wondered what was going on; but they were astonished in the morning when they saw a tower higher than the fort, and a swarm of men on the top firing through loop-holes, and picking off with their rifles every man who showed his head above the parapet. Lord Rawdon had not come, and Lieutenant M'Kay saw that he would soon lose all his men, and that he must surrender. Before noon the Americans were in possession of the fort and all its supplies.

Chapter 31
EUTAW

ABOUT forty miles north-west of Charleston, near the line between Charleston and Orangeburg counties, are some wonderful springs. The water boils up from the ground, clear and pure. It is a subterranean river that appears upon the surface, and that winds through the lowlands north-west for about two miles, and empties into the Santee at Nelson's Ferry.

Beneath the grateful shade of the surrounding forest, Colonel Stuart, in command of the British forces in South Carolina, was encamped on the 8th of September, 1781. Lord Rawdon had returned to England, worn down by the fatigue of the campaign. Colonel Stuart had twenty-three hundred men. General Greene was only sixteen miles distant, on the high hills of the Santee, north of the river. There were no boats on the Santee by which he could cross it to attack Stuart, and he had only twenty-six hundred men, of whom, however, not more than sixteen hundred could be of any account in a battle, for a thousand were poorly armed, or were sick, or were required to bring in supplies. Yet General Greene determined to strike a blow at the British.

He broke up his camp on the 22d of August, marched north-west about twenty-five miles, almost to Camden, and crossed at the Camden Ferry; then turned south, and marched rapidly to the Congaree, about twenty-five miles, and crossed it at Friday's Ferry; then turned south-east toward Eutaw Springs, twenty-five miles away; making a march of seventy-five miles to get sixteen. Rain had been falling, the swamps were filled with water, and all the low-lands were flooded, making the march a difficult one. The sun was hot, and at midday the army rested; but from day-break till mid-forenoon, and from four o'clock till late in the night, the soldiers plodded their weary way.

General Greene learned that General Stuart intended to erect a fort at the springs, from which parties could go out in all directions to rob the Whigs, and stir up the Tories to enlist in the king's cause, and he determined to strike a blow that would frustrate the design, even if he were defeated in battle. He had few stores, and would not risk them. He prepared for a retreat, if a retreat should be necessary, by sending all his heavy baggage to Howell's Ferry, on the Congaree, where it could be taken across the river at a minute's warning.

General Marion knew all the country—every lonely path through the woods, as well as every highway; and so vigilant were his men, that Stuart's spies, scouts, and foraging parties were captured one by one. Stuart, having no suspicion that Greene was making such a roundabout movement, was resting in security in Eutaw Springs.

Stuart's camp is a few rods south of the springs, in a field at the junction of the great road leading south-east to Charleston, with the river road running east and west. There is a brick two-story house on the north side of the road at the junction, with a garden behind it reaching down to the springs. West of the house, and north of the road, is a cleared field; and there is another field across the road, and opposite the first. In these fields Stuart had pitched his tents. There are fences around the garden and fields. It is only a mile north in a direct line to the river. The swamp and creek in that direction will prevent Greene from flanking Stuart on the north. The woods around the field are thick, the trees tall and large, and the gray moss hangs in long, trailing, sombre masses from the timber. The clearing is on a hill thirty feet or more above the level of the springs. It is a strong position; but General Greene determines to attack it, nevertheless.

General Greene is at Burdett's plantation, seven miles west of Eutaw, on the 7th of September. The men go into camp, cook their supplies, and lie down beneath the trees for a few hours' rest before marching to battle. Stuart does not know that they are there; but during the night two North Carolina men, who have been forced into service against their will, take revenge by deserting.

"We come from the American army. It is only seven miles distant, and you are going to be attacked in the morning," t h e y say, when brought b e f o r e General Stuart.

The British general does not believe it. Greene c a n n o t h a v e reached that position undiscovered. The men are spies, and he o r d e r s them under guard. If he finds that they are s p i e s, they will dangle from the limbs of one of the live-oaks in the morning. He will see, however, if there are any Americans lurking in the vicinity; and orders

The Diggers Throw Down Their Hoes, and Flee Toward Eutaw.

Major John Coffin, brother of Admiral Isaac Coffin, and refugee from Boston, who sailed with General Howe to Halifax in 1776, and who is now in Carolina fighting for the king, to beat them up.

By daylight Greene is on the march with about twenty-three

hundred men. At the same time, Major Coffin, with four hundred men, is pushing out to see if there is any truth in the report of the deserters, and also to dig sweet-potatoes in a plantation not far away. He suddenly finds himself face to face with Major Armstrong, of Lee's cavalry, who is leading the advance of Greene.

"There are some Whig militia," is the word in Coffin's ranks.

"Charge!" is the order of Coffin, and his troops come riding down the road to scatter the Whig militia; but the Whig militia do not run. They sit in their saddles, take deliberate aim, and one after another of the British troops tumbles to the ground.

"Charge!" It is Lee who gives the command, and his men, with drawn swords, sweep down the road, scattering the British in an instant. Forty prisoners are captured, and several are killed and wounded.

The potato-diggers, protected by a body of infantry, are close at hand; but the diggers throw down their hoes, and flee toward Eutaw.

General Greene, seeing the British infantry, directs his aid to ride toward them, and inform them that if they do not surrender he will be under the necessity of cutting them to pieces; and the British give themselves up. Major Coffin's party is utterly routed. A sudden but effective blow has been struck already upon Stuart.

There is commotion in Stuart's camp—drums beating, soldiers springing to their arms. Some of the soldiers take position behind the garden fence, others place logs around the brick house, and in a short time make it a strong fort. The walls are thick, and Greene, with his two three-pounders and two six-pounders, will have to batter them a long while before he can make them crumble. From the windows Stuart's marksmen will pick off the Americans as they approach.

Stuart could hardly believe that Greene was at hand with his whole force, or that he would dare attack him in so strong a position. He did not strike his tents, for he was sure of driving the rebels pell-mell up the road in a very few minutes. He formed his men in a single line in the edge of the woods by the field, four hundred feet from his tents.

On the north side of the road, west of the garden, he placed the Third regiment, or "the Buffs," as the soldiers called them. Colonel Cruger, with the fragments of several battalions and companies, is placed in the centre across the road, and the Sixty-third and Sixty-fourth on the south side. Behind the Buffs, he placed a battalion of light-infantry, under Major Majoribanks. The major had his troops in a thicket of black-jack. Some of his soldiers were posted by the spring. Major Coffin, with his cavalry, was placed in the field south, to guard the left flank. The artillery was stationed in the road, while a detachment of infantry was sent out a mile to skirmish with Greene as he advanced.

Greene formed his men in two lines. In the front line, which he placed south of the road, on the right, was a battalion of South Carolina militia, under General Marion; then came two battalions of North Carolina militia, under Colonel Malmedy. On the north side of the road was another battalion of South Carolina militia, under Colonel Pickens. The whole front line was under Marion. He planted his two six-pounders in the road between the North Carolinians. A short distance behind them he stationed three small brigades of Continental troops. On the south side of the road, behind Marion's South Carolinians, he placed the North Carolinians, three battalions of them, commanded by Lieutenant-colonel Ashe, Major Armstrong, and Major Blount. General Sumner commanded the brigade. In the centre were two battalions of Virginians, under Major Snead and Captain Edmonds—both under Colonel Campbell. On the north side of the road were the Marylanders—one battalion under Lieutenant-colonel Howard, the other under Major Hardman, and both under General Williams. He gave General Lee charge of the right flank, and placed some battalions of State troops, commanded by Colonel Wade Hampton, Colonel Polk, and Colonel Middleton—the whole under Colonel Henderson—to protect the left. General Greene had still a few troops left. He would not extend his lines, and so held them in reserve.

They were Lieutenant-colonel Washington's cavalry, and a battalion of Delaware troops, under Captain Kirkwood.

General Greene believed in double lines and in a reserve, and he placed his best troops in the second line, as at Guilford Courthouse. If the first line of militia gives way, as possibly it may, there will be some old soldiers behind to receive the shock. At Guilford he was the party attacked; but now things are reversed, and he is about to attack a superior force. What chance has he of success? Not much. Why, then, does he attack? Because, even if he is defeated, he can strike a blow which will be almost equivalent to a victory. If he can give an effective blow, he will compel Stuart to leave the interior and take refuge in Charleston, and so free the upper country. He will take care that a defeat shall not be a rout, as he did at Guilford. That battle, though he was driven from the field, compelled Cornwallis to retreat to Wilmington, and it was the turning-point of the war in the South. If he can compel Stuart to retreat to Charleston, it will be a victory. To complete his arrangements, he places his two three-pounders in the front line, and the two six-pounders in the second line. He will begin the battle with the militia and the three-pounders, but will end it with the Continental troops and the six-pounders. Stuart will find the contest hardest at the close, and not at the beginning.

It is nine o'clock. The sky is cloudless, and the day is hot, but the men are sheltered by the foliage of the trees. They are in the woods, and the trees will be a shelter not only from the burning heat, but also from the bullets of the enemy.

The army was still a mile from the Eutaw, moving slowly, when it met the detachment which Stuart had sent out. Lee was in front. He concluded that he was near the main body of the British. There was the roar of a cannon, and a ball came whirling through the woods. Lieutenant Gaines unlimbered his three-pounders; and when the British sent a shot, Gaines returned two; and in a very short time the British fell back to Eutaw. The troops filed right and left, and took position in the order of battle. Gaines unlimbered his three-pounders again and opened fire, and the British artillery replied. Gaines was a good gunner, and he very soon dismounted one of the British guns, but not long after had both of his three-pounders disabled. The militia were getting used to the sound of the cannon. The cannon-balls of the British made havoc among the trees, but flew harmlessly over the heads of the soldiers.

Through the under-brush the militia in the front line can see now, as they advance, the bright-red uniforms of the British regulars. It is about a quarter-past nine when the musketry begins. The success of the morning has stirred the blood of the militia. They have got used to the roar of the cannon; they are partly sheltered by the trees, and they take steady aim. They fire, load, step forward a little, fire again, and so advance. The British are firing, and the air is filled with the whistling bullets.

Over on the right, General Lee's infantry is engaged with the Sixty-third British. The Sixty-fourth, in turn, is pressing the North Carolinians in the centre, under Malmedy; but the North Carolinians, anxious to wipe out the stain of the panic at Guilford, hold their ground till they have fired seventeen rounds; then, and not till then, do they yield. They do not flee panic-stricken, but fall back behind the Continentals, under Sumner.

Stuart has resolved to break Greene's centre. He will strike a great blow there by moving straight down the road. He will throw in his reserve, and it shall be like a wedge driven into a log: by such a movement he will rend Greene asunder, and cut him up piecemeal. The fight goes on more fiercely, and at close quarters. The three-pounders are disabled; but the six-pounders open with a louder roar. Henderson, on the north side of the road, can not advance against Majoribanks on account of a thicket; but he holds his ground, and Lee is holding his, on the right flank. Stuart presses on his men in the centre, and the North Carolina Continentals retreat in confusion. But there are two cool-headed men on horseback in the rear who are watching the battle. One is the man from Rhode Island, whom Washington long ago selected as the fittest general of the army to be his successor, in case he should fall—General Greene. Close by is Otho H. Williams, who has been Greene's right arm all through the Southern campaign.

"Advance and sweep the field with your bayonets!" is Greene's order; and the Virginians and Marylanders, under Campbell, with loaded muskets and fixed bayonets, advance. On, on, slowly and steadily, they move, till they are not more than one hundred feet from the British. So near, and no faltering on either side! It takes courage for men to stand still and look into the muzzles of a line of muskets so near, knowing that the next moment a murderous storm will burst forth—a lightning flash, a cloud of blinding smoke and roar of thunder, and that there is certain death for scores of men behind it all. Face to face stand the Continentals and the veterans of England. There are two flashes of lightning, two thunder-peals, and the ground is strewed with the dying and the dead.

The Continentals do not stop to reload; they do not flee, not even falter; but, with a wild hurra, burst through the cloud and rush upon the British, who flee in confusion through the woods and across the field.

There is a panic in Stuart's camp. Men are fleeing in haste down the Charleston road, horsemen crying, "We are defeated!" Some of them ride forty miles to Charleston. The Americans secure two cannon. The field is won—so the soldiers think. They are in possession of Stuart's camp. Tents, provisions, all are theirs. Provisions! Rum! What soldier can refrain from halting and taking a dram, a big drink, after such a triumph? They rend the air with their shouts. They drink, and shake hands over the victory. Lee is following the British, but suddenly comes to a halt, for the brick house is a fortress. The British are inside, as in the Chew house, at Germantown, and pour a murderous fire from the windows. The British outside have not all fled. In the thicket below the house, and around the spring, is their right wing, protected by the thicket, the garden fence, and the defenses which Stuart has thrown up. The battle is not over, nor is the victory won. How shall the British be dislodged? Colonel Washington sees a place down by the creek where his cavalry can dash through in sections, and get in their rear. The attempt is made, but the troops go down one by one. Washington's horse is shot under him, and before

ON, ON, SLOWLY AND STEADILY, THEY MOVE.

he can disentangle himself he is captured. Hampton and Henderson and Kirkwood advance, and the British, under Majoribanks, are compelled to fall back to the garden. The fence has been made so strong that the garden and the house make together a formidable fortress. Stuart and Coffin are behind the house rallying the fugitives. What! British veterans flee before a motley crew of countrymen! For shame!

Rum, rum—things good to eat, plunder—what wonder that the countrymen never before in battle, never before under discipline, should stop to eat and drink, and secure the baggage? But while they are doing it, the British, chagrined and burning to recover their lost encampment, are rallying. Gaines has been trying his six-pounders upon the house, but the walls are thick, and the balls do not pierce them. One by one his gunners fall, and now Majoribanks makes a rush, drives the Americans, and seizes the two British guns again, and brings them back to the house. Stuart has reformed his men. He is in possession of the house and the garden, and General Greene can not dislodge him. The British have a small cannon in the house, and fire it from a window, sweeping down the Americans. The success, the rum, the plunder, the heat, all have told on them. The battalions are disorganized; brave officers have been lost. Greene sees that it will not be possible to get possession of the house, and that it is useless to attempt it. He has struck a telling blow, and is confident that Stuart will soon retreat to Charleston. It is nearly one o'clock: the men have marched seven miles, fought four hours, and they are not demoralized; on the contrary, feel that they have won a victory. He places Hampton in position to guard the rear, and draws off the troops, taking one British cannon, though leaving his own in their hands; but two of them are disabled and of no account. Campbell is dead. Howard and Henderson are wounded. One hundred and thirty privates have been killed, and the loss, all told, is five hundred and thirty-five, or nearly one-fourth of the army. The British have lost, in killed and wounded, six hundred and ninety-three. Back to the camp of the night before Greene marches, taking with him over five hundred prisoners.

The morning of the 9th dawns, and Stuart is marching toward Charleston. He has lost half of his army. He has destroyed every thing that he can not take away. Lee and Marion are hanging on his rear, picking up stragglers. So the defeat, as at Guilford, becomes a victory, and people all over the country and across the water in England said, that of all the American commanders, next to Washington, stood Nathaniel Greene, of Rhode Island.

Chapter 32
FORT GRISWOLD

NEW LONDON was an important town on the west bank of the Thames, in Connecticut. Privateers were fitted out there which captured many British ships. The shipmen and sailors of New London were brave and daring. One day in May, 1779, a British fleet of twenty-one vessels, under convoy of a frigate, and the *Lady Erskine,* of ten guns, was passing along the Sound, when three sloops sailed out of the harbor and captured the *Lady Erskine.* So energetic were the New London sailors, that nine Tory privateers were captured between the 1st of March and the 13th of June, 1779. British ships arriving from England and sailing up the Sound to New York, almost at the end of the voyage, were suddenly pounced upon and captured by the New London sailors. In August, 1781, the ship *Hannah,* from London, with the richest cargo brought to America during the war, was captured by the *Minerva* and taken into that port.

The capture exasperated Sir Henry Clinton, and he determined to make New London pay for it. Perhaps he thought also that a movement of a force into Connecticut would trouble Washington, who was closing around Cornwallis at Yorktown. An expedition of thirty-two vessels—eight of them war-ships— was fitted out. Two thousand men were sent from New York, and General Arnold was made commander. He was born close by New London. His home was on the bank of the Thames, between New London and Norwich, and he was just the man, Sir Henry thought, to be let loose upon his old neighbors.

The people of New London looked out upon the calm waters of the Sound on the evening of the 5th of September, and saw a great fleet of vessels sailing close under the Long Island shore; but many a fleet had sailed the Sound during the war, passing by New London; and so, thinking that no harm was nigh, they went to bed as on other nights.

The vessels were steering eastward. Little did the sleepers in New London dream that, when darkness came on, all the vessels turned their prows northward, shook out all their sails to the gentle breeze blowing from the south-west, and sailed for the harbor of New London. General Arnold intended to land before daylight. Gradually the fleet approached the harbor. It was one o'clock. Another half-hour, and he would drop anchor before the town; but suddenly the wind shifted north, blowing directly out of the mouth of the river; and instead of going straight into the harbor, the vessels had to tack this way and that way, getting a little nearer at every turn.

Day dawned. The people of New London were astounded. A great fleet, with eight war-ships, was just ready to enter the harbor. The meeting-house bell was rung. Boom! boom! went two guns from Fort Griswold. That was the signal which had been agreed upon as an alarm. Three guns were to be a signal of rejoicing over the news of a great victory. As soon as the echoes had died away, boom! boom! boom! came from the fleet. A Tory had told Arnold what the signals were. The people out in the country had heard the two cannon-shots, and were ready to seize their guns; but what was the meaning of the three?

The people leaped from their beds in terror. Out on the Sound were the ships of the enemy. In a short time British, Hessians, and Tories would be landing. Men harnessed their horses; there was a quick packing-up of things most valuable. Men, women, and children, half-dressed, were running through the streets, crying and wringing their hands. Women, laden with bags and pillow-cases, with infants in their arms, hastened out of the town. They had no time to stop to get breakfast. Hungry, barefoot, bare-headed, with dishevelled hair, they hastened into the fields and pastures, or on to the country-houses,

WOMEN, LADEN WITH BAGS, WITH INFANTS IN THEIR ARMS, HASTENED OUT OF THE TOWN.

where the kind-hearted neighbors gave them breakfast and shelter.

There was a fort on each side of the river: Fort Trumbull, on the west or New London side; and Fort Griswold, on the Groton side. Captain Shapley commanded at Fort Trumbull, which was simply a battery facing the water on three sides, open behind, and only designed to be used against ships in the harbor. Captain Shapley had but twenty-three men. There were eight cannon in the battery, but two of them were dismounted. Fort Griswold was a stronger work. It had stone walls ten feet high. There was a ditch outside, and on the walls were pickets projecting twelve feet; and there were one hundred and fifty men, most of them farmers and citizens of Groton, who seized their guns and hastened to defend the fort, when they heard the booming of the cannon.

Colonel Ledyard was in command of New London and Groton. He sent messengers out into the country to carry the alarm, and men rode on foaming horses, as Paul Revere rode on the 19th of April, 1775. Colonel Ledyard hoped that the people from the country would arrive in season to help him defend the forts, and he resolved, come what would, to hold Fort Griswold.

"If I must lose to-day my honor or life, you who know me can tell which it will be," he said, as he stepped into the ferry-boat and crossed the river to defend the fort.

Although Arnold had hoped to land before day-break, it was nearly ten o'clock before the ships could get into the bay. They dropped anchor, the boats were lowered, and about one thousand men entered them: the Thirty-eighth British regiment; a regiment of Tories, under Colonel Beverly Robinson (the man who owned the house near West Point); a regiment of New Jersey Tories, under Lieutenant-colonel Upham; and sixty Hessian Yagers. The boats pulled toward a little cove, where there was a sandy beach. The men leaped into the water, waded to the shore, and formed quickly, as if about to face a great army. The first movement was toward Fort Trumbull. The twenty-three men, under Captain Shapley, saw them advancing, and loaded the six cannon with grape-shot.

"Be ready to spike the guns," said Captain Shapley. A cannoneer stood by each piece, waving the port-fire.

"Let them have it!" shouted the captain. The guns blazed. A half-dozen men dropped in the British ranks.

"Drive in the spikes," said Captain Shapley. The spikes were driven into the vent-holes, and the twenty-three ran to their boats, leaped into them, and started for Fort Griswold; but they were so near the British fleet, that the boats were fired upon, and seven of the men wounded and captured.

Arnold hastened on to the town. On the common by the meeting-house was an old iron cannon. Some of the citizens loaded it, and fired at the approaching British, and then fled. Other citizens fired from behind fences; but the few could not do much against a thousand men.

Over on the Groton side, at Fort Griswold, a brave fight is going on. Lieutenant-colonel Eyre has landed, with two British regiments—a battalion of New Jersey Tories and some Hessians, with two cannon. Colonel Eyre is able to get within four hundred feet of the fort without being exposed, by leading his men along under the shelter of a ledge south-east of the fort.

It is noon. He sends a white flag toward the fort.

"I demand an instant and unconditional surrender," is his summons.

Colonel Ledyard summons the officers—Captain Avery, Captain Stanton, and Captain John Williams. They are farmers, and live near by, and have rushed into the fort to defend it.

"Defend the fort!" they say; and the officer goes back to Lieutenant-colonel Eyre, who sends a second summons: "If obliged to storm the works, martial law shall be put in force," is the message. That means that no quarter will be given.

Captain Shapley has reached the fort, and Colonel Ledyard sends him out with the reply of the brave men: "We shall not surrender, let the consequences be what they may."

Colonel Eyre prepares to advance. He will make a rush, leap the ditch, climb the walls, and get inside before the garrison can reload after firing once.

Captain Halsey stands by an eighteen-pounder. He is an old sailor, and has been in many a fight. He rams home two bags filled with grap-shot.

The British move on toward the fort. Captain Halsey runs his eye along the cannon. They are in range.

"Fire!" he shouts. The cannoneer touches it off. The air is filled with the whirring shot, and twenty men go down. A wide gap has been made in the British ranks, and the entire line is thrown into confusion.

"On! on!" shout the officers, striking the reluctant soldiers with their swords.

From every embrasure a stream of fire bursts forth, and the ground is quickly strewed with the killed and wounded. Colonel Eyre falls mortally

Samuel Edgecomb Picks Up Cannon-balls and Hurls Them Down.

wounded, and three other officers of the Fifty-fourth regiment are disabled. The Fortieth regiment, under Major Montgomery, swings round toward the east and north. His men rush to the ditch. Now they are so near that the cannon can not harm them. Joseph Woodmancy stands behind the parapet, and

loads and fires his musket right down into their faces. Samuel
Edgecomb thinks there is a better way than that, and he picks
up cannon-balls (nine-pounders) and hurls them down upon the
heads of the British, smashing their skulls.

The British, to get into the fort, must tear away the pickets
which run out from the walls over the ditch. A soldier climbs
upon the back of a comrade, reaches up and seizes one of the
pickets; but before he can wrench it away, Edgecomb dashes
out his brains.

But other soldiers are climbing up. Their heads appear above
the pickets. Oh for more men! If there were three hundred,
instead of only one hundred and fifty, in the fort, those heads
would drop in a twinkling.

Major Montgomery is a brave officer. He climbs up through
the pickets, but Jordan Freeman, a negro, is as brave as Major
Montgomery. He has no gun, only a long-handled spear, which
he plunges into Montgomery's side, and the Briton falls, mortally wounded, into the ditch upon the heads of his men.

The British are swarming through the embrasures. It is the
many against the few—seven to one. A British soldier leaps
from the parapet inside, and rushes to unbar the gate, but a shot
brings him down. Another succeeds. He unbars the gate, and
the British rush in.

"Stop firing!" shouts Colonel Ledyard. He sees that the fort
is lost, and his men cease the contest, all except Captain Shapley
and the few men with him over in the south-west bastion, who
do not know what has taken place.

The British wheel a nine-pounder, and pour a volley of grape
into the men. Captain Shapley and Lieutenant Chapman are
killed, and the men throw down their arms and stand before
their captors. Now that Colonel Eyre and Major Montgomery
have fallen, Major Bromfield commands the British.

"Who commands here?" he shouts.

"I did, but you do now," is Ledyard's reply, handing out his
sword.

Major Bromfield takes it, draws back his arm, and plunges
the weapon to the hilt through the body of the brave man. He

withdraws the bloody blade, and the commander falls dead to the earth.

Captain Peter Richards, and Captain Ledyard, a nephew of the colonel, see that no quarter is to be given, and resolve to sell their lives as dearly as possible; but in a moment they are cut down, and hacked to pieces.

The British platoons enter the fort, and fire into the unresisting Americans. Some of the Americans rush to the magazine, but the British fire into it, and the fugitives fall in heaps. Major Bromfield is afraid that the magazine will explode, and stops the firing; but the living are pulled out and bayoneted. Some rush into the barracks, but the British stand by the door and windows and shoot them as if they were sheep in a pen.

Mr. Mallison is a strong man. He rushes to the parapet, leaps over the pickets, lands in the ditch outside the fort, and, though a dozen muskets blaze at him, escapes to the woods.

William Seymour is lying upon the ground, with his knee shattered by a ball, and the British soldiers give vent to their fiendish passions by stabbing him thirteen times. Lieutenant Avery has had an eye shot out, his skull broken, and his brains are spattered upon the ground. A soldier stabs him in the side; and yet he breathes, recovers, and lives forty years to narrate the horrors of the day.

For the credit of humanity, let it be said that one British officer is tender-hearted. "Stop! stop! In the name of God, stop! My soul can't bear it!" he shouts, and rushes upon the soldiers with his sword to stop the butchery.

It stops because there are no more to be butchered. There were one hundred and fifty at the outset. Captain Shapley came with about twelve men, making one hundred and sixty in all; but General Arnold, in his report, says that eighty-five were killed, and sixty wounded, most of them mortally—one hundred and forty-five butchered!

Sir Henry Clinton sends home this indorsement of the massacre:

"The assault of Fort Griswold will impress the enemy with every apprehension of the ardor of British troops, and will hereafter be remembered with the greatest honor to the Fortieth and Fifty-fourth regiments and their leaders."

Major Bromfield was promoted for his conduct. So the massacre was indorsed by the general, by the ministers, and the king.

The British soldiers stripped the dead, plundered the living, picked up the wounded, tossed them, bleeding and fainting, into a cart, and ran the cart down a hill over the stones. It came against a tree with a terrible jar. Some died; others fainted. They took them from the cart to a house, and left them there; dug a ditch, threw their own dead (about forty) into it; and left a party to lay a train to the magazine; set a house on fire, and marched to their boats, for from every road men were hastening with their guns.

While the massacre was going on, Arnold was in New London. One party under Colonel Upham, with the New Jersey Tories, marched up Cape Ann Lane to Mr. Latimer's house. It was so far out of the village that a great many of the people had moved their goods into it. A house so far out of the town certainly would be spared, they thought; but it was soon in a blaze, and all the goods were consumed.

Arnold, with Lord Dalrymple, who acted as aid to him, rode up to a hill overlooking the town, where he could see every thing that was going on. In the river he sees the ships trying to escape up stream to Norwich, and people are running from the town. And now the flames of burning buildings ascend to heaven. The soldiers are going in all directions with fire-brands, setting fire to houses, stores, ships, and boats.

An English officer comes to Captain Richard's house, where the captain's daughter is lying, too ill to be moved. He is humane enough to bid the soldiers spare it; but all the other houses and stores in the vicinity are set on fire. Arnold, sitting on his horse, issues his orders. "Soldiers, do your duty!" he shouts.

A Tory leads the British, and pilots them to the homes of the Whigs. Houses, stores, piles of lumber, ships, boats, wharves, and goods are given to the flames. The soldiers stave in the heads of hogsheads filled with molasses, and a river of molasses runs down one of the streets. They rip open bags of coffee, destroy hogsheads of rum, and drink themselves drunk. The market-house, the Episcopal church, the jail, all are set on fire. The harbor is a sea of fire. All the fishing-boats and ships are in flames. The fire burns the hempen cables, and the ships are blown by the wind hither and thither, burning to the water's edge, and then the blackened hulls disappear beneath the waves. While the flames are wildest, Arnold is eating dinner in the house of an old acquaintance, helping himself to the best the house affords. While eating, the house takes fire and he is forced to leave. So almost to the spot where he was born the traitor brings the torch and the sword to the homes of those who have honored and trusted him.

The sun descends the western sky. Evening comes. But what a scene! Blackened ruins in New London; many mangled corpses in Fort Griswold; and out upon the hills hundreds of homeless men, women, and children, stripped of every thing— their husbands, brothers, fathers slain!

Down to the beach march the British, who leap into their boats and row out to the ships. They have left a train of powder in Fort Griswold, and soon they expect to see a grand explosion of the magazine—a lighting-up for a moment of the heavens, and then a shower of burning timbers, followed by total darkness. That shall be the close of this day's work. But Major Peters, of Norwich, has reached the fort. The barracks are on fire. He sees the train laid to the magazine. There is a pump, but the British have knocked out its spout. He can only find an old cartridge-box, but he uses it for a bucket, gets at the water, moistens the train of powder, and prevents the explosion. Other men come to his aid, and they put out the fire.

The British ships are sailing down the bay, and the women and children are coming to see how it fares with their husbands and fathers. There they lie—eighty-five of them—cold in death, massacred and mangled. Calm and serene the features of the brave commander. There lies Daniel Williams, only fifteen years old. He fought for freedom, and was massacred in cold blood.   Near by him lies Thomas Avery.   His father was a lieutenant.   They fought side by side.   "Tom, my boy, do your duty," said the father, when the fight was hottest.

"Never fear, father," Tom replies; but the next moment is cut down.   He is only seventeen.

"It is in a good cause, my boy," says the father; and a moment later he lies by the side of the son, pierced through and through by British bayonets.

With torches in their hands, women move amidst the slain in search of their husbands.   One wife wipes the gore from the faces of thirty of the dead before she finds the one dearer than all others on earth.   Never more will the glazed eyes beam upon her, never more the loving arms clasp her to his heart.   A wail of anguish rends the air.

The people are coming now from all parts of the country. Far away the farmers have seen the pillar of cloud ascending to heaven, and are rushing with their guns.   And women are as brave-hearted as their husbands.   "John, don't get shot in the back!" shouts a wife to her husband, as he starts with his rifle.

They are too late.   The massacre is finished, the burning accomplished, and the enemy sailing back to New York.   They can only gaze with swelling hearts upon the scene of blood and woe, lend helping hands to those so sorely stricken, or, lifting them to heaven, swear anew their allegiance to the cause they have espoused.   Never, never will they lay down their arms till America is free and independent, and the last British soldier driven from the land.

Chapter 33
YORKTOWN

THIS is the way the men stood upon the checker-board: Sir Henry Clinton was in New York; there was a body of troops on Long Island, and a fleet in the harbor; Lord Cornwallis was in Virginia, and there was a small fleet in Norfolk harbor; British troops were in possession of Charleston and Savannah. The South was pretty much conquered, and Sir Henry hoped that in a very short time Cornwallis would bring Virginia to terms.

On the other side, the American army was at North Castle, at White Plains, and Dobbs's Ferry, and the French army also. General Washington and Count Rochambeau had their headquarters at the house of Mr. Livingston, near Dobbs's Ferry, a large mansion with an ell, a piazza, and delightful grounds around it. General Lafayette was down in Virginia, at Williamsburg, with a handful of men, watching Cornwallis. In the West Indies was a French fleet, under Count de Grasse. General Washington expected that about the middle of August Count de Grasse would suddenly make his appearance off Sandy Hook, and that, with his aid, he could besiege Sir Henry, capture the troops on Long Island, and eventually take New York. General Clinton had his spies in Washington's army, and they reported to him that such was the plan.

Sir Henry became alarmed. He dispatched a vessel to Virginia, and ordered Cornwallis to send him three thousand men. Cornwallis could spare them, and then be able to drive Lafayette out of the State. A day or two after the vessel set sail, Sir Henry's heart was gladdened by the arrival of a fleet from England with three thousand Hessians. On August 13th, General Washington and Count Rochambeau, Robert Morris (the man who could obtain money when every body else failed), and Mr. Richard Peters, Secretary of the Board of War, were talking over the plans of the campaign at the Livingston house, when letters were brought in for Washington and Rochambeau. A vessel had arrived at Newport, bringing a mail from Count de Grasse, who said that he had decided not to sail to New York. This upset all their plans. Washington was disappointed. The French fleet, under D'Estaing, had failed Sullivan at Rhode Island, and now De Grasse was overturning all his plans.

Another messenger came from the South with letters from Lafayette, with the information that Cornwallis was embarking a portion of his army at Portsmouth for New York.

Another messenger arrives from the East, bringing a letter from Count de Barras, in command of a French fleet at Newport, who has received another letter from Count de Grasse, who has concluded not to stay at the West Indies, but will sail, on the 13th of August, for the Chesapeake, with twenty-eight ships of the line, and thirty-two hundred troops, under General St. Simon, and will be ready to co-operate with the Americans in any movement. Joyful news this! But it is a long distance for men to travel on foot from the Hudson to Norfolk. There are great rivers to cross—the Hudson, the Delaware, the Susquehanna, the Potomac, and many other streams—a long, weary, tedious march over poor roads. It is three hundred miles. It will take a month. A vessel from New York, with a fair wind, will make the run from Sandy Hook to the Chesapeake in forty-eight hours; and Sir Henry Clinton can move his whole army to Virginia before Washington can cross the Susquehanna.

General Washington reads the letter, and turns to Judge Peters. "Sir, what can you do for me?"

Judge Peters is the man selected by the Board of War to consult with Washington.

"With money, every thing; without it, nothing," Peters replies.

"What sum do you want?" asks Mr. Morris, who is already thinking where he can obtain the money.

Twenty thousand dollars hard cash will do something. Count Rochambeau can spare so much from his military chest till the 1st of October, and Robert Morris will be sure to pay it then. The matter is quickly arranged.

There is activity in the American army. Orders are issued to clear the road to Kingsbridge. The army is going to attack New York. A company of men go down toward New York to clear away the trees, so that the army can march; and Sir Henry expects an attack from the north. A body of

A Rebel Is Brought into Sir Henry's Camp.

men go down on the Jersey side and mark out a place for an encampment, and erect ovens for baking bread. General Washington has a large number of boats or vessels. Is he going to launch them below Paulus Hook, and make a movement for Staten Island, and erect batteries which will drive the fleet out of the Narrows?

General Clinton is keeping a sharp lookout for such a movement. Now that three thousand Hessians have arrived, he does not need any troops from Cornwallis, and has sent a vessel countermanding his order, but requesting Cornwallis to continue to harass the rebels in Virginia.

A rebel is brought into Sir Henry's camp. He is a young Baptist minister, Rev. Mr. Montaigne, who was arrested by the Cowboys at Ramapo, on the west side of the Hudson. He was carrying dispatches from Washington to one of his officers, and it is very evident, from some things in the dispatch, that Washington has a scheme for the capture of New York.

On the 19th of August the American army was under arms; but, instead of marching down to Kingsbridge and crossing Harlem River, the troops turned north, marched to King's Ferry, crossed the Hudson, and moved down the west bank. It was evident to Clinton that General Washington had changed his plan, and was going to march down to Newark or Amboy, and cross to Staten Island.

And now, for a few days, Sir Henry can not find out exactly where Washington is, or what he is doing. He can get no information; every avenue leading to the city is guarded, and his spies can not get in.

The Americans were marching south, making eighteen or twenty miles a day. On the 1st of September they crossed the Delaware at Trenton. The next day they passed through Philadelphia. When the French troops arrived, dressed in their gorgeous uniforms of white broadcloth faced with green, their bands of music playing, the inhabitants were wild with excitement. Congress was sitting there, and the troops passed in review before the President, Hon. Thomas M'Kean.

On the 4th the troops were at Wilmington; on the 5th, at the head of the Elk, on the Chesapeake. General Washington has had men employed in collecting all the vessels in the bay at that point, and no fewer than eighty are in waiting; and the troops embark.

Let us take another look at the chess-board. At this moment Cornwallis was throwing up intrenchments at Yorktown. He would leave a small force, and then fall upon Lafayette, who was at Williamsburg, the capital of Virginia, only twelve miles distant, with his quarters in Raleigh Tavern. Williamsburg was a rebellious town. It was the head-quarters of the rebellion in Virginia, and had been from the first. It was there, in the House of Burgesses, that the young lawyer, Patrick Henry, astonished the Tories and electrified the patriots by his speech in March, 1775, advocating the separation of the colonies from England.

"There is no retreat," he said, "but in submission and slavery. Our chains are forged; their clankings may be heard on the plains of Boston. * * * I know not what course others may take; but, as for me, give me liberty, or give me death!"

Cornwallis has seven thousand men, and as soon as his intrenchments are completed he will finish the war in Virginia.

Up in New York are Sir Henry Clinton, Admiral Graves, and Admiral Hood. The last named has just arrived from the West Indies. Admiral Rodney, in command of the British fleet there, has discovered that Count de Grasse has sailed for the American coast, probably for New York, and has sent Hood with fourteen ships to co-operate with Admiral Graves, who has four ships of the line, and together they will be a match for Count de Grasse.

Admiral Hood is surprised not to find De Grasse at Sandy Hook. Where can he be? At New York? No; for word comes that Admiral de Barras has sailed with the French fleet from Newport southward.

Light begins to dawn upon Sir Henry. Count de Grasse and Barras are to meet in the Chesapeake. Washington and Rochambeau, instead of attacking New York, have outgeneraled him, and are on their way south to attack Cornwallis! It is clear as day now.

Whatever is to be done must be quickly done. Perhaps, if a movement were made into Connecticut, General Washington would turn about and hasten back. General Arnold was therefore sent on an expedition to New London, as we have seen. But General Washington had laid his plans, and no movements of General Arnold to pillage and burn the defenseless towns would call him back.

Admiral Graves and Admiral Hood spread their sails for the Chesapeake. On the 5th of September, at sunrise, the Count de Grasse, looking eastward from Lynn Haven Bay, at Cape Henry, saw a fleet of vessels. It must be Count de Barras, he thought, coming from Newport; but soon he discovered that it was an English fleet under Graves. He was ready for a fight, but wanted more sea-room, and sailed out upon the Atlantic. It was four o'clock when the fight began. Only a part of the two fleets got into action. The battle went on till sunset. Graves could not get all of his vessels into action, and hauled off to wait till morning. During the engagement, the *Terrible,* one of his ships, was so much damaged that, after taking out the men and stores, she was set on fire and burned. The French lost two hundred and twenty men, killed and wounded; the the English two hundred and forty-six. Morning came, but Graves was not quite ready to commence the battle. Nor was De Grasse, who hoped soon to see the topmasts of Count de Barras's fleet dotting the horizon. For five days the fleets stood on and off, sometimes close inland and then out upon the sea. On the 10th of September, Count de Grasse sailed back to the Chesapeake, and a glad sight met his eyes, for there was De Barras with his fleet and troops and transports, with heavy siege-guns and military stores. Admiral Graves hastened back; but there, blocking his way, were the combined fleets getting ready to sail out and sink him. There was but one thing to be done—and that to spread his sails for New York. On the 11th of September, while the American army was at Annapolis, Admiral Graves was fleeing from the Chesapeake.

Cornwallis sees a net drawing around him. The fleet has gone. He can not fight his way inland past Williamsburg, for Lafayette blocks his way there. If he were to attempt it, whither could he go? Nowhere, and be safe. Washington and Rochambeau and Lafayette would soon be upon his track, or cutting him off. He can only throw up strong defenses and stand a siege till Sir Henry Clinton hastens to his relief. Sir

Henry should have hastened with half his army when Admiral
Graves sailed. Then was his golden opportunity.

Down past the mouth of York River, where the French ships
were blockading Cornwallis, into James River, and up the James
to Jamestown, sailed the ships from Elkton, landing on the 25th,

and marching to Williamsburg. On the 28th, the combined
army of twelve thousand men marched from Williamsburg to
Yorktown.

Yorktown was a small place of about sixty houses. One of
the best was owned by Governor Nelson, who was with Washington, in command of the Virginia militia.

The York River is about half a mile wide, and lying in the stream were several British ships.

Major Elijah Favor's services were called for to lay out the lines. He rode over the ground and reconnoitred it. He saw that the ground was for the most part level, that the soil was a sandy loam, and that it would be an easy matter to dig intrenchments. South of Yorktown, a little more than a mile, was a large field, and immediately south of that a little brook had its rise, which ran southward. The brook was the dividing line between the French and American armies. The French occupied the ground from the brook north-west to York River. Washington and Rochambeau had their marquees pitched on the west side of the stream. Crossing the brook, he came to General Knox's head-quarters, with the artillery around it. By the roadside was Baron Steuben's tent. He had command of the Pennsylvania, Virginia, and Maryland Continental troops. Next were the New York, Rhode Island, and New Jersey troops, under General James Clinton, also the sappers and miners. The tents of the troops reached to the road leading east from Yorktown to Hampton.

Crossing this road and riding north-east, Major Favor came to Lafayette's tent. Under his command were the Virginia militia, and in advance of them was General Lincoln, with the light-infantry. General Lincoln's tent was close by Wormeley's Creek, almost over to York River. Riding back, he took a view of the French lines. Nearest Rochambeau's quarters were the French brigades, commanded by Baron Viomenil and Viscount Viomenil. Beyond them were the troops from the West Indies, under General St. Simon.

Out in the river he could see the British ships, the *Guadaloupe* and *Charon,* of forty-four guns each, and several transports. Over on Gloucester Point there were nearly one thousand British, under General Tarleton and Lieutenant-colonel Dundas. But Count de Grasse had sent the French marines on shore, and the Duke de Lauzun, with his brigade, and General Weedon, with a body of Virginia militia, the whole under General de Choisé, were sent across York River to lay siege to Gloucester.

Major Favor now lost one of his best friends, Colonel Scammell, the adjutant-general of the army. He was from New Hampshire, and had been in the battle of Bunker Hill, under Stark. Scammell had seen service all through the war, and had been wounded at Stillwater. He rode out to reconnoitre Cornwallis's lines close by the York River, west of the town. He did not know that behind a knoll covered by thick bushes was a body of Hessian cavalry. Suddenly a squad of Hessians was upon him. He saw that he could not escape, and held up his hand; but a Hessian wantonly fired at his breast. He fell from his horse, mortally wounded, and was taken prisoner.

General Cornwallis saw that he could not hold his outer lines against the great army, and abandoned works which had cost him a great deal of hard labor to construct. All the horses in the American army were set to work hauling cannon, ammunition, and supplies from Jamestown. General Washington was anxious to hasten the siege, for he had received word that Admiral Digby had arrived at New York from England with a fleet. He knew that Graves and Digby would soon make their appearance, and probably Sir Henry Clinton, with his army, to rescue Cornwallis. Day and night the soldiers worked.

The night of October 6th was very dark, but Elijah Favor had looked over the ground in front of the British out by Wormeley's Creek, and knew just where to drive down his stakes for the soldiers to begin their intrenchments. He went with a body of soldiers within a quarter of a mile of the British lines. A part stood guard while the others worked. No one was allowed to speak. In silence they toiled—so silently that the British sentinels heard no sound. In the morning they had a breastwork so high that it sheltered them from the British guns. The next night they dragged up several twenty-four pounders, and placed them in position. On the night of the 10th, the artillery was ready. Colonel Lamb, the brave man who had lost a jaw at Quebec; Lieutenant-colonel Ebenezer Stevens, who had fought under Arnold on Lake Champlain in '75, and in Canada in '76, and who had commanded the artillery at Stillwater; and Colonel Carrington—took turns in directing the artillery.

The batteries opened and sent their solid shot and shells into Cornwallis's lines. Cornwallis's guns replied, and all night long there was a roaring of cannon and bursting of bombs. The French fired hot shot across the water at the *Guadaloupe,* the *Charon,* and the transport-ships. The *Guadaloupe* had to cut her cable and creep away. The *Charon* was set on fire and burned, and also three of the transports. The lurid flames lighted up the heavens, and gave courage to the besieging troops. Captain Stevens made it so hot for the British that they ceased firing, and the British gunners lay down behind their intrenchments to find shelter.

On the night of the 11th, Elijah, with a party of men, got within almost nine hundred feet of the British, and threw up a new line of redoubts. They soon had guns mounted in them, and pounded away at the British with more effect than ever. But there were two batteries of the British—one east of the town, down by the river, and another a little farther west— which partly enfiladed the new intrenchments. It was decided to capture them. The American light-infantry, under Lafayette, would capture the one by the river, and the French grenadiers and chasseurs, under Baron Viomenil, would take the other.

Colonel Alexander Hamilton, the young captain who commanded two pieces of artillery at Harlem when the British undertook to cross the Bronx in 1776, is appointed to command the American detachment. Captain Ogden, of New Jersey, has command of the advance. Cornwallis has erected a strong abatis. The troops move out silently in the darkness. No word is spoken. They approach the redoubt. The British cannon blaze. The British soldiers fire over the intrenchments at the dusky forms which they see approaching—not marching now, but rushing on up to the abatis, tearing it away, and leaping over the embankments. Short the contest. In a minute they are victorious, having thirty-nine killed and wounded. The British lose eight killed and wounded, and about twenty are captured. General Washington, General Lincoln, and General

Knox are in one of the redoubts awaiting the result. The shout that goes up when the victory is won is sweet music to their ears.

Not so successful are the French. One hundred and twenty soldiers garrison the redoubt which they are to attack. The French march bravely up to the abatis, but halt there, and fire in the darkness. For an hour the fire goes on, and one hundred are killed and wounded before the British in the redoubt, after having eighteen killed and wounded, call for quarter. Forty-one are captured, but the rest make their escape. And now the captured guns are turned and aimed at Cornwallis's main line.

The night of the 14th comes. Cornwallis resolves to make a sortie. The British troops march out just before day-break and surprise the French, driving them from their lines; but the troops in the rear come up and drive the British back again into the town. Now the cannon of the allies are so near that they can pour a cross-fire into the British camp. There is only one safe place inside of Cornwallis's lines, a cave under the bank by the river; everywhere else the shot and bombs are falling.

Cornwallis conceives the idea of taking his army across York River to Gloucester Point, surprising the allied troops, hemming them in, and then seizing all their horses and marching north through Virginia, Maryland, and Pennsylvania to New York. He thinks that he can get horses and mount his men. He does not think of the rivers he will have to cross, nor that the news will go a great deal faster than he can march, nor that he will find the people rising to block his way, nor that the fleet can sail up the Chesapeake with the army and be at Baltimore in advance of him. It is the wild idea of a man driven to desperation by the prospect of defeat and humiliation. There is no reason in it, yet he endeavors to carry it out. All night long the boats at his command are transporting troops to Gloucester Point. In two more nights he will have them all north of York River. But the winds and waves are high, and the boats can not pass. He sees that the project must be given up.

Cornwallis is in General Nelson's house, which he is using for his head-quarters. The morning of October 17th dawns, and with its dawning the cannon-balls begin to plow their way through the house, and the British commander is forced to leave it. The first shot is fired by General Nelson himself. All the morning the uproar goes on. Few shots can Cornwallis send back, for the American riflemen are picking off his gunners. His troops are exposed everywhere. The killed are increasing, and everywhere the wounded multiplying. Amidst the uproar the Americans hear the roll of British drums beating a parley. The cannonade ceases, a white flag is raised on the British works, and an officer comes out. General Cornwallis proposes a suspension of hostilities for twenty-four hours, and the appointment of commissioners (to meet at Mrs. Moore's house) to negotiate a surrender.

Twenty-four hours! By that time Admirals Digby and Graves and General Clinton may appear. No; General Washington can not give so long a time. Lord Cornwallis will please send his propositions in writing before the commissioners are appointed; there shall be no fighting for two hours. Lord Cornwallis assents.

Out in Mrs. Moore's house the commissioners meet. Colonel Laurens for the Americans, and the Viscount de Noailles for the French; Lieutenant-colonel Dundas and Major Ross for the British; and the terms are agreed upon. The gunners may extinguish their port-fires now, the soldiers may throw down their arms, for nearly a century will pass before there will be any more fighting at Yorktown.

At two o'clock on the afternoon of October 19th, the surrender takes place on the field, not far from Washington's and Rochambeau's quarters. The Americans are paraded north of the Hampton road, the French south of it, the lines extending more than a mile. Washington, on his bay horse, is at the head of the Americans, and Rochambeau at the head of the French. The officers of both armies have put on their best uniforms. The Stars and Stripes float above the Americans, while above the French are the lilies of France. Out from Yorktown come the British. In silence and in sadness they march. Upon many a bronzed cheek there are tears, for it is humiliating to surrender. Between the lines they march, and lay their guns upon the

ALL THE MORNING THE UPROAR GOES ON.

ground. The standards, twenty-eight in number, are to be delivered up. Ensign Wilson, of Clinton's brigade, receives them. He is the youngest officer in the service, only eighteen; but well does he perform his part—receiving them from the British captains and handing them to the twenty-eight sergeants appointed to receive them.

Cornwallis is not there. He is heart-sick. His disappointment, grief, and mortification are too great to be borne. He has sent for O'Hara to deliver up his sword. General Washington has appointed General Lincoln, who had to surrender to Cornwallis at Charleston, to receive it. General Lincoln holds it a moment, and gives it back to O'Hara, to be returned to Cornwallis.

The scene is over. Eleven thousand men, including soldiers, sailors, and Tories, are surrendered—a little over seven thousand being British and Hessians. Seventy-five horses, one hundred and sixty-nine iron cannon—all the supplies and ammunition, tents, camp equipage, eleven thousand dollars in money, are among the spoils.

Joy, joy, joy everywhere! Lieutenant-colonel Tilghman is sent by Washington to carry the news to Congress at Philadelphia. It is midnight when he arrives. The watchmen are going through the town; the slumbering people hear them crying the hour of midnight as never before—louder, quicker, and more joyfully. *"Twelve o'clock, and Cornwallis is taken!"*

Out from their beds they spring. Women in night-caps appear at the windows, people rush into the streets to hear the news—Cornwallis taken! Cornwallis taken! No news like that since Burgoyne laid down his arms at Saratoga.

Chapter 34
CONCLUSION

WITH the surrender of the British army at Yorktown the king's ministers lost all hope of conquering the Americans. It was a terrible blow to Lord North. When he received a letter informing him of the surrender of Cornwallis, he threw up his hands as if a bullet had struck him, and said, "O God, it is all over!"

The king was for sending more armies, but the British people were tired of the war. They had seen one army after another melt away; taxes were more burdensome than ever, and they saw that the Americans never could be conquered; that men who would throw down the axe and hoe, and leave the plow in the furrow, and hasten to capture an army, would maintain their liberties against the king's attempts to subjugate them. There were many Englishmen who from the beginning stoutly maintained that the Americans were right, and that they ought to be free; and there was so much opposition to a continuance of the struggle, that Lord North resolved to give up all further effort, for it had already cost England five hundred million dollars and fifty thousand lives.

There were still British soldiers in America. In South Carolina the Whigs continued to fight the British and Tories. Sir Henry Clinton was in New York, and General Washington with the American army was on the Hudson at Newburgh, with his head-quarters in a Dutch farm-house. It was a quaint old building. The dining-room had seven doors, and only one window. The fire-place was large, the walls low, and there were great beams overhead; but there the commander-in-chief entertained his officers and their wives. Mrs. Washington was with him, and many pleasant dinner parties assembled in the spacious dining-room.

It was nearly two years after the surrender of Cornwallis at Yorktown before the war was wholly ended; but on the 3d of September, 1783, a treaty was made at Paris between the English and American commissioners, and the United States was recognized as a free and independent nation.

So, after fighting more than seven years, after suffering untold hardships and privations, the Boys of '76 obtained their liberties, established the United States as a nation, and secured to mankind a government of the people and for the people forever.

THE END

Historical Reprints

from Maranatha Publications

The Story of Liberty *originally published in 1879.*

The secular humanists have edited God out of history! Now you can read what they cut out. Reprinted from the original 1879 edition, *The Story of Liberty* tells you the price that was paid for our freedom and how it was won. An excellent historical resource for your library. Quickly becoming a best seller among home schools and Christian educators. paperback, illustrated, 415 pages, $14.95 ISBN 0-938558-20-X

The Story of Liberty Study Guide

Steve Dawson's study guide for Charles Coffin's *The Story of Liberty* contains three main features designed to provide a comprehensive moral understanding of the people, main events and ideas contained inside Coffin's valuable book. Each chapter of the 98 page guide contains fill-in-the-blank questions to help facilitate personal and group study sessions or home schooling classes. Priced at $10.95, the 8-1/2"x 11" guide comes with a separate answer booklet.

Sweet Land of Liberty

originally published in 1881 as Old Times in the Colonies

Sweet Land of Liberty, sequel to *The Story of Liberty*, tells the historical highlights of colonial America with a Providential view. Written by civil war correspondent and children's author Charles Coffin, *Sweet Land of Liberty* has now been faithfully reproduced exactly as it was originally printed in 1881. paperback, illustrated, 458 pages, $14.95 ISBN 0-938558-48-X

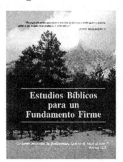

MARANATHA PUBLICATIONS, INC.

P. O. BOX 1799 • GAINESVILLE, FL 32602 • 352-375-6000 • FAX 352-335-0080

Bible Study Books — *by Bob and Rose Weiner*

BOOK NAME	PRICE	QUANTITY	TOTAL
Firm Foundation	$ 11.95		
Overcoming Life	$ 11.95		
Lovers of God	$ 9.95		
Life of Excellence	$ 9.95		
Preparation of the Bride	$16.95		
One Set of Above Studies (5)	$55.75		
Jesus Brings New Life	$ 5.95		
Spanish Firm Foundation	$ 11.95		

Christian History Books

BOOK NAME	PRICE	QUANTITY	TOTAL
The Story of Liberty (A Christian History Text)	$14.95		
Story of Liberty Study Guide - by Steve Dawson	$ 10.95		
Sweet Land of Liberty (Sequel to Story of Liberty)	$14.95		
The Boys of '76 (Sequel to Sweet Land of Liberty)	$16.95		

Booklets

BOOK NAME	PRICE	QUANTITY	TOTAL
— by Bob and Rose Weiner			
How to Become a Dynamic Speaker	$ 2.50		
Mightier Than The Sword	$ 2.50		
The Bed Is Too Short	$ 2.50		
Christian Dominion	$ 2.50		
— by Lee Grady			
Defending Christian Economics	$ 2.50		
A Vision For World Dominion	$ 2.50		
War of the Words	$ 2.50		

VISA and MasterCard Accepted

Sub Total	
Shipping	
Add FL sales tax	
TOTAL US Dollars	

Ship To:

Name _____

Address _____

City _____

State _____ Zip _____

Phone (_____) _____

❑ Check enclosed, payable to Maranatha Publications, Inc.

❑ Charge to my: ❑ VISA ❑ MasterCard

Card No. _____ Expires ___/___

Shipping & Handling:

Less than $10.00	$3.50
$10.00 - $24.99	$4.50
$25.00 - $49.99	$5.50
$50.00 or more	9%

Mail Order To: **Maranatha Publications, Inc., PO Box 1799, Gainesville, FL 32602**